# NAME THAT SUCCULENT

'According to some sixteenth century chronologists the world was created by fiat from aboriginal, chaotic nothingness during the week of October 18 to 24, 4004 B.C. . . . . Although the biblical cosmogony was reported as colossal and inclusive, some nominal chaos, nevertheless, remained. Things and processes were nameless, and in consequence man, on emerging as a conscious being, aware of his environment and gifted with the power of speech, began to identify persons, things and phenomena by name, thus ordering his own thoughts and facilitating discussion of matters with his fellows. The animals, so the story runs, were brought before Adam to be named, but there is no record that he was commanded to name the plants. Botanists have been diligently attending to this project . . . When Eve and Newton dally beneath apple-trees sin and science are imminent. As a result of the scientists' curiosity the world is gradually being analysed, dissected, named, classified and the how, if not the why of it, understood.'

R. W. BROWN in *Composition of Scientific Words* 1956: 33–34.

# Name that Succulent

Keys to the Families and
Genera of Succulent Plants
in Cultivation

With illustrations by the author

## Gordon D. Rowley

Department of Agricultural Botany, University of Reading

Stanley Thornes (Publishers) Ltd

First published in 1980 by:
Stanley Thornes (Publishers) Ltd
Educa House
Liddington Estate
Leckhampton Road
Cheltenham GL53 0DN

British Library Cataloguing in Publication Data
Rowley, Gordon
  Name that succulent,
  1. Succulent plants—Identification
  I. Title
  582'.14.  SB438




ISBN 0-85950-447-6

Printed in Great Britain by The Pitman Press, Bath, Avon

# A Cactus by any other Name . . .

Oh, call me a cactus—but what shall I call?
    What titles, what names, or what manner of terms?
For 'wot's-it' and 'thingummy' won't do at all
    For Dicotyledonous Angiosperms.

There are names of a kind that the family favour:
    'Pincushion' and 'Peanut' and 'Queen of the Night';
'Golden Barrel' and others of similar savour,
    All very familiar—so hardly polite.

For a cactus essentially needs a cognomen
    In sesquipedalian syllables scored,
In language exotic, archaic and Roman;
    How else can its spines be refreshed and restored?

Of names of this kind I can give you a quorum:
    Like *Cereus* and *Wittia,* just for a start,
And *Thrixanthocereus blossfeldiorum*—
    The very delight of the botanist's heart!

When a cactus you see looking languid and lame,
    Speak kindly, and do not provoke it or trounce it.
It's merely obsessed by the thought of its name,
    How to spell it, and write it, and how to pronounce it!

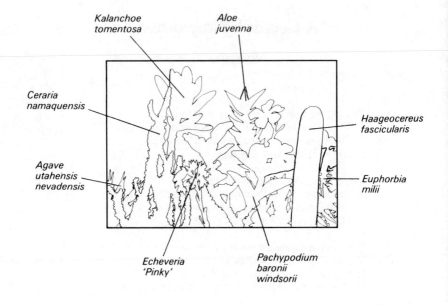

Kalanchoe
tomentosa

Aloe
juvenna

Ceraria
namaquensis

Haageocereus
fascicularis

Agave
utahensis
nevadensis

Euphorbia
milii

Echeveria
'Pinky'

Pachypodium
baronii
windsorii

**Key to the jacket design.**

# Contents

# Contents

# Preface

Although there are already many books on succulent plants—in particular on the cacti—they mostly concentrate on cultivation, giving a selection of pictures to help in establishing identities. Illustrations are certainly a boon (especially now that good-quality colour has come to be the accepted norm), but only a small sample of the many thousands of succulents can be shown, and one can easily misidentify a tiny seedling as the giant saguaro or an echeveria leaf rosette as a flower. At the other end of the scale there are the floras and monographs, written by botanists for botanists, which are of little help to the average collector because of their scarcity, high price or uncompromising style. How plants are named, how they are classified, and how they can be identified remain subjects veiled in a mystique of technical terms: small wonder that the average author shrinks from attempting to explain them. Yet there is a need for such information: I have never yet met a collector or nurseryman who did not lament the confusion over naming and the lack of helpful books on identification. A plant that loses its label may well be damned to anonymity for evermore.

Many everyday subjects involve getting to know technical jargon. The newspapers bristle with novel terms and initials, and even a knitting pattern has to be deciphered before it can be put to use. Just as a knowledge of musical notation can add an extra dimension to a listener's enjoyment, so the hobby of collecting and growing succulents can gain interest and impetus as we discover how the plants are related one to the other, wherein lie their distinctions, and what is the significance of their often formidable names.

This explains the thinking behind this book, which is (I believe) the first attempt in any language to bridge the amateur–professional gulf and provide a mechanical means for 'running down' any cultivated succulent to the generic level and at the same time introduce the mysteries of taxonomy and nomenclature. The core of the book is a major key to

Families followed by separate keys to the succulent genera of each Family. These, so far as possible, use easily observed characters and assume minimal botanical knowledge. Line drawings and a glossary explain all terms used.

Twenty-eight Families are treated alphabetically and for the most important a full page plate of line drawings explains flower structure and diagnostic features. Following a description of each Family and reference list is the alphabet of 266 genera, each with citation of place of publication and type, locality, approximate number of species, brief description emphasizing distinctions from other similar genera and reference to specialist books on the genus, especially noting keys to species.

The first dichotomous key for identifying succulents was produced in 1668 by John Ray, the leading botanist of the seventeenth century. My own first key to succulents was compiled in student days in 1941. Since then it has been many times revised, abandoned as hopeless, and resurrected; it appears in print now only with the realization that perfection always eludes us, and a patched and torn blanket is better than no blanket at all. All commonly-encountered Families and genera of succulents are covered, as well as a fair number of rarities. For the names of species, references are given to specialist books and revisions, where these are known to exist. For many large genera such as *Aloe*, *Euphorbia*, *Portulaca* and *Ruschia* no modern key to species exists; nor is one likely to be attempted until much more field work has sorted out the tangle of species. Descriptions of nearly all the known species of succulents will be found in the two *Lexicons* of Backeberg and Jacobsen*, to which the present book is intended as a primer.

Having had to make a choice between various competing names and classifications, I have tended to be conservative—few, large genera rather than many, finely split—since I believe that 'inflation' bedevils the botanical world every bit as much as it does our everyday lives.

In the opening chapters I have dealt with the procedure whereby plants are named and the two Codes of nomenclature because there seems to be a special need for enlightenment here, with so few other books touching on these matters. Growers deserve an explanation of why the same plant may be encountered under different names, and how to go about deciding which among these is the right one for them. Furthermore, since

---

*References to literature cited in Part I will be found on pp.60–61; to Part II on p. 259.

amateurs often feel impelled to plunge in and have their own say amid the welter of opinions, it is only right that they should do so fully armed with the tools of their adopted trade. If these chapters can do something to stem the flow of ill-formed, surplus or illegitimate names given to the world every year, they will indeed have served their purpose. Those already familiar with botanical procedure will no doubt be happy to skip these opening chapters and go straight to the main key on p. 71. Even so, attention is drawn to the Hints and Pointers on p. 67, and to p. 233, in case your efforts get nowhere at first attempt.

Identifying plants is not a task for the faint of heart. It is a skill that grows with experience: only the mechanics of it can be taught. It requires access to technical literature, familiarity with terminology and, sooner or later, with foreign languages also. And it requires a propensity, amounting to passion, for looking closer and still closer at the small things of life, seeking out similarities and differences. To the dedicated enthusiast all these aptitudes are within reach, and many of them— especially the last—bring satisfaction out of all proportion to the time and effort expended.

It is a real pleasure to acknowledge the help given me by friends during the long period when different formats for keys and text were being tried out. It is not possible to list in full all those, including colleagues on the staff at Plant Sciences, Reading University, who read and criticized various sections. I would, however, like to thank especially Prof. W. T. Stearn who read most of the text and made many refinements to the wording of complex nomenclatural points.

It was an especial source of delight that Stanley Thornes (Publishers) Ltd. of Cheltenham agreed to add this book to their list. Later on, when revision is needed, as it assuredly will be, the possibility is open for an enlarged edition with colour plates. To that end, the author would welcome constructive criticism from practical users of the keys.

Gordon Rowley<br>
Cactusville<br>
1 Ramsbury Drive<br>
Reading RG6 2RT<br>
May 1980

# PART ONE

# What you Need to
# Know to Name a Plant

# CHAPTER 1

# What Succulents Are

'The real purpose of books is to trap the mind into doings its own thinking.'
*(Christopher Morley)*

**Succulents** are defined as flowering plants in which the leaves, stems or roots have become more than usually fleshy by the development of water-storing tissue. Along with this go a number of other features not exclusive to succulents, associated with retention of water: reduced surface, thickened impermeable epidermis, mutual shading of one part by another, fewer breathing pores (**stomata**), and so on. These features are collectively termed **xeromorphic**, and **xerophytes** are characteristically plants of hot, dry, sunny regions where the annual rainfall is low and long periods of drought occur.

To the layman, all strange-looking and prickly succulents are cacti; but to the botanist, cacti are members of one Family only: the Cactaceae. These are native to North and South America and are characterized by the presence of areoles and floral peculiarities, as set out in full on p. 103. There are at least 27 other Families that are wholly or in part succulent, demonstrating quite extraordinarily convergent evolution in the plant bodies although flowers and fruits show them to be unrelated. It is the function of this book to bring out these differences.

The situation is not helped by popular insistence on 'cacti and other succulents' or—even worse—'aloes, cacti and other succulents' as is fashionable in South Africa now. The botanist maintains that 'all succulents are born equal', and that practice is followed here, throwing emphasis instead on the diagnostic characters of the Families under which they are grouped.

While the more extreme manifestations of succulence are easy to recognize—indeed, they evoke wonderment or strike terror at first glance—the limits of the group are more difficult to state. This is because

1

the tendency to store water has evolved independently in many plants faced with water stress in habitat, and in many and varied ways. Frequently we are confronted by a complete series of life forms from species with thin, easily wilting leaves requiring ample water (**meso-phytes**) up to highly xerophytic succulents. Such series can be seen in *Senecio, Euphorbia, Ceropegia, Pelargonium, Peperomia*, and elsewhere. Hence there are problems for writers on succulents: just what do they include and what do they omit?

Since the object of this book is practical—to identify the genera actually represented in people's glasshouses and gardens—it is here that guidance must be sought. The amateur grows anything that in looks and cultural requirements blends with his cacti, agaves, crassulas and unquestionable succulents, frequently stretching the limits where rarity or novelty is involved. The motivation and logic (if any) behind his choices would be a fascinating subject for analysis by itself, but here I merely sketch out a few home truths on how he decides what to cherish and what to evict:

1. The fleshier and more obese-looking the better—but, if the plants are not very fleshy, then at least they should be xerophytic and tolerate life in hot, dry conditions.
2. Perennial plants are favoured more than annuals. (Love is long-lasting.)
3. Tender plants are favoured more than hardy. (Love is all-attentive.)
4. Exotics are more attractive than the native flora. ('Distance lends enchantment . . . .')
5. Weird appearances count for much, especially the ultra-spiny. Resemblances to modern sculpture or to objects more basic in attractiveness weigh heavily. ('Beauty is in the eye of the beholder.')
6. Plants over-familiar, obviously pretty and too accessible appeal to a different aesthetic sense and do not blend well in a succulent house. This rules out cyclamens, begonias, bulbous flowers and many conservatory favourites, but admits the ultra-delicate, the ungrowable, the near-extinct and those with flowers so small, infrequent or ill-favoured that even plant encyclopaedias speak of them as 'of botanical interest only'.
7. Genuine succulence occurs among the orchid Family, Orchidaceae, and to a degree in the pineapple Family, Bromeliaceae. These

two very large groups have a following of their own, their special societies and journals, and are best treated separately.

8. A few bona-fide succulents defeat all efforts so far at acclimatization away from the habitat and are also omitted here. This goes for the whole of the Family Zygophyllaceae.

The keys that follow cover the whole Family Cactaceae and most of the genera listed in Jacobsen's *Lexicon of Succulent Plants*, excluding a few that seem to stretch the definition of succulence too far, and including a few extra genera now represented in cultivation. Since the scope is 'succulents in cultivation', another difficult decision to make is just how many specimens need to be around to qualify as 'in cultivation'? A single import in a botanic garden can hardly be counted, especially if it resists attempts at propagation or proves impossible to maintain alive. However, the mere mention of a plant as difficult or rare (or 'not included in Rowley's keys'?) is sufficient to stamp it as top priority for acquisition and set pulses racing among more avid collectors. Hence in cases of doubt I have usually included the genus, if only as a small-type addition at the point in the key where it would key out, marked as 'Unc.' to indicate uncultivated or for various reasons rarely to be encountered. Assuredly some revisions will be needed if later editions ever are called for.

## Distinguishing Features

A modest knowledge of botany is needed in order to work the keys: an understanding of the organs of plants, how they lie in relation to one another, and how they may have been transformed. Technical terms needed to describe them will be found in the glossary on p. 235. Succulents come in all shapes and sizes. The diversity is bewildering, but a source of endless joy to the collector. Some succulents look little different from conventional plants except for a thickening of the leaves (Figs. 1.1, 1.2). Others may have become so altered in the course of evolution that it is hard at first to realize that they are living plants at all, and they may be fancifully likened to futuristic sculpture, lumps of rock, clusters of fruit or pebbles, and so on. Yet all these are derived by modification of the same three basic organs, *leaves*, *stems* and *roots*, plus a fourth source, *surface appendages*.

Leaves may be packed tightly on a shoot so as to overlap like tiles (Fig. 7.3) or like the scales of a pine cone; they may be spiralled in rosettes

**Figs. 1.1-1.7  Supposed lines of evolution of the main life forms in succulents: 1.2-1.4 water stored in leaves; 1.5-1.7 water stored in stems**

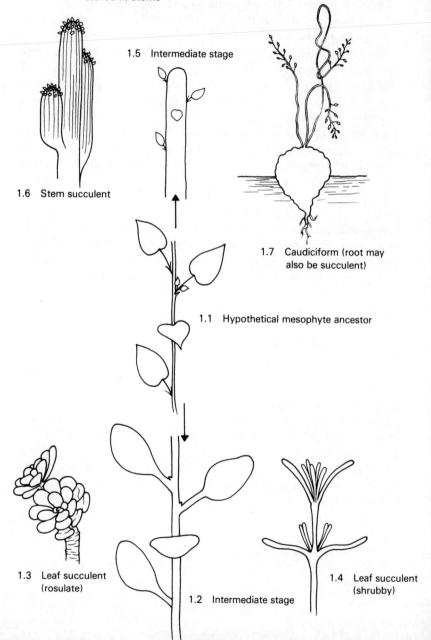

1.5  Intermediate stage

1.6  Stem succulent

1.7  Caudiciform (root may also be succulent)

1.1  Hypothetical mesophyte ancestor

1.3  Leaf succulent (rosulate)

1.2  Intermediate stage

1.4  Leaf succulent (shrubby)

(Figs. 1.3, 7.4) which have a flower-like form. The more nearly an object approaches a sphere in shape, the smaller will be its surface to volume ratio, and hence the less water it will evaporate. We see all stages of this, ending up in solid, chunky single leaves (Fig. 7.5) and united leaf pairs (Fig. 7.6).

In all these types the water-storing tissue is concentrated in the foliage and the stems remain relatively slender or undeveloped. We call such plants **leaf succulents**, and they comprise the first of three main life forms in succulents. The second is **stem succulents** (Figs. 1.5–6, 7.7–10) derived by progressive reduction of foliage and transfer of water storage to the enlarged stems, which are also green when young and take over the function of leaves as factories for manufacturing food in sunlight. All stages can be recognized down to the complete suppression of leaves, and again the climax development is a spherical body. The flattened, fleshy stems (**phylloclades**) of *Epiphyllum* and some species of *Rhipsalis* and *Euphorbia* are often mistaken by the uninitiated for leaves. They can be distinguished by their incipient buds around the edges or over the surface, from which can arise further stems or flowers. No leaf produces a flower, or buds of any sort, except for a few kalanchoes, which produce tiny vegetative buds round the margins. But here we have no doubt that the organ is a leaf because of its blade (**lamina**) and leaf-stalk (**petiole**) which separates freely at the base when the leaf drops.

The third main group, **caudiciform succulents** (Fig. 1.7), exploits a division of labour: short-lived, non-succulent, leafy shoots during the growing season, combined with a non-green, perennial basal storage organ (**caudex**) at or partly below ground level. Once more there is a diversity of forms (Figs. 7.11–14): each of the three groups in its own way meets the necessities for water economy and a short burst of growth between long rests.

A few plants combine features of two or all three of the above groups. These cause trouble in the making of keys, but if the reader is unable to decide in which section a particular plant fits, he should try either lead: the answer will appear under both. In dealing with living organisms we expect to find exceptions to most man-made rules.

## Flowers

Whereas the vegetative body of succulents is often very distinct from that of mesophytic plants, the flowers have few unique features that set them apart. They are pollinated by the same range of insects, birds and sometimes bats and they display the same range of attractive and protective devices. To anyone unfamiliar with dissecting flowers and learning the names of their parts, a start can well be made with the bloom of *Crassula* (Fig. 1.8) or other genus of Crassulaceae—structurally one of the simplest. Each flower is seen to be composed of four concentric whorls of parts, successive whorls alternating with one another in their insertion, and containing the same number of parts (**isomerous**), in this case five. The parts are all free—that is, not joined to one another (**connate**).

Commencing at the outside we have the **receptacle** (Fig. 1.9) supporting the floral envelope or **perianth** (**perigon**). If its members are all alike we call them **tepals**, but here we have a **calyx**, which serves as protection for the bud, made up of green and more or less leaf-like **sepals** (Fig. 1.10), and an inside **corolla**, coloured and attractive to insects, made up of **petals** (Fig. 1.11). Next come one (or two) alternating whorls of **stamens**, the male organs of the flower (Fig. 1.12). Each is composed of a stalk (**filament**) bearing at its top an **anther** (Fig. 1.13) which splits to release the dustlike **pollen grains**. At the centre stands a single whorl of **carpels**, the female organs (Fig. 1.14). Each is like a miniature pea pod (Fig. 1.15): the husk is the wall of the carpel and the peas are the eggs or **ovules** (Fig. 1.16) inside. The apex is drawn out into a **style** tipped by a usually brushlike and adhesive receptive area, the **stigma**. For seed to set, pollen must be conveyed from the anther to stigma (preferably on a different plant of the same species) where each grain germinates, pushes a tube down the style and into the ovule, where fertilization is effected by union of its nucleus with one inside the ovule. After fertilization the floral parts wither and fall, and the carpels enlarge as the ovules within them develop into **seeds**. In some succulents (most Cacti, Fig. 14.4, or Vitaceae) the fruit is fleshy and attractive to animals, who eat the flesh and inadvertently distribute the seeds, either by rejecting the 'pips' *in situ*, or by swallowing them and voiding them undamaged at some distance from the parent plant. In most, however, as in all the Crassulaceae (Figs. 18.4-5), the fruit is dry and breaks apart (**dehisces**) allowing the fine seed to be thrown out to the wind. Mesembryanthemaceae have a water-dispersal mechanism all their own (Figs. 28.3-5).

The Crassulacean flower is described in some detail because it can be taken as basic in interpreting the flowers of other Families, some of the most distinctive of which are figured here alongside the appropriate description of the Family. Although so varied in appearance, even the most complicated blooms can be related back to the same prototype, from

**Figs. 1.8-1.16   The parts of a typical flower (based on *Crassula*)**

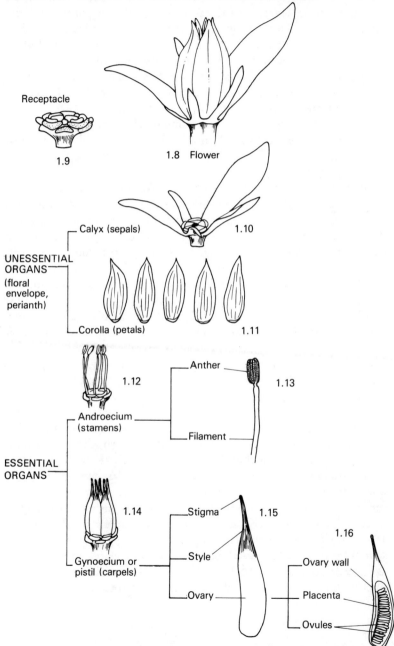

Receptacle

1.9

1.8   Flower

Calyx (sepals)

1.10

UNESSENTIAL
ORGANS
(floral
envelope,
perianth)

Corolla (petals)

1.11

1.12

Androecium
(stamens)

Anther

1.13

Filament

ESSENTIAL
ORGANS

1.14

Gynoecium or
pistil (carpels)

Stigma

1.15

Style

Ovary

Ovary wall

1.16

Placenta

Ovules

which, presumably, they evolved. The sequence of parts is unvarying, with the female organs in the centre surrounded by males and the perianth outside; but there can be alterations to function and symmetry:

    (1) Adjacent parts can unite, sepals and petals can join to form a tube to which the stamens may also be attached.

    (2) Parts can be variously transformed—stamens can lose their anthers and function as stiff hairs (**staminodes**) or become adapted as scales secreting nectar (**nectaries**).

    (3) A radially symmetrical (**actinomorphic**) flower can become lop-sided (**oblique-limbed**) and finally bilateral, divisible into two mirror-image halves only in one, usually vertical, plane (**zygomorphic**).

To examine samples of increasingly specialized flowers, we can compare our *Crassula* with the flower of Commelinaceae (Fig. 15.1–4), which has parts in threes (**trimerous**) rather than fives (**pentamerous**). Here the three carpels are united into a single, three-celled **ovary**. A further modification in Dioscoreaceae (Figs. 21.1–10) is separation of the sexes. One plant will bear flowers with only stamens and a tiny knob where the ovary would be expected to stand; another has a functional ovary but six tiny knobs representing rudiments of missing stamens. We call this condition **dioecy**, and two plants of opposite sex are needed if you hope to set seed. Elsewhere we find separate male and female flowers borne on the one plant, as in some Cucurbitaceae: this is called **monoecy**.

In Liliaceae (Figs. 27.1–3) the flowers of *Aloe* are also trimerous, but the perianth is tubular and pendent, usually bright red or yellow, and copious nectar is secreted—an adaptation to bird pollination.

Portulacaceae (Figs. 34.1–3) have open, bowl-shaped flowers, un-selective as regards visitors, but markedly **anisomerous**—that is, having different numbers of parts in each whorl: typically two sepals, five petals, numerous stamens, and three stigmas. The carpels are not only united with one another, but the whole ovary is more or less sunken below the level of insertion of the calyx and corolla: we call it **perigynous** when half-sunken, as in the *Portulaca* illustrated, and **epigynous** when completely inferior. By contrast, the condition where the carpels stand above the level of insertion of the floral envelope is called **hypogyny**.

In the two largest Families of succulents, the Mesembryanthemaceae (Fig. 28.1) and Cactaceae (Fig. 14.2), the most noticeable floral feature is the large and indefinite number of petals and stamens. In some cacti the stamens

**Figs. 1.17-1.18  A complicated insect-trap flower:**
              *Ceropegia distincta* ssp. *haygarthii*

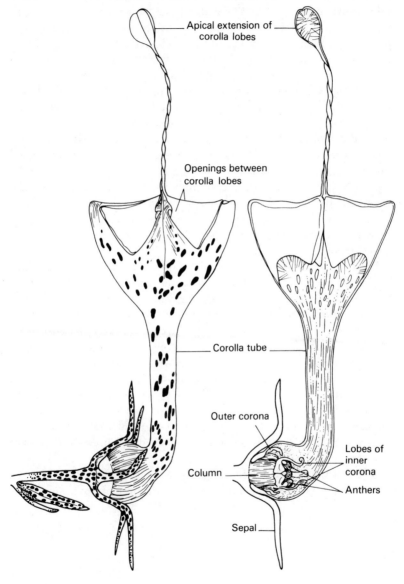

Apical extension of corolla lobes

Openings between corolla lobes

Corolla tube

Outer corona

Lobes of inner corona

Column

Anthers

Sepal

1.17   Flower in profile ( × 3)                    1.18   Flower halved ( × 3)

run to thousands in a single bloom. Both Families have an epigynous ovary, and in most cacti there is a tubular extension above it (**receptacle tube** or **hypanthium**) (Fig. 37.63) that bears numerous spirally arranged organs, beginning as tiny scales near the bottom, and grading imperceptibly through sepals into white or coloured petals at the mouth of the bloom. A unique feature of the Family is the presence of hairs and sometimes bristles, spines and areoles on this receptacle tube.

An altogether more complicated flower structure is to be found in the stapelia Family, Asclepiadaceae (Figs. 11.1–5), associated with pollination by flies. At first sight, a *Ceropegia* bloom (Figs. 1.17–18) has little in common with that of *Crassula*. The only similarity is the five obvious narrow sepals at the base of the bloom. The five petals are joined into an elaborate vase- or lantern-like structure with five small slits at the top by which the flies gain access, and sometimes a further tassel-like extension that no doubt makes the flower more visually attractive and recognizable. The five stamens are carried up on a **column** that arches over the top of the two, free carpels. The pollination mechanism is discussed more fully on p. 87.

Finally, mention should be made of two very large and successful, worldwide Families in which floral evolution has taken a different turn. What looks like a single bloom (Figs. 16.1–6) turns out to be made up of a large number of tiny flowers (**florets**) massed into heads and surrounded by a protective envelope of floral leaves (**bracts**). We call such a structure a **pseudanthium** ('false flower') and in popular parlance it should be referred to as a flower-head, not as a flower. Biologically it has certain advantages over a single large bloom. In the Compositae we even find actinomorphic and zygomorphic florets in the same flower-head, the latter contributing a petal-like effect round the outside. In Euphorbiaceae (Figs. 22.1–4) the bracts are often coloured and petal-like. The structure of both these is discussed in more detail under the relevant chapters.

The functioning of flowers as agents of fertilization and seed set is a fascinating subject, but outside the scope of the present work.

# CHAPTER 2

# How Plants are Classified

'Knowing things means bringing things under classes. To classify things you must define what is essential to them, what is their idea or form.'

*(Farrington)*

A **taxonomist** (or **systematist**—the word means much the same) is one who arranges things in order, forming in the process what we call a **system**. Classification is thrust upon us in all walks of life where we encounter similar objects too numerous to remember individually. The bibliophile reaches a point when he can no longer find the book he wants, so he sorts them into groups, perhaps according to author or perhaps to subjects—fiction and non-fiction—the latter being sub-divided as historical, scientific, and so on. In either case he is selecting properties that would help him most to find the book he wants: 'maximum retrieval' we would say. Another type of collector might arrange the same volumes according to century of publication, or style of binding, to suit his own special interests. These we refer to as **special purpose classifications,** or **artificial systems** where a single feature like colour of binding is given greater weight than all the others. Of all possible classifications, the best all-round one (i.e., the one most suited to a reference library) would be the one that serves as many readers as possible. In practice, a combination of subject matter and author name usually meets this need. It has the advantage that a single author usually writes on one topic, and a single subject often brings together the works of one author.

Similar principles apply to the classification and identification of plants. The first Peruvian who noticed that tomatoes with red or yellow fruits were good to eat, and that others with purple or white fruits were distasteful or poisonous, was recognizing a taxonomic character and making a simple classification into two groups. A **character** (strictly

11

speaking, a **characteristic**) is any property that is considered sufficiently constant and definable to serve as a means of distinction. The same set of plants can be classified in many ways: as annuals or perennials, as alpines, aquatics, succulents, and so on. But the most universally useful (or **natural**) classification is that which brings together plants having most features in common with one another, and separates one group from another with which it shares fewer characters. Thus attention is directed to the search for as many characters as possible to enable our classification to store the maximum amount of information. The better the classification, the more closely it will reflect the natural similarities and differences in nature as we see them, and the greater its value will be in the retrieval of information. The closer, too, will our system be likely to reflect lines of descent during evolution, for two groups that have diverged from each other relatively recently can be expected on average to show more features in common than others of earlier divergence. A system built upon observable features of the living plants is called a **phenetic** system, as distinct from a **phylogenetic (phyletic)** system which purports to show lines of descent from fewer common ancestors. In succulents we are almost wholly concerned with the former, since we have no fossil record and are as little able to retrace actual genealogies as we would be able to recreate a tree by merely seeing the tips of the branches.

## Units and Hierarchy

A glance at the English countryside will reveal that the different kinds of weeds and wild flowers do not intergrade, but fall into groups of different levels of distinctness. Primroses are distinguishable from cowslips, although they have many features in common. The creeping jenny is rather different, and dandelions much more so, although all are herbs with yellow flowers. In botanical language, primroses all belong to the one species, *Primula vulgaris*, and cowslips to another, *Primula veris*, although both are within the same genus, *Primula*. Creeping jenny belongs to an allied genus, *Lysimachia*, but all three are members of the primrose Family, Primulaceae. Finally, dandelion (*Taraxacum*) because of its completely different flower structure belongs to an unrelated Family, Compositae. Features of flower, fruit and seed are most valued in classification because they change less than, say, leaf size and shape under different growing conditions.

Species, genus and Family are successive ranks up the hierarchy of categories whereby the botanist classifies and pigeonholes the animate world around him. It is this limitation of the human brain that we cannot take in a random array of objects that leads to a 'box-within-box' method of filing our images. A table of the main categories and their names will be found on p. 19 and will be further discussed when considering nomenclature. Here we need consider only the definition of these categories or **taxa**, as they are called, a **taxon** being a taxonomic group of any rank. None of them can be precisely defined, although the majority of taxonomists throughout the world come to pretty much the same average concepts.

The **species** is taken as the basic unit—the brick from which classifications are built. Typically it is made up from one or usually many populations in which the individual plants interbreed and are completely interfertile; when cross-pollinated to individuals of another species no seed is set or, if it is, the hybrid nearly always shows reduced fertility— sometimes total sterility. Species come true from seed with all characters regarded as diagnostic, although overall there may be great diversity among individuals. Thus they persist in time as well as in space. For the remaining levels of the hierarchy it is wisest merely to say that a **genus** is a 'group of species more closely related to one another than to the species of any other genus', and so on up the scale, without being more precise about degrees of difference.

## How do we Classify?

Whereas there is general agreement on the merits of an all-purpose phenetic classification, the size of units adopted is controversial. This arises from basic differences in approach, as the following example will show. Suppose we recognize in the genus *Furniture* two species: *chair* and *bed*. There will be many and diverse examples of both species, but the system works well until we encounter something that has the characters of both a *chair* and a *bed*. What is to be done? There are four possibilities. If the phenomenon is rare, expediency may best be served by including it as a 'variety' of a *chair* or a *bed*, stretching the definition of either in order to include it. Another opinion would claim that the occurrence of an intermediate shows that the two species *chair* and *bed* are not really distinct after all, and must be lumped together into a single, large and

## Conflicting Attitudes to Classification

| Splitting | Lumping |
|---|---|
| *Advantages*<br>1. Units small, more easily recognized and defined.<br><br>2. Differences emphasized rather than similarities.<br>3. Attractive to nurserymen and collectors. | *Advantages*<br>1. Units larger and fewer, with fewer names to remember (especially binomials).<br>2. Similarities emphasized rather than differences.<br>3. Attractive to writers of encyclopaedias and floras.<br>4. Space-saving in books, which are accordingly cheaper. |
| *Disadvantages*<br>1. Tendency to magnify minute or inconsistent characters in order to justify segregations.<br>2. Surfeit of names, difficult to grasp and remember.<br><br>3. Danger of inflation and general debasing of hierarchy whereby everything ends up with higher rank than before.<br>4. Books become weightier, more expensive and more difficult to consult. | *Disadvantages*<br>1. Tendency to ignore or overlook real points of difference.<br>2. Units composite and definable only on combinations of characters; exceptions must be allowed for.<br>3. Difficult to do consistently and know where to draw the line. |

variable species. The fourth approach is to split off a new 'species' for the intermediates: *sofa* or *settee* perhaps.

There are merits and demerits in all four procedures. Which one adopts depends on personal preference and an overall knowledge of each particular situation. The larger the taxon, the more difficult it becomes to comprehend and the greater the search for characters by which to break it up. But where does one draw the line, and what constitutes a 'good' character? We can segregate botanists into two opposing camps, the 'lumpers', who favour a few, broadly defined units, and the 'splitters' who prefer many, small, atomic units. Since this division of opinion underlies much of the controversy over rival classifications today, the table opposite sets out in some detail the points in favour of each, and those against.

In seeking for guidelines, about the only one we can find is that we should try to be consistent, avoiding finely divided units in one taxon if its neighbour is much less finely divided. Thus, in Cactaceae, it would be illogical to accept the splitting up of *Borzicactus* into *Matucana*, *Arequipa*, *Loxanthocereus*, *Hildewintera* and all the other fine segregates if at the same time one accepted *Echinopsis* in the broad sense to include *Trichocereus*, *Helianthocereus* and so on. Uniformity across the board should be the watchword.

It so happens that in the past, for a variety of reasons, succulents have suffered more than their share of extreme splitting by comparison with related non-succulent Families. Thus the *Cactus Lexicon* of Backeberg (1978) recognizes no less than 233 'atomized' genera—nearly three times as many as in the moderately conservative synopsis of Hunt (see Chapter 14). Since this oversplitting is now being increasingly recognized, in the present book the more conservative classifications have been favoured, indicating in synonymy the names split off by others.

## Stability or Flexibility?

A botanical classification is in a way a summation of all the knowledge we have about the plants involved. The more facts we know, the better fitted we should be—with or without the aid of computers—to arrange the units to show similarities and differences. And the more data that are inbuilt in the system, the greater its predictive value becomes. The present century has seen dramatic increase in the raw materials of classification—not only in numbers of plants available for study, but in the kind of data we can extract from them. Evidence is now sought from many disciplines: morphology, anatomy and phytogeography; cytology can provide chromosome data; light and electron microscopy reveal small features and surface patterning, and biochemistry can add further information at the molecular level. Classification is never static: perfection always eludes us, and we have to accept that new advances mean adjustments to the system. Unfortunately, as we shall see, they often also mean changes of names and supplanting of the familiar by the unfamiliar.

Much of the next chapter is devoted to the evaluation of these changes of classification as manifest in renaming.

Perhaps the extent of name-changing is exaggerated. There is always an outcry at the rechristening of a favourite garden flower, while many hundreds of others suffer no change. In defence it might be pointed out that plant names are not the only ones to change. An atlas today is out-of-date almost before it is published because of alterations in names of countries, and in everyday life ladies expect to have their names changed at least once—an event that rarely arouses hostility or insistence that Mrs. Brown continue to be called Miss Smith, but is usually celebrated with universal rejoicing!

**Fig. 3.1** *Lophophora williamsii* ( × ½ )
A cactus by any other name . . .

# CHAPTER 3

# How Plants are Named

'If you know not the names, the knowledge of things too is wasted.'

*(Isidorus)*

The names given to plants are recognized as being of three types. Consider the following: dumpling cactus, peyote, peyotl, Rauschgift-kaktus, Schnapskopf, *Lophophora williamsii* Coulter, *Lophophora williamsii* var. *diffusa*, *Lophophora williamsii* 'Cristata'. All these refer to one botanical species, as defined on p. 13, and illustrated in Fig. 3.1. The first five are **common** or **colloquial names**, part of the language of the country in which they are used. Peyote and peyotl are the old Mexican names for our plant in its country of origin. English-speaking races call it the dumpling cactus because of its appearance. The fourth and fifth names ('intoxicant cactus' and 'brandy head') are favoured by the Germans in allusion to the intoxicant alkaloids it contains. All these names are of national rather than international usage, although peyote is understood in many countries outside of Mexico now. There are many more common names and variant spellings on record for this one species.

In theory, there is no reason why common names could not be coined and standardized in just the same way as is described below for scientific binomials. Indeed, several attempts to do this have been made: see, for instance, the book by Kelsey and Dayton (1942). But English is much less concise and convenient than Latin for coining words, and the objection would always arise that such a method favoured one nationality more than others.

For universal acceptance we refer to the **scientific name**: *Lophophora williamsii* Coulter, which is understood by botanists throughout the world. It is **binomial**—that is, composed of two parts: a **generic name** (*Lophophora*) followed by a **specific epithet**, *williamsii*. The former comes from the Greek *lophos*, a crest, and *phoreo*, to bear, and refers to the hairy crown of the plant. The latter commemorates C. H. Williams, an English plant collector in Bahia in the 1860s. 'Coulter' is J. M. Coulter, the botanist first responsible for this binomial; the author of the name, as we would say. This binomial method of naming plants is not unlike our own system of Christian and surnames, except that the order is reversed—a plant's surname comes first—and 'John Smith' applies to one individual person, whereas *Lophophora williamsii* covers the whole species—millions, no doubt, of individual cacti.

A species can, if desired, be subdivided into smaller units to give recognition to distinct patterns of variation within it. Thus, *L. williamsii* var. *diffusa* is based upon an isolated community of plants from the State of Queretaro that are distinct in the shape of their tubercles and biochemically, but not sufficiently so to warrant status as a separate species. A species is taken to be the sum of all its included subspecies, varieties and forms, etc.

The third type of name is the **cultivar name**, illustrated here by *L. williamsii* 'Cristata'. 'Cultivar' is a shortening of 'cultivated variety' and applies to plants artificially maintained in horticulture but not (usually) established in the same way as species in the wild, although they may have been found there in the first place (p. 38). This is an uncommon, crested or fasciated variant of the dumpling cactus which has little future in the wild but can be multiplied by grafts or cuttings and kept going indefinitely for the benefit of collectors. Cultivars are often mutations, such as *Echeveria gibbiflora* 'Carunculata' (with curious excrescences on the leaves) or *Senecio kleinia* 'Candystick' (with decorative pink and cream-striped foliage). Others are hybrids, as for example *Echeveria* 'Perle von Nürnberg' (*E. gibbiflora × potosina*).

Note that the three types of name are distinguished typographically: the common names are written and treated like ordinary nouns without a capital initial (in English, at least); scientific names go in italics with a capital to the generic name only (capitalization is permissible for specific epithets derived from personal names, but very few do this nowadays); cultivar names go in Roman type with an initial capital and are either enclosed in single (not double!) quotes or preceded by the abbreviation 'cv.' (but not both!).

## Scientific Names and Categories

Scientific names are in Latin or Latinized form—that is, adapted from Greek or any other language, with appropriate endings and connecting vowels. A knowledge of Latin is immensely helpful in understanding the meaning and formation of plant names. Indeed, it is essential to the taxonomist since much of the older literature and all new descriptions are in Latin. Latin is less frequently taught in schools than formerly, but there is an excellent handbook by Stearn (1966) designed especially for the botanist and covering all the terminology and grammar he is likely to need. It can be highly recommended, along with the books by Ivimey-Cook (1974) and Smith and Stearn (1972).

The 'box-within-box' system of classification, explained in Chapter 1, requires names at different levels up the hierarchy, and to some extent the rank of the name is indicated by a standardized ending (suffix). Thus *-ales* indicates an Order and *-aceae* a Family, and so on. There are eight exceptions to the Family rule, sanctioned by long usage: the only two likely to interest lovers of succulents are Compositae, for which the alternative Asteraceae can be used by those who prefer uniformity, and Labiatae, with alternative Lamiaceae.

A synopsis of the main taxa is set out below, taking our dumpling cactus as an example.

|  |  |  | *Suffix* |
|---|---|---|---|
| KINGDOM | Vegetable |  |  |
| DIVISION | Spermatophyta | Flowering Plants | — phyta |
| ORDER | Caryophyllales |  | — ales |
| FAMILY | Cactaceae | Cactus Family | — aceae |
| SUBFAMILY | Cactoideae |  | — oideae |
| TRIBE | Cacteae |  | — eae |
| SUBTRIBE | Cactinae |  | — inae |
| GENUS | *Lophophora* | Dumpling cactus |  |
| SPECIES | *L. williamsii* |  |  |
| VARIETIES | *L. williamsii* var. *williamsii*, var. *diffusa*, etc. |  |  |

Additional categories can be interpolated into the above system where needed. For example, a large genus can be divided up into subgenera, a subgenus into sections and a section into series. But the sequence is immutable: a species must not be divided into tribes, and so on. It should be noted that certain much-used words have a special significance in systematic botany: 'family', 'tribe' and 'form', for instance. Others, such as 'kind', 'sort' and 'group' have no such special rank. Gardeners frequently use the former words in a loose sense, speaking of 'the dahlia family' when they mean the genus *Dahlia*; the dahlia Family is the whole of Compositae. One should be careful when writing to use the former words only when their precise meaning is wanted, and to stick to neutral words of the latter type everywhere else.

The name of a species, as we have seen, is binomial; names of higher taxa are uninomial, a single word, but mostly with a special ending declaring the rank. Names below specific level are of three or more words and can become quite a mouthful. Too much faith should not be placed in names like *Sedum album* L. subsp. *gypsicolum* Maire var. *glanduliferum* Ball forma *purpureum* Pau & Font y Quer. Although the Codes place no restriction on the number of subordinate categories that can be recognized, human perceptibility does, and the botanist who claims to be able to perceive so many fine shades of difference below species level is as much an optimist as the composer who marks his score ppppppp and pppppppp! In normal usage, the above name is abridged to *Sedum album* f. *purpureum*, but it must never be rendered as '*Sedum purpureum*'.

## The Botanical Code

Mention of Codes leads naturally to a formal introduction to them. The naming of wild plants is governed by the International Code of Botanical Nomenclature, known as the Botanical Code or I.C.B.N.; that of cultivated plants by the International Code of Nomenclature for Cultivated Plants, usually referred to as the Horticultural Code (p. 38).

The Botanical Code begins with six Principles epitomizing its main features, followed by seventy-five Articles—the 'rules' themselves—and sundry Recommendations. The Articles are obligatory and, unless otherwise stated, retroactive—that is, they must be followed by present-day workers and any past names not in conformity with them must be adjusted. The Recommendations, as the word implies, are not obligatory, but should be heeded as far as possible. One cannot be prosecuted for disobeying the Codes; the penalty is merely that your efforts can be ignored and may have to be done all over again—usually by someone else with better things to do.

Zoology has its own Code, and the same binomial can be used for a plant and for an animal; confusion is unlikely. But within the Plant

Kingdom, the aim is one name and one name only for each taxon—within the bounds of the system of classification in use.

## Linnaeus and the Binomial

1753 is taken as the starting point for scientific names of flowering plants, corresponding to the publication of the first edition of Linnaeus's *Species Plantarum*. Since this contains no descriptions of genera, the species described in it are associated with the separate generic descriptions in his *Genera Plantarum*, Edn. 5, of 1754. Carl Linnaeus (Carl von Linné) was a great Swedish naturalist who was born in 1707 and died in 1778. He brought order out of chaos by devising a simple classification system for all plants based on flower parts; he standardized terminology and nomenclature, and provided convenient binomials which have stood the test of time to this day and eventually replaced the older, cumbersome and haphazard multiverbal names. Thus, the 'Stonecrop with flattish, serrated leaves, a leafy corymb and erect stem' (*Sedum foliis planiusculis serratis corymbo folioso caule erecto*) was shortened by Linnaeus to the much more convenient *Sedum telephium* L. The greatest asset of a binomial is the amount of information it conveys in a minimal space. Consider one example: *Crassula arborescens* (Mill.) Willd. A botanist encountering this name for the first time in a book could pick up the following information:

1. It is a taxon of the rank of species.
2. It is a member of the genus *Crassula*, which gives him a mental image of herbaceous leaf-succulents with corymbs or panicles of small, often starlike flowers—in other words a rough idea of the sort of plant to expect.
3. It is a species distinct as *arborescens*—tree-like, so must be a good deal larger than average among crassulas.
4. It was named by Miller and subsequently reclassified by Willdenow, probably by transfer from another genus. 'Mill.' to a botanist means Philip Miller of the Chelsea Physic Garden, and a reference to his *Gardener's Dictionary* of 1768—the only edition of importance for binomial names—so at once we have a clue where to look for information. Similarly, 'Willd.' means Carl Ludwig Willdenow, a German botanist flourishing at the start of the nineteenth century, whose enlarged edition of Linnaeus's *Species Plantarum* would be the obvious starting point to search for further facts about this name.

Of course, not all binomials are as informative as this—I have chosen a good example—but one can see what a time-saver they can be.

The citation of authors' names following that of the plant gives extra precision where it is desirable to distinguish the same name used in different senses. Thus, *Agave paucifolia* Baker (1878) is a different species from *Agave paucifolia* Todaro (1877). Both names may be encountered, although only one—the earlier—is acceptable. To make things doubly clear one can write *Agave paucifolia* Bak. (1878) non Tod. (1877) or Tod. (1877) non Bak. (1878). In non-technical contexts, authors' names can be dropped.

The double-author citation quoted above—the former name in brackets followed by another—indicates a change of some sort, usually a transfer from one genus to another, or a change of rank. *Crassula arborescens* was first published as *Cotyledon arborescens* by Miller. Willdenow subsequently assigned it to the genus *Crassula*. Again, for brevity, the latter name is taken to be the more important and the former can be dropped.

Various other forms of citation will be encountered. A few examples suffice to explain some of the commonest:

1. *Pilocereus lateralis* Web. in Bois.

   Weber supplied the description and name, but it was published by Bois in his Dictionnaire d'Horticulture. Here Weber is acknowledged as the publishing author and his name should be retained if the citation is abridged.

2. *Digitorebutia* Frič & Kreuz. ex Buin.

   Buining here is the publishing author and provided the full description, but he credited the name to Frič and Kreuzinger who had suggested it earlier.

3. *Echinocacteae* K. Sch. emend. Buxb.

   Buxbaum amended this Tribe of Cactaceae from Karl Schumann's classification, retaining the type genus *Echinocactus*, but paring away others to narrow its scope. 'Sensu' meaning 'in the sense of' can alternatively be used when a name has been interpreted in different ways and one wants to indicate one particular author's concept of it.

4. *Portulaca grandiflora* hort. non Hook.

   What gardeners grow as 'Portulaca grandiflora' is considered by some as distinct from the wild species originally described by Hooker. 'hort.' means 'of gardens' and is best written with a small 'h' to distinguish it from the name of Sir Arthur Hort.

5. *Lobivia famatimensis* auct. non B. & R.

   'Auct. non' means 'of authors other than' and alludes to the fact that many people have misinterpreted Spegazzini's original 1921 description of *Echinocactus famatimensis*, on which this name is based. So we have two species: *Lobivia famatimensis* (Speg.) B. & R., and *L. famatimensis* auct. non B. & R. which was subsequently shown to be *L. densispina*.

6. 'Comb. nov.' or 'Stat. nov.' following a binomial means that it is a new combination, or a change of status, appearing in print for the first time. In all subsequent references to the name, these words are omitted: a name can be 'new' only once!

## Choosing the Name

Plant names can come from any source, although, as we have seen, they are treated as if Latin. Obviously it is best if the name is in some way descriptive of the plant's unique attributes: *Glottiphyllum* for a plant with tongue-shaped leaves, for instance, and *G. fragrans* for a species with scented flowers. The species epithet can be an adjective, which agrees in gender with the generic name, or a noun, which is either treated as indeclinable, or provided with a genitive ending. The name *Sempervivum* is a neuter word, hence *Sempervivum hirtum*; when this is transferred to the feminine genus *Jovibarba* the name becomes *Jovibarba hirta* accordingly. Deciding the gender of generic names can be a problem if it is not obvious from looking at past lists of the included species. Recommendation 75A of the I.C.B.N. gives helpful pointers, and the *Dictionary* of Smith and Stearn (1972) should also be consulted. It is not just a matter of giving the epithet the same ending as the generic name.

An especial pitfall is *Sedum rosea* DC., which looks as if it ought to be 'Sedum roseum': the pink stonecrop. Yet the name is correct. The explanation is that *rosea* is not an adjective here but a noun: the old pre-Linnaean genus *Rosea*, the name by which herbalists knew the roseroot. Linnaeus took it up and used it as a specific epithet to preserve the ancient connection, but it remains a noun and indeclinable. If written *Sedum Rosea* a clue to its origin would have been given—one of the rare instances where capitalization of specific epithets is advantageous.

Names can be commemorative, as in the *Lophophora williamsii* referred to above, or geographical, indicating the place of origin, as for example *Glottiphyllum buffelsvleyense*. Already we can sense dangers that names acceptable and easy to pronounce in one language may not be so in others! Since the supply of good descriptive names, and even of persons and places to honour, soon runs out, botanists may have to resort to other sources. Even anagrams are permissible, and good examples like *Lobivia* (from Bolivia) and *Mila* (from Lima in Peru) are at least better than long or ugly-sounding names (caconyms) like *Sempervivum dzhavachischvili* Gurgenidze, wished upon a hapless houseleek in 1969, or *Austroboreoheterocephalocereinae* Y. Ito, a subtribe of cacti proposed by a Japanese botanist, apparently in revenge for having such a short name himself. Although there are copious Recommendations that names should be short and easy to pronounce, the above cannot be rejected if in other respects they comply with the I.C.B.N. Thus the 'South/North' contradiction at the start of the second does not invalidate it, but, happily, the fact that it turns out to be a *nomen nudum* (p. 35) does, and we can safely dig a very long grave and bury it. These examples—and there are many more like them—serve as a dire warning to use care and forethought before rushing new names into print.

Again, the Code does not allow us to alter existing names just because they are incorrect: *Cereus peruvianus* does not come from Peru, but the name stands. We are allowed to amend only typographic or orthographic errors. Just what is meant by this can be seen from the examples cited under Article 73. *Opuntiaeflora* should be changed to *opuntiiflora* because the connecting vowels are wrong: the root is *opunti-* plus *-i-* plus *-flora*. But the generic name *Heurnia*, commemorating Justus Huernius, for evermore commemorates also Robert Brown's bad spelling. Only if the author himself subsequently calls attention to an error of this sort are we free to accept the change.

## Commemorative Names

Certain recommendations relate to the way in which commemorative names should be made. The following table summarizes some approved endings.

For generic names, the original spelling must be retained even when it contradicts these guidelines, as in, for example, *Stayneria* (not *Staynera*), and *Tillaea* (named after Tilli; not *Tillia*). For specific epithets, Art. 73 Note 3 treats variants as orthographic errors which should be corrected:

## Derivation of Commemorative Names

|  | Generic name | Specific epithet | |
|---|---|---|---|
|  |  | Named after a man | Named after a woman |
| Following a consonant (-er excepted) | Add -*ia* <br> *Duvalia* <br> (after Duval) | Add -*ii* or -*ianus*† <br> *bolusii* or <br> *bolusianus* <br> (after Harry Bolus) | Add -*iae* or -*ianus*† <br> *bolusiae* or <br> *bolusianus* <br> (after Mrs. H.M.L. Bolus) |
| Following -er or a vowel | Add -*a* <br> Exceptions: <br> Add -*ea* after -*a*; <br> Make no <br> addition after <br> -ea. <br> *Bursera* <br> (after Burser) <br> *Fockea* <br> (after Focke) | Add -*i* or -*anus*† <br><br> *meyeri* or <br> *meyeranus* <br> (after Rev. G. Meyer) <br> *herrei* or <br> *herreanus* <br> (after Hans Herre) | Add -*ae* or -*anus*† <br><br> *meyerae* or <br> *meyeranus* <br> (after Mrs. Meyer) <br> *bravoae* or <br> *bravoanus* <br> (after Helia Bravo Hollis) |

†Declined -*us*, -*a*, -*um*, as appropriate, to agree with gender of genus.

*craigi* to *craigii*, *herreianus* to *herreanus*, and *kupperianus* to *kupperanus*.

Note that the new name for a genus takes a feminine ending, even when named after a man: *Buiningia* rather than *Buiningius*.

Many other longer commemorative names are possible: *Herreanthus*, for instance, meaning 'Herre's flower', and *Meyerophytum*, meaning 'Meyer's plant'. In choosing a new name it is important to look around and avoid one that could readily be confused with existing names. A slip of the pen could so easily convert *Rebutia muscula*, for example, into the much commoner *Rebutia minuscula*. Other examples are *Opuntia polyantha* ('many-flowered') and *O. polyacantha* ('many-spined'); *Ferocactus hamatacanthus* ('hook-spined') and *F. haematacanthus* ('bloodred-spined'). A classic case is the two species of *Mammillaria* commemorating two different people named Schwartz and Schwarz respectively. So similar are these that the I.C.B.N. allowed the later published binomial, *Mammillaria schwartzii*, to be changed to avoid confusion with the earlier *Mammillaria schwarzii*. Similarly, the cactus genus *Winteria* could well be taken for *Wintera*, a South American shrub, both names being derived from the same personal name. Hence the former was renamed (pp. 34–35).

On the other hand, we are compelled to retain *Adenia* and *Adenium* (which can look very alike when not seen in flower), and *Echinopsis*, the cactus, and *Echidnopsis*, the stapeliad; also *Ruschia meyerae* and *Ruschia meyeri*, since they were named after a lady and gentleman respectively.

## Pronunciation

A mention is needed regarding the pronunciation of scientific names—a subject not covered by either Code and especially embarrassing to those who have not studied classical languages. Although we are assured that Latin is the language of science because it is dead (and hence favours no one nation more than another), logical, concise and universally acceptable, it is far from being uniformly spoken, as any delegate to an international botanical conference soon finds out. There are certain rules of thumb; they can be studied in Stearn's *Botanical Latin* pp. 53–56. But if strictly applied they give unfamiliar accents to some well-known names, and those derived from the names of people follow no rules at all excepting general euphony. Who, for instance, would know that *Caralluma dalzielii* is named after Dalziel who pronounced his name 'deel'? And in any case, which way should his plant be spoken?

## Publication and Priority

It has been an intrinsic feature of nomenclatural practice for over a century that strict priority is observed. Where two or more names compete, it is the earliest published that must be retained or reinstated, the remainder falling into synonymy. Whether this desire to avoid bias by honouring the first author was wise or not is open to question. Often it has led to a scramble to be first to name a desirable novelty, and the winning description may turn out to be the most scrappy and slipshod. However, this is not the place to argue the ethics of the Codes but to explain how they work in practice.

Priority depends upon time of publication, which next calls for our attention. First, publication must be **effective**. The Code tells us that 'publication is effected . . . by the distribution of printed matter (through sale, exchange or gift) to the general public or at least to botanical institutions with libraries accessible to botanists generally.' The number of copies is not specified: the original publication of the names *Gasteria* and *Haworthia* goes back to a pamphlet of 1809 of which only one copy is known to survive, but since more were undoubtedly circulated the publication is effective. Since 1953, publication in tradesmen's price-lists and non-scientific newspapers is not accepted, but mimeographed or photocopied magazines are. However, since easy access for consultation is prerequisite, it is obviously better if new names appear only in the better-class printed journals of wide circulation.

The exact dating of publications can be a problem. For instance, in 1973 two authors on opposite sides of the Atlantic published the same cactus name within four days of each other! It is often not enough to accept the date as printed on the title page. Jacobsen's well-known Lexicon was not effectively published until late April 1975, despite the date 1974 at the front. In critical cases one has to search around for review articles, or annotated copies in the larger libraries which sometimes give clues to the exact date. A most valuable work in this connection is Stafleu's *Taxonomic Literature*, which gives dates for many key works, including several published originally in parts.

**Valid** publication is publication according to the Articles of the Codes: a Latin diagnosis (after 1953) and citation of type (p. 29) (after 1958) for new taxa, and a full reference to the basionym (p. 33) in the case of a name change.

A **legitimate** name is one that is both effectively and validly published, and hence to be taken into account in considering issues of priority. If any of the above requirements are not met, the name is **illegitimate**. A species can have two or more legitimate names (p. 28), but only one—the **correct** name—applies at any one time within the framework of the classification in use.

Priority applies to taxa of all ranks from the level of Family downwards, but only within each rank: if the rank is changed, the name competes for priority at the new level. Ignorance of this is one of the commonest blunders and leads to vast wastage of efforts and confusion. To give an example, an author decides that *Lobivia rossii* Boed. 1933 is no more than a variety of *L. pugionacantha* Rose & Boed. 1931, so publishes the new combination *L. pugionacantha* var. *rossii* (Boed.) Rausch. However, in the synonymy he lists *L. rossii* vars. *carminata*, *salmonea* and *sanguinea*, all of Backeberg (1956). By changing the rank of *L. rossii* from species to variety, he should have taken up the earliest epithet available at the new rank—in other words, one of the above three varietal epithets. (Where two or more names are published simultaneously, as here, the first author who makes a choice must be subsequently followed.) Hence the combination *L. pugionacantha* var. *rossii* is illegitimate and a new combination must be made on the lines indicated.

Whereas insistence on conformity with this rule is the only way of avoiding nomenclatural anarchy, it must be admitted that it can lead to epithets with inappropriate meanings being forced upon a group. Thus the new variety of *L. pugionacantha* may not have flowers all carmine, pink or blood-red as the above three epithets imply. But in all such circumstances the meaning of names has to be treated as secondary.

Note that in no case does a binomial have priority—each of its components, the generic name and the specific epithet, is treated separately. *Graptopetalum paraguayense* (N.E.Br.) Walther has been variously classified as a *Cotyledon*, a *Sedum*, an *Echeveria* and a *Byrnesia*, and under various specific epithets: *arizonica*, *byrnesia*, *paraguayensis* and *weinbergii*. The correct name is arrived at by combining the earliest available specific epithet with the name of the genus to which the botanist (Eric Walther in this case) judged the plant to belong.

A further example of a change of rank is provided by the genus *Haworthia*, which is at present divided by Bayer into three sections. One of these, centred around *H. margaritifera*, has stout, almost aloe-like stalks supporting the flowers and is called, aptly if clumsily, Section Robustipedunculares. Suppose that a botanist decided that this section were so distinct that it merited recognition as a genus by itself. He would first have to hunt around and see if any name already existed at the rank of genus. As it happens, there is one: *Tulista* of Rafinesque 1840, with type *H. margaritifera*, which would therefore need to be taken up.

Since 1953 the following rule has applied: if two or more names are published simultaneously by the same author for one taxon (that is, based upon the same type), none of them is validly published. If a new *'Kalanchoe ruritanica'* were described, but referred to in the notes or picture captions as *'Bryophyllum ruritanicum'*, the author's indecision as to which genus he recognized would invalidate both names (such things do happen!). If, on the other hand, he headed the article *Kalanchoe*

*(Bryophyllum) ruritanica*, since *Bryophyllum* is regarded by some as a subgenus of *Kalanchoe*, this could be taken to mean that the real binomial is *Kalanchoe ruritanica* but that the author was indicating to which subgenus it referred, so there is no ambiguity.

Special circumstances apply when a new taxon is considered to be so distinct that it warrants a new, monotypic genus to itself, as for example *Tacitus bellus*. Here the author has a problem in describing the genus, since, until other species are discovered, he doesn't really know what its diagnostic features are as apart from those of the species. Hence the I.C.B.N. allows that a single description can cover both the genus and the species. But if two or more species are included, a separate description of the genus is obligatory.

It will be evident that an early need in the taxonomic study of any genus of plants is a list of all the binomials associated with it (synonyms and transfers to other genera, too) and the references to where they were originally published. This determines the application of the names. Access to a large library, such as those at Kew, the Royal Horticultural Society, the Linnean Society or the Natural History Museum in London, is essential. First publications of all names of genera and species of flowering plants can be located in the *Index Kewensis* (1895 and later); for succulents at any rank published since 1950 there is the annual *I. O. S. Repertorium* (1951 and later). Illustrations, up to 1940, can be traced in the *Index Londinensis* (1929–31, 1941), but under the name as published, which may not be correct now.

## The Type Concept

A valuable stabilizing influence in nomenclature is the type concept, introduced into the I.C.B.N. in 1930 but originating much earlier in the U.S.A. It works like this. When a modern author describes a new species or lower taxon for the first time, in addition to the diagnosis in Latin and whatever description he sees fit to add, he is obliged (since 1958) to cite an actual specimen of the species and where it is deposited. A living plant in somebody's collection will not do: it must be a herbarium specimen on a sheet or, since succulents resist compression into two dimensions, pickled or dried material. The reason for this is that it makes it very much easier for subsequent botanists to check the name if they see an actual specimen: the description alone may be ambiguous or lack vital details.

In the event of the species being later split up into two or more, the name always remains with that element selected as type.

The actual specimen chosen is called the **holotype**. Many such are lodged in herbaria of famous botanical gardens and museums, and because of their value are carefully documented and stored. Duplicates (**isotypes**) may be distributed to other herbaria. Where an author has specified no type, or the holotype is lost, one of his specimens or one from the original collection can be selected as **lectotype**, or, if no authentic material is available, a substitute (**neotype**) can be prepared. Once selected, the choice must be followed by others unless an error can be demonstrated. A change of type is normally possible only by conservation (p. 36).

A **clonotype** is a living clone (p. 39) propagated vegetatively from the same stock that provided the author with his holotype. Although, as we have seen, living types have no standing nomenclaturally, a clonotype should be especially treasured above unpedigreed specimens, and could provide a replacement in the event of loss of the holotype. The clonotype of *Sempervivum soboliferum*, the 'Hen and Chickens Houseleek', from Linnaeus's garden at Hammarby, is still in cultivation after more than two centuries.

Some very wrong ideas are current regarding the nomenclaturist's use of types. One is that the whole scheme is an anachronism based on the idea of fixity of species: everyone now knows that at any one time a species is the sum of all variations among many populations, so how can one specimen be selected as 'typical'? This is a confusion of ideas. A type specimen is not the same as a typical specimen; it may even be rather aberrant. This does not matter. Its sole function is as an anchor for the name. It must belong to some taxon, large or small, and that is the one with which the name is permanently associated.

Another bizarre notion is that an author selects his holotype first and then describes it in as minute detail as possible. This would really put the cart before the horse, and I think it will be evident from what has already been said that every individual plant would be in danger of ending up as a new species. Not even the most ardent splitter has so far demanded this!

The type of a species or any taxon below specific rank is an actual specimen. But the concept also extends up through the hierarchy, so that the name of a genus is tied to a single selected species, that of a Family to one genus, and so on. This is reflected in the names of certain ranks—

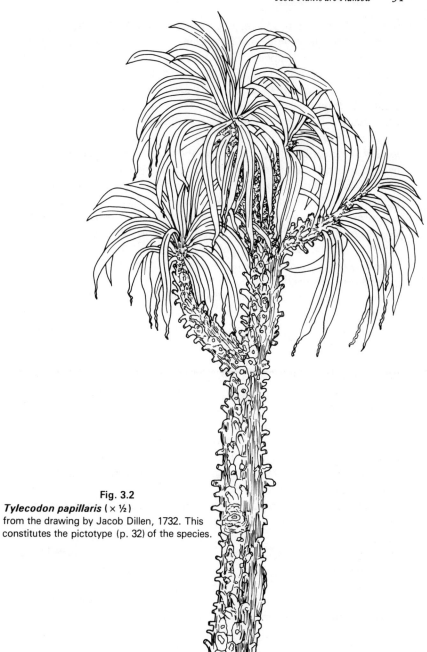

**Fig. 3.2**
*Tylecodon papillaris* ( × ½ )
from the drawing by Jacob Dillen, 1732. This
constitutes the pictotype (p. 32) of the species.

notably the subgenus and section within a genus and the ranks below specific level. Here the name of the element including the type repeats the name of the rank above, without an author citation. It works in this way. *Conophytum* Subg. *Conophytum* Sect. *Conophytum* tells us that we are dealing with that Section that includes the type species of the genus, *C. truncatum* N.E. Br., which hence retains its name no matter what changes are made to other sections and subgenera.

When Buining in 1968 first published the species *Notocactus uebelmannianus* Buin., he noted that about 15% of the plants observed had yellow flowers, the remainder red. There were other differences in fruit shape and seed size. He therefore named the yellow-blooming plants as forma *flaviflorus* Buin. Although he did not state as such, this act automatically created a second form, *Notocactus uebelmannianus* f. *uebelmannianus* for those plants with red flowers. Whatever other forms of *N. uebelmannianus* might subsequently be recognized, f. *uebelmannianus* remains attached to the type of the species.

Surprising discoveries can come to light when old and long-accepted names are checked back to their origin. For instance, collectors of succulent Compositae have long searched in vain for *Senecio papillaris* Sch. Bip., described in Jacobsen and many other reference books as having curiously tuberculate stems and long fleshy cylindrical leaves. Yet nothing in Compositae matching such a plant has been found anywhere in collections or in the wild. Is *S. papillaris* extinct, then, or long lost and awaiting rediscovery? Neither, as a search for its type revealed. The name is founded upon a species first described by Linnaeus in 1753, of which the type turns out to be not an actual specimen but a fine large engraved illustration (a **pictotype**, permissible under the Code in certain special circumstances) in a folio book of 1732 (Fig. 3.2). This picture is instantly recognizable as a plant long familiar in many collections and not even remotely related to *Senecio: Tylecodon* (or *Cotyledon*) *cacalioides*. In the absence of flowers Linnaeus had associated it with *Senecio kleinia*, a rather similar looking plant on the adjacent plate, and assumed it to belong to the same genus, and his error had gone undetected for over two centuries! Despite this, the epithet *papillaris* is validly published, and antedates *cacalioides* by 28 years, necessitating a rechristening for the plant as *Tylecodon papillaris* (Rowley 1979).

A name is illegitimate if it was superfluous when first published—that is, if it includes the same type as a taxon already named. For instance,

*Gymnopoma* N.E.Br. (March 1928) is a superfluous name for *Skiatophytum* L. Bol. (Jan. 1928), both being monotypic genera based upon the same type, *Mesembryanthemum tripolium* L.

## Name Changes

As pointed out on pp. 15-16, an inherent drawback of the binomial system is that a change in classification may necessitate a change of name. This can also result when names are found to have been published in contravention of the codes. Since anyone can reclassify plants, a species can accumulate a number of names, any one of which may be correct according to the system followed. Thus our *Lophophora williamsii* was first described as *Echinocactus williamsii* in 1845, was reclassified as *Anhalonium williamsii* in 1886, *Mammillaria williamsii* in 1891 and finally became *Lophophora williamsii* in 1894. Several other 'species' were meantime described under various of these generic names, although most people now agree to associate them all under the one name *L. williamsii*.

Normally when a species is transferred from one genus to another its specific epithet is retained unchanged, except for any necessary alteration of ending to make an adjective agree in gender with that of the new genus. However, this is impossible if the new binomial already exists for another plant. For example, when it became clear that *Frerea indica* was only a species of caralluma with leaves, the new combination *Caralluma indica* could not be used since there already existed another species, *Caralluma indica* N.E.Br. In the absence of any other available epithet, it was rechristened *Caralluma frerei* to preserve the original association with the naturalist Sir Henry Frere.

When a transfer or name change of this sort is made for the first time nowadays, the I.C.B.N. requires that after 1953 the older name (**basionym**) must be 'clearly indicated and a full and direct reference given to its author and original publication with page or plate reference and date.' (Art. 33.2). These are the commonest sources of nomenclatural transgressions if the above is not scrupulously adhered to. To take an example of what is required as a minimum, when it became apparent that *Stapelia margarita* was no species but a form of the long-familiar *S. pulvinata*, to legalize the new name a published statement was made to this effect:

**Stapelia pulvinata** Masson forma **margarita** (Sloane) Rowley
Syn. *S. margarita* Sloane in White & Sloane 'The Stapelieae'
Edn. I: 165, 1933.
*(Nat. Cact. Succ. J.* 28: 4, 1973)

Interpretation of the wording of Art. 33.2 has, unfortunately, given rise to differences of opinion. Some maintain that the basionym does not have to be actually stated but only indicated (i.e. with a reference, but the binomial need not be quoted). Some even reject the transfer if more than one page is cited, as for example '165-168' to cover the whole length of the first description. However, the important words to heed are 'clearly indicated' and with a 'full and direct' reference—that is, traceable and unambiguous. In any case, where there is doubt, the final sentence 'Bibliographic errors of citation do not invalidate the publication of a new combination' can be invoked to avoid rejection of 'near-misses'. Prior to 1953 the rules were less strict and one may have to be quite a detective to hunt out basionyms.

When two genera are merged, it is the earlier published name that must take priority. This can cause problems. Many cactophiles feel that *Eriosyce ceratistes* is nothing more than an outsize *Neoporteria* and that the two genera should hence be combined as one. However, the very small (perhaps monotypic) genus *Eriosyce* has fifty years priority over *Neoporteria* as a name, so this move would necessitate renaming over 60 species of *Neoporteria* as *Eriosyce*! The only way round this would be by conservation of the former name (see p. 36).

Where the same name has been independently given to different taxa, these duplicate names are referred to as **homonyms**. Thus, a Mexican stonecrop was named *Sedum platyphyllum* ('broad-leaved') by Alexander in 1942 and a Chinese one *Sedum platyphyllum* by Fu in 1951. By the rule of priority (Art. 11.3), the former name stands, and the later homonym had to be renamed (*Sedum fui*).

A **synonym** is a superfluous name, based either upon the same type (**nomenclatural synonym**) or on a different type (**taxonomic synonym**). In the latter instance personal judgement decides whether or not the two taxa are so much alike that they are best considered as one. Reference to any systematic work on succulents will often reveal long lists of synonyms, mostly a sorry reflection of too hasty publication of 'new species', or a conflict over the interpretation of genera. An example of nomenclatural synonyms is provided by *Winterocereus* Backeberg 1966 and

*Hildewintera* Ritter 1966, both being substitute names for *Winteria* Ritter (non *Wintera*, p. 26). Rejection of the later published of the two is automatic under the Code: *Hildewintera*, which appeared in print in January 1966, has precedence over *Winterocereus* which was not out until May 1966.

*Neoporteria nidus* B. & R., *N. multicolor* Ritt. and *N. senilis* Back. were described originally from different samples and therefore have different types. Although originally seen to be distinct-looking, subsequent exploration has revealed them as all belonging to one large and variable species. They are therefore treated as taxonomic synonyms and can be united under one name, for which the first-mentioned has priority. But this is not obligatory: a splitter can retain two or all three names, or alter the last two to subspecies, varieties or forms if desirable. Since we are already overburdened with names and synonyms, wilful tinkering is discouraged and changes involving names should be made with restraint and only if based on ample evidence—not merely to satisfy personal whims.

It would take up too much space to enumerate all the reasons why names sometimes have to change. Often a long-familiar name of a species is found upon checking to be a *nomen nudum*—that is, it has never been validly published but has come into use by the back door, so to speak. If, in the meantime, another name for the same species has been validated, that has to be reinstated, even although it may be less familiar or appropriate.

It will be evident from what has been said about the two types of synonym—nomenclatural and taxonomic—that one needs to know something of the background history before judging the spate of new names pouring from the press each year. Merely looking at them one has little idea which should be taken up at once, and which merely express flights of fancy or variations upon a theme. Well-documented nomenclatural changes, of the sort mentioned above, are best swallowed gracefully, however unpalatable at first, since if properly researched they are likely to be generally accepted and incorporated in future standard reference works. Changes for taxonomic reasons are more difficult to assess. A preference for large or small units (p. 14) comes into play. For growers and nurserymen content to follow an existing handbook the question hardly arises. As for the newly described species, a glance at the enormous lists of long-dead synonyms in genera such as *Melocactus* should be a

warning that all with prickles is not gold, and today's novelties soon
become tomorrow's deadwood.

## Name Conservation

Previous to 1900 it was recognized that slavish application of the Code
would lead to a large number of name changes and loss of many familiar
names because others, long forgotten, were found to have been
published earlier. In order to avoid this, it was decided to make it
possible to waive the rules in certain cases where a strong enough case
could be made for retaining the later, but invalid, name. As a result of
this, about two-thirds of the bulk of the present I.C.B.N. consists of lists
of *nomina conservanda* (conserved names), both Family names and
genera—among them a sprinkling of succulents: *Anacampseros*, *Bowiea*,
*Haworthia*, *Mammillaria*, *Melocactus*, *Pectinaria*, *Pedilanthus*, *Rhipsalis*,
and others. The present policy is to accept additions to the list only if a
large upheaval of names would result from reinstating the earlier name or
if the plants concerned are of considerable economic importance. Conservation can also be used to retain a particular spelling of a name, or to
exclude the type.

The procedure is to make out a case, giving full documentation and
pros and cons, which is published (usually in *Taxon*). It is then assessed
by an international committee and, if approved, comes up for final
judgement at the next Botanical Congress, held at five-year intervals. The
example of *Eriosyce* v. *Neoporteria* (p. 34) could be resolved if the latter
name were conserved. But an earlier proposal to conserve the name
*Malacocarpus* for use in Cactaceae (invalidated by the identical name in
another Family) came to nothing.

Unfortunately it has never been found practicable to conserve the
names of species, despite many efforts and numerous suggested methods.
Most of the changes needed have already been made, and most of the
early literature searched; it is hoped that the number of future changes
will steadily diminish. However, an innovation in the 1978 I.C.B.N.
(Art. 69) reads: 'A name must be rejected if it has been widely and
persistently used for a taxon not including its type. Names thus rejected
shall be placed on a list of *nomina rejicienda*.' This is at least a first step
towards eliminating names that have been a lasting source of confusion.
Procedure for proposing such names for rejection is the same as that set
out above for conservation.

# Hybrids

Hybrids are a problem to the taxonomist because they break down the lines of demarcation between species. They are no less of a problem nomenclaturally, since a hybrid obviously cannot be placed under the same binomial as either of its two parents. Hence special provision has to be made for the naming of hybrids, and since they can be of either wild or man-made origin, both Codes are involved.

A hybrid between two species can be represented by a formula name, thus: *Sempervivum arachnoideum* × *montanum*, where '×' is the sign of hybridity. For many purposes this name is adequate, and requires no formal publication. If, however, the cross is an important element of the flora, or horticulturally valued, it can be given a new binomial similar to that of a species but with the epithet prefixed by the sign '×'. For the above-mentioned cross the collective name is *Sempervivum* × *barbulatum* Schott. Such a name requires formal publication and typification just as does a species. It covers all descendants from the original, including back-crosses to either parent.

Since these two houseleeks are variable throughout their wide range, spontaneous hybrids from different areas where both grow together may look dissimilar and merit naming. In order to reserve terms like sub-species, variety and form for non-hybrid plants, the term **nothomorph** (abbreviated nm.) is used, so we have *Sempervivum* × *barbulatum* nm. *barbulatum* (the type), *S.* × *barbulatum* nm. *delasoiei*, *S.* × *barbulatum* nm. *noricum*, and so on. If it should be proved experimentally that *S.* × *barbulatum* is not, in fact, of the parentage stated, the Code requires that the name is retained in the new sense, and a fresh name would be needed for *S. arachnoideum* × *montanum*. If a species is proved to be a hybrid, or vice versa, the name remains but the '×' sign is added or removed as appropriate, without change of author citation.

Succulents differ from most other flowering plants in the ease with which plants of different genera can be crossed. Again, a formula name is often adequate: *Echeveria agavoides* × *Graptopetalum paraguayense*, for example. A new generic name can be coined, which must combine elements of the accepted names of the two parent genera—in the present case, × *Graptoveria*. All individuals of the above pedigree then fall under × *G. haworthioides*. Note the position of the sign of hybridity: it immediately precedes that part of the name that is 'hybrid'. '*Graptoveria* × *haworthioides*' would be wrong, as would '× *Sempervivum barbulatum*'.

Since it is not possible to draw up a description of a 'hybrid genus' like *Graptoveria* in anticipation of knowing all the crosses that might be made, hybrid generic names are treated as formulae and require only a statement of parentage to validate their publication.

Hybrid generic names have to be altered if the names of the parent genera change. If *Nopalxochia* is included in *Weberocereus*, × *Epixochia* (*Epiphyllum* × *Nopalxochia*) and × *Heliochia* (*Heliocereus* × *Nopalxochia*) will need to be rechristened.

In the epicacti, combinations of three, four and more genera occur, and combining all these generic names would lead to long and ugly-sounding words. If a name is needed, the I.C.B.N. prescribes the termination -*ara* added to the name of the breeder or a person associated with the plants. As yet there are no examples to cite from the succulents, which is perhaps just as well. Even more so than among wild plants, great restraint is needed in naming hybrids. One can easily touch off an explosion of naming as each and every possible combination becomes christened, as has happened in Orchidaceae. The literature becomes glutted with names, many of which are stillborn because the hybrid exists only as a single individual which is never propagated. Hence the right to name hybrids should be exerted only when they are important botanically or superior horticulturally and there is reasonable certainty of their being propagated and marketed.

## Names for Cultivated Plants

By comparison with the I.C.B.N., the horticultural Code is slimmer, easier to digest, and less stringent in its rulings. This reflects its readership of gardeners, florists and foresters rather than academics and professional botanists. Originally it formed a chapter of the botanical Code, but since 1953 it has led an independent existence since it was felt that cultivated plants differ in so many ways from their wild ancestors that their names and naming should be as different as possible to avoid confusion.

This explains the concept of the **cultivar** as the basic unit (p. 18), which is defined in full as 'an assemblage of cultivated plants which is clearly distinguished by any characters (morphological, physiological, cytological, chemical or others) and which, when reproduced (sexually or asexually), retains its distinguishing characters' (Art. 10). Another relevant term is **clone**, which is used for a group of individuals propagated vegetatively from a single individual and presumed to be all genetically identical. Thus a cultivar can be a single clone, or sometimes many; species, on the other hand, are by their nature only rarely a single clone. Cultivars with double flowers, or non-flowering crests, can only be multiplied asexually, and this is true of hybrids, sterile or fertile, which do not come true from seed. A cultivar is the lowest recognized category bearing a name; if two or more elements seem worthy of receiving names, they are treated as separate cultivars.

As an example we may cite *Gymnocalycium* 'Jan Suba', a fertile hybrid of unrecorded origin which has apparently been raised from seed for several generations and now breeds more or less true to type. Should any seedling prove superior and be taken up for commercial distribution, it is treated as a new cultivar, although it helps if the new name reflects its derivation, as 'White Jan Suba' or 'Striped Jan Suba', for example.

The cultivar is approximately the equivalent of the variety in botanical classifications, and the latter word is sometimes used in the sense of cultivar. But the practice should be discouraged in the interests of precision.

Sometimes we need a collective epithet for a group of cultivars having features in common—the outcome, perhaps, of one breeding programme. For these we can coin a group or **grex** name (*grex* means literally 'a flock'). Thus we speak of × *Echinobivia* Paramount Hybrids for a batch of *Echinopsis* × *Lobivia* crosses emanating from Johnson's Nursery in California. For maximum precision, individual cultivars can be cited in full as × *Echinobivia* (Paramount Hybrid) 'Stars and Stripes', and so on.

## Names of Cultivars

Since 1959, it has been the rule that names of cultivars must be fancy names differing from those used for wild plants. Latinized words like 'Grandiflorus' are out. Not more than three words are allowed in one name, and botanical terms like variety and form are banned, as are botanical names of genera and species. Various recommendations refer to the best method of setting out commemorative names. Thus, *Euphorbia* 'William Denton' is preferred to 'Wm. Denton', and 'Denton's Variety' would be rejected as a name.

In the discussion on the naming of hybrids (p. 37) it was indicated how wild hybrids of the same parentage could be named as nothomorphs under a common hybrid epithet. A parallel system operates for hybrid cultivars, which can be separately grouped under one blanket name. Thus all crosses between *Echeveria agavoides* and *E. elegans* fall under the collective name *E.* × *gilva* Walth. Since no cultivar name was given by Walther at the time, his clonotype was subsequently named 'Gilva', to distinguish it from a new mutation with bluer leaves called 'Blue Surprise'. For brevity one can write *E.* 'Gilva' or *E.* 'Blue Surprise'. But note that *E.* 'Gilva' is a single unvarying clone; *E.* × *gilva* covers several clones.

Prior to 1959, many cultivars were described and given scientific names as forms, varieties and even species, although not known to occur wild and of garden origin only. This is especially true of succulents, where the temptation to erect 'new species' often overrides the need to know where they came from in the first place. In order to avoid abundant renaming, the Code allows us to retain such names in Latinized form, but they are written as if cultivar names. By way of example, *Echeveria hoveyi* Rose was validly published with full honours as if it were a wildling, whereas we now know it to be a cultivar of uncertain, probably hybrid, origin. The name is therefore written *Echeveria* 'Hoveyi', without author citation. All variegated succulents originally named *variegatus*, and fasciations named *cristatus* or *monstrosus*, are best treated as cultivars. Adjectival names of cultivars of this type agree in gender with that of the genus. Thus, if *Senecio articulatus* 'Variegatus' is treated as a *Kleinia*, the name becomes *Kleinia articulata* 'Variegata'.

Just as the status of a taxon can be changed from species to cultivar, so the same name can be used both as a specific epithet and as a cultivar name. *Nopalxochia ackermannii* is a rather delicate and rare wild species of epiphytic cactus from Mexico; × *Heliochia* 'Ackermannii' is a vigorous intergeneric hybrid (*Heliocereus speciosus* × *Nopalxochia phyllanthoides*) of similar appearance that for a long time passed as the true species in collections until the distinction was pointed out.

## Publication

Conditions for the publication of new cultivar names are not so strict as for scientific names. No Latin diagnosis or type specimen is demanded (although the latter is undoubtedly desirable), and the only restrictions on the medium used are that, after 1958, it must be dated, at least as to year, and carry a description (in any language). Recommendations are parallel to those applying to species epithets, stressing the value of illustrations, notes on distinguishing features, and so forth.

A name that is a *nomen nudum* in the botanical sense can still be preserved as a cultivar name if appropriate to do so. The popular white-flowered glottiphyllum has been around for many years under the unpublished name *'Glottiphyllum album'*. It is probably a hybrid and unknown in the wild; we can therefore refer to it as *Glottiphyllum* 'Album'. Names cited as 'hort.' (p. 22) can be treated in similar fashion.

Unlike the situation for wild plants, where only one scientific name is allowed at any one time, with cultivars 'commercial synonyms' are permitted. These may be straight translations to suit different nationalities, or substitute or abridged names for ease of memorizing and pronunciation. The original name of the cultivar, however, takes precedence. Thus the red, chlorophyll-free mutant of *Gymnocalycium mihanovichii* var. *friedrichii* originated in Japan where its first cultivar name was 'Hibotan'. Introduced in the West as 'Rubra', it is now usually known in the U.S.A. as 'Mr. Redcap' and in Great Britain as 'Ruby Ball'.

Another difference from the I.C.B.N. is that a name can be used over again for a different cultivar, ten years or more after the previous bearer of the named is known to be extinct. Thus the name 'Magnificus' for an epicactus raised by Graessner in 1928 can stand provided that no plant comes to light of an earlier nineteenth century hybrid also called 'Magnificus'.

## International Registration Authorities

To lighten the burden on the user, trying to sort out proper usage of cultivar names, and to provide a central authority and court of appeal for conflicts over names, international registration authorities have been set up for many of the major groups of cereals, crop plants and flowers. They are charged with the publication of lists of approved names, and are authorized to make a choice when two or more names compete. Relatively few succulents have so far had the distinction of such official recognition. The international registration authority for aloes is in South Africa, that for epicacti in California, and the Sempervivum Society in England covers *Sempervivum* and *Jovibarba*. Prior to 1959, listing of a name by such a body is adequate to validate it even if no published description exists—the plants, presumably, do.

## A Great Future for Hybrids

As yet, hybrid succulents have received all too little attention compared, for example, to hybrid orchids, for which there is a separate expanded version of the Codes (*Handbook on Orchid Nomenclature and Registration*) and an elaborate procedure for the registration of new crosses under acceptable generic and grex names. Although some growers are actively opposed to the hybridization of succulents, it is inevitable that as time goes on more and more hybrids will appear. The pattern of past horticultural history supports this. And public tastes may well change to favour hybrids for their superior vigour, hardiness or freedom of flowering, especially as the supply of material from the wild dwindles. Hence it is important to have foresight and maintain a methodical and practical means of fitting such novelties into the nomenclatural system. The two Codes provide just that framework.

Since intergeneric hybrids are commoner in succulents than in any other group of flowering plants except the orchids, special prominence is given here to the available hybrid generic names, which are included in the alphabetical listing of genera as well as referred to under each parental genus.

## Chimaeras

In botany, a chimaera is a plant in which there are two or more genetically distinct tissues, each of which preserves its identity indefinitely. Variegated plants provide a good example, having localized areas of tissue that lack green pigment, chlorophyll. The subject is too great to enter into detail here; those interested are referred to the excellent book on the subject by Neilson-Jones. We have no proven examples from succulents, and chimaeras are mentioned here only because the horticultural Code includes four Articles (Nos. 20–24) devoted to their naming.

The most stable chimaera is one having a thin skin of one tissue overlying a core of the other, much like a glove covering a hand. Such plants exist only in cultivation, since only one component (that beneath the epidermis) contributes to sexual reproduction. Proof that a plant is such a chimaera comes only from breeding tests and from separating out and growing the two components. Raising a chimaera from root cuttings isolates this core component, since growth buds then arise from deep down in the tissues. Segregation may happen spontaneously and show up as strikingly different branches or parts of branches on the same plant. I described in *Nat. Cact. Succ. J.* 35: 22, 1979 a plant of *Echinopsis* 'Haku-Jo', with its curiously felted ribs, in which one side has grown out into a normal unfelted *Echinopsis*. Similar 'reversions' have been reported in *Echeveria* 'Hoveyi' and *Harrisia jusbertii*. But we must be cautious in proclaiming them chimaeras until experimental proof has been tried; similar changes could be the result of mutation or virus infection.

## Changes to the Rules

The Codes have gone through many editions. The Code for wild plants goes back to Linnaeus's first guidelines on plant naming in 1736 and 1737, and is still reviewed at successive botanical congresses held at five-year intervals. Proposals for amendments should be published (*Taxon* is the favoured journal) and are open to all, although it is anticipated (and hoped) that future alterations will not be great. There is always the danger that, in attempting to spell out the facts in full and cover every eventuality, the text will become so verbose that it defeats its own ends.

## Back to the Codes

It is important to stress that the summary of the two Codes as given above omits many details, minor rulings, highly technical and legalistic matters. This is therefore no substitute for consulting the actual Codes, and anyone contemplating serious taxonomic work should lose no time in acquiring their own copies and reading them in full.

Compared with the fevered rush to name new species, there has been comparatively little attention paid to the naming of cultivars of succulents. Cultivar names could well be used as temporary tags on novelties pending full taxonomic evaluation; they are easy to publish, and require no Latin diagnosis—just a good description and illustration for preference. There are many desirable hybrids around worthy of naming, and cultivar names would be ideal for distinguishing, for instance, the solitary and offsetting races of *Aloe aristata* and *Mammillaria plumosa*.

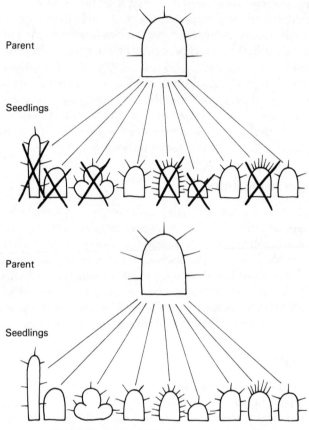

Parent

Seedlings

Parent

Seedlings

Fig. 4.1   The species as in nature (above) and
cultivation (below).
In nature plants marked X are
eliminated as unfit by natural
selection; only those nearly like the
parent will survive. In cultivation
artificial care ensures survival of
seedlings showing a greater range
of variation, but they are still all the
same species.

# CHAPTER 4

# How to Taxonomize

*'Beauty from order springs.'*
*(W. King)*

The fascination of building up a large collection of succulents over the years often leads the owner to seek new ways in which he can justify his lavish care and industry. Many advanced hobbyists are content merely to have *objets d'art*, deriving their satisfaction from the plaudits of visitors and the prizes from exhibition judges. To some, conservation is the prime incentive, and no-one will question that they do real service in acclimatizing rare species and learning how to propagate them. Others, driven no doubt by desperation at the chaos reigning in catalogues and labels, veer towards an interest in taxonomy, and it is to them that this book is especially addressed. Elsewhere (p. 58) a strong case is made out for discouraging amateurs, however well-meaning, from plunging in at the deep end without being fully aware of what is involved in proposing new classifications or naming new species. However, there are many other fields in which the observant cactophile can do useful work and fill gaps in our present knowledge.

Taxonomy is greatly concerned with the study of variation. Individuals of a species may differ from one another as much as individuals of the human race (Fig. 4.1). It is wrong to imagine that each must exactly match the type description, or else qualify to be described as new. Variation can be examined scientifically only by recording it in some way so as to allow direct comparisons to be made. It is easy to say that 'A usually has longer stalks to its flowers than B', but this means little unless you have both in front of you in flower at the same time. What we need to be able to say is 'A: pedicels 3–7 mm' and 'B: pedicels 5–15 mm', and that involves patient recording of a number of specimens, perhaps over several years. But only in this way can we arrive at a clearer picture of species boundaries and, incidentally, provide a ready means of checking identities.

A start can be made with the plants themselves: are they really what the labels lead us to believe? Plants received direct from the habitat, or raised from wild-collected seed, are much to be preferred botanically to those raised from open-pollinated seed in a glasshouse (and perhaps hybrid) or of unrecorded origin. Hence it is necessary to keep an index—on cards, or in a looseleaf album—of specimens, with full data on where they came from, when, and their subsequent performance and propagation. A sample layout is shown below. It is just a sample

**The layout of a sample record card for documenting living plants in a collection. When designing your card put the most-needed data in the top right hand corner for easy access. The status (see p. 48) can be indicated by the letters A, B, C, D, or by a coloured dot as on the plant label.**

| Family | Accepted name<br>Checked | | Accession number |
|---|---|---|---|
| Dead or<br>disposed of | Name as received<br>Checked | | Status (see p. 48)<br>A    B    C    D |
| Supplier | Source | | Date |
| Received as plant or seed - - - - sown<br>germinated<br>distributed | | | |
| Performance<br>Flowers ¦ Fruits | | Propagation<br>Vegetative¦    Seed<br>Sown          Germinated | |
| self-compatible<br>-incompatible | | | |
| Notes — Overleaf | | | |

and each grower will want to modify it to suit his own special interest. For instance, keen photographers will want to note if pictures have been taken, and perhaps even include prints.

## Status Symbols

A scheme has been put forward (Rowley 1979) allocating status to individual plants in a collection according to how closely they represent the species as it was originally described. This is something of prime interest to botanists and conservationists, and should be seriously considered by all who, having spent time and money amassing a collection, seek ways of making it more than a mere *objet d'art*.

The categories and their appropriate number and colour codings are shown on p. 48.

Naturally occurring hybrids, if of known provenance, and clonal propagations from such plants, can be rated in the same way as species. Seedlings from them, if any, are not expected to come true, and at best can rate only 4 (D), as do all hybrids of garden origin.

Note that a plant without a name, but with a collector's number, rates higher than a cultigen, however grand its name may sound. The vital link is the field number, like 'FR789', which allows us to trace back to the original collector and where he collected in the field. This should always be recorded—even after the plant has received an official name.

## How to Score your Plants

The scheme is that each plant in your collection bears on its label either a number or a coloured dot indicating its status. The same is recorded in the record file, index card or whatever written record is kept of the collection. There also one can record fuller details of source and habitat. Colours can be marked cheaply with crayon, paint or waterproof felt pens, or expensively with self-adhesive plastic tape or dots (Brady Quik-Dots).

Begin by ignoring all unlabelled specimens—or, better, check out their names so that they can qualify for D status. Then allocate the same status to all labelled specimens lacking provenance. I am assuming that your labels are correct (being a habitual optimist by nature). If in doubt, you can express different levels of certainty by writing: '*Rebutia* sp.', or

Status Symbols for Succulents in Cultivation

| Received as plants | Raised from seed | Main value | Status symbol | Numerical index | Colour code |
|---|---|---|---|---|---|
| **Clonotype.** Vegetatively propagated from the actual plant designated as type by the publishing author. | | Anchor for the name; replacement of type specimen in the event of loss. | A | 10 | Red |
| **Topotype.** Plant collected in the type locality, and clonal propagations from it. | Seed from type locality, or from hand-pollination of Status A/B plants. | Revaluation of old and confused species for which no type is known. | B | 8 | Blue |
| **Indigen.** Plant of recorded wild provenance (field data or collector's field number). | Seed from specified wild habitat, or from hand-pollination of Status C plants. | Assessment of species variation in the wild. | C | 6 | Yellow |
| **Cultigen.** Plant lacking field data or a collector's number. | Seed from unrecorded source, lacking habitat data, or from open-pollination. | Assessment of species variation in cultivation. | D | 4 | Black |
| Unlabelled plants of any kind. | | Horticultural only. | — | 0 | — |

'*Rebutia* sp. (Sect. Aylostera)', or '*Rebutia* sp. aff. *deminuta*', or '*Rebutia ?deminuta*'. But for purposes of status scoring, emphasis is on documentation rather than identity; the accession number rather than the name on the label, which is liable to change.

The remaining plants, usually a small minority, will qualify as status C unless your records show that they come from the type locality (B) or from the actual type plant itself (A).

## Value of Status Symbols

Why have a number as well as a colour code? Not just for colour-blind cactophiles: the colour dots look good on labels, but with numbers you can do sums. They can be added together and averaged to give an overall rating for the collection: the higher the rating, the greater the botanical content. Alternatively, the percentages of C, B and A plants can be calculated. Such information could well be included in future editions of the *I. O. S. Register of Collections* (Rowley and Hunt 1975).

If the owner of a collection dies, it would be immediately apparent to anyone charged with disposing of the plants which of them deserve especial care, irrespective of size or condition.

Finally, a word of cheer to those whose plants all qualify for the bottom category. Not everyone demands a pedigree dog for a pet, and a cultigen often beats an indigen hands down for looks and show appeal. A plant that matches the species description has botanical value even if its origin is unknown. Some species have not been recollected from the wild for many years, and the only living material available for study may be that nurtured in collections.

## Characters, Major and Minor

The characters used by the taxonomist are of two sorts. **Major** or **discontinuous characters** are those that exist in two contrasted states, without intermediates. An example is whether the fruit is a berry or a capsule. Berries rely on animal agency for dispersal; capsules eject the seed mechanically. Here an intermediate condition would be neither attractive to animals nor efficient by itself so would have disappeared long since in the course of evolution. Major characters like this are ideally simple to recognize and measure, but are quite rare. There are even exceptions to the rule of berries and capsules—*Astrophytum* and some other genera of cacti, for instance, in which the fruit starts fleshy but subsequently splits open.

**Minor** or **quantitative characters** are those where there is overlap, as in the pedicel lengths cited on p. 45. Frequently these are the only characters available, so means must be devised for recording and making use of them. Rib number in Cactaceae is a good example: at the ends of the range an absolute separation is possible between genera, as in the key entries for *Borzicactus* and *Rathbunia* (see key p. 110). Two or more quantitative characters can be taken together to ensure distinction, as seen in the separation of *Echinopsis* and *Harrisia* (same key, p. 109).

Suppose, let us say, that we are setting out to score the number of spines per areole in a group of related cacti. It will be immediately apparent that the total differs from one areole to another, the variation increasing as the total goes up. Thus, whereas *Opuntia vulgaris* fairly consistently lives up to its synonymous name *monacantha* by having one spine to each areole (rarely 2 or 0), in *O. aciculata* the number may be as low as 40 or over 100. We need to devise a series of categories of increasing size, for example:

Spines 0; 1–2; 3–5; 6–10; 11–20; 21–40; over 40.

The number of such arbitrary categories depends on how much importance the observer attaches to spine count, how constant or variable the number is with age, cultivation and so forth, and how much effort he is prepared to put into making counts. A minimum of six randomly selected areoles per plant might provide a working basis. Similar principles apply to other numerical characters like the number of ribs and stigma lobes. A useful shorthand way of summarizing the counts is thus: 'Spines (3–)5–8(–13)' which means: 'Spines normally between 5 and 8, but exceptionally as low as 3 or as high as 13'.

More difficult to assess are features that vary continuously from one extreme to the other, like colours or shapes of leaves. Often there are several components, as in the areole of a cactus and its various appendages (Figs. 4.2–15). If the components can be disentangled and treated separately, this helps a great deal. Thus leaf shape can be analysed into

1) overall outline, 2) shape of apex, and 3) shape of base.

The outline can be further distinguished as

i) widest midway, ii) widest below the middle, iii) widest above the middle.

**Figs. 4.2-4.15 Scoring cactus morphology: Areoles and areolar productions**

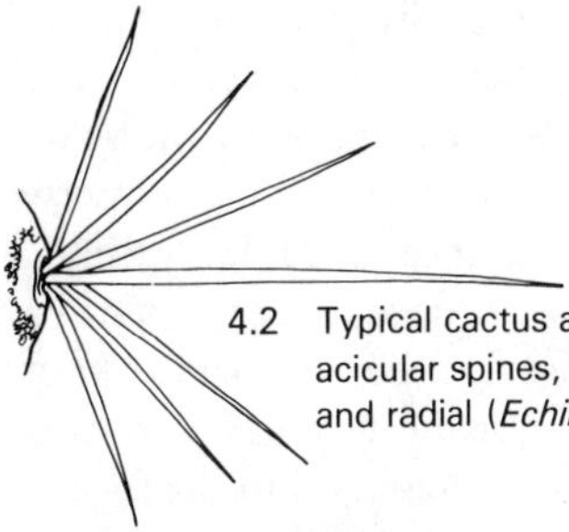

4.2 Typical cactus areole with acicular spines, central and radial (*Echinopsis*)

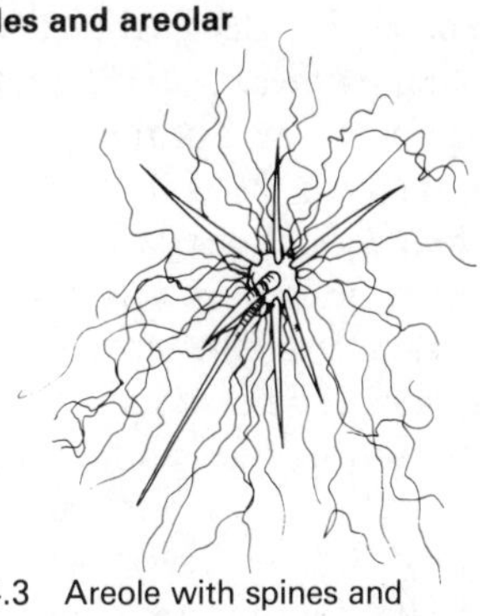

4.3 Areole with spines and hairs (*Borzicactus celsianus*)

4.4 Spineless areole with enlarged felted hairs (*Lophophora*)

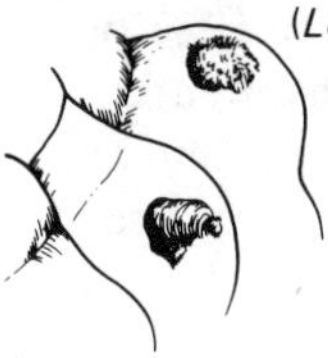

4.5 Spineless areole with glochids (*Opuntia microdasys*)

4.6 Glochids (enlarged) showing barbs

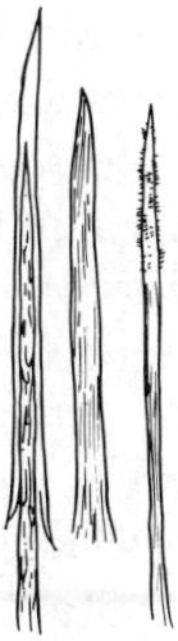

4.7 Sheathed spine (*Opuntia tunicata*)

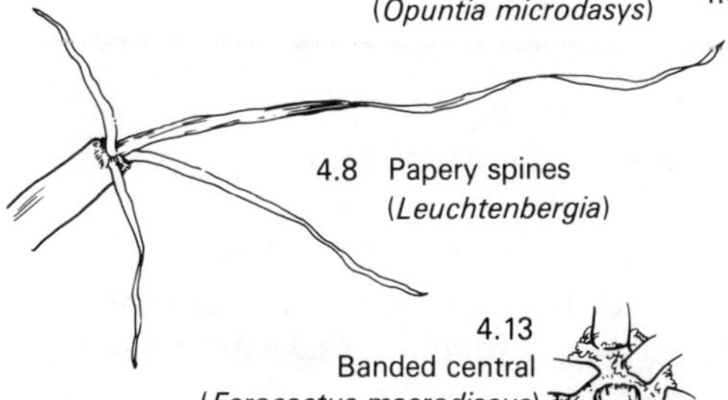

4.8 Papery spines (*Leuchtenbergia*)

4.9 Conic spines (*Myrtillocactus*)

4.13 Banded central (*Ferocactus macrodiscus*)

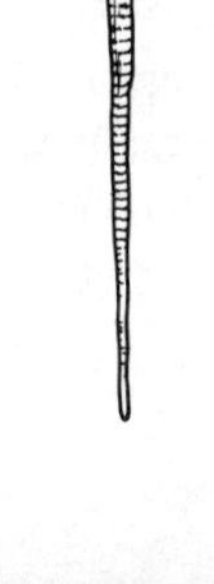

4.11 Hooked and banded central (*Ferocactus acanthodes*)

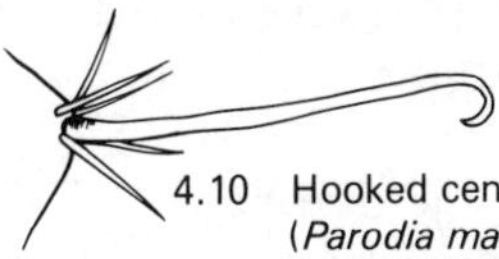

4.10 Hooked central (*Parodia maassii*)

Pectinate spines (*Pelecyphora aselliformis*)

4.15

4.12 Plumose spines (*Mammillaria plumosa*)

4.14 Pectinate spines (*Echinocereus reichenbachii*)

For an excellent tabulation of outline shapes of plane (and solid) bodies, see Stearn (1966), summarized here on p. 238.

For many parts of the plant there exists an extensive terminology, and one then has the task of trying to locate the right term. A leaf apex may be **rounded, obtuse, acute, mucronate, acuminate, cuspidate**, and so on. Dictionaries are not very helpful here, since they proceed in the opposite direction, from the term to the definition. Lawrence (1955) has excellent diagrams of types of indumentum, leaf shapes, inflorescence types and so forth, so that one can match the plant against the pictures and read off the right term. Colours can be matched against the Royal Horticultural Society's Colour Charts, which are conveniently presented in the form of four fans; for the terminology of colours see Dade (1949).

If terminology frightens you, learn to draw! Simple line sketches of the outlines of seeds as seen under a lens, for example, require close observation but little artistic skill. You can make up a master set of outlines to serve as a standard, numbering them 1, 2, 3, 4 . . . and recording just the number as each plant is matched against it. Matching to a standard is one of the best techniques for coping with complex or indefinable characters: corona shape in Stapelieae, or placentation and cell shape in Mesembryanthemaceae, and the like. To classify the many fruit types in the latter Family you can single out the most striking and record them as 'Delosperma type', 'Conicosia type', and so on.

Of course, there will always be the odd plants that do not exactly fit any of the categories available. Nature simply does not oblige so readily! The system has to be flexible enough to allow for extra categories, or one for 'other types'.

A sample score sheet for recording Mesembryanthemaceae is shown on p. 53. The back of the sheet could be used for additional notes, or could carry the plant record as set out on p. 46. Considerable ingenuity can be exercised in designing a score sheet to be as compact and informative as possible, and it is as well to spend some time in trial and error since once the sheets have been duplicated it is difficult to make changes.

For example, to make a complete record of the distribution of all possible types of surface appendage (**indumentum** or **vestiture**) throughout the plant, simply list the organs in one column, the indumentum types in another, allocate symbols to each and mark up the sheet as follows on p. 54.

The layout of a sample score sheet for documenting species of Mesembryanthemaceae. Suitable terminology can be separately listed as shown on p. 54.

| Family: Mesembryanthemaceae | | | | Name: |
| --- | --- | --- | --- | --- |
| | | | | Accession number: |

| | | | | Dimensions |
| --- | --- | --- | --- | --- |
| Habit | | | | |
|   Duration | | | | |
| Indumentum type | | Localisation | | |
| Roots | | | | |
| Stems | | | | |
|   Extension | Branching | Internodes | Colour | |
| Branches | | | | |
|   Extension | Inclination | Internodes | Colour | |
| Leaves | | | | |
|   Phyllotaxy | Homo- or heterophylly | Disposition | Base Connation | |
|   Petiole | Texture | Surface colour | Surface topography | |
|   Shape (or shape of leaf-pair if united into a body) | | | | |
|     Plan | | Profile | Cross-section | |
|     Apex | | Base | Margins | |
| Inflorescence | | | | |
|   Bracts | | Peduncles | Pedicels | |
| Flowers | | | | |
|   Season | Opening times | Duration | Scent | |
| Sepals | | | | |
|   Number | Form | Equality | Connation | |
| Petals (outer staminodes) | | | | |
|   Number | Shape | Colour | Connation | |
| Inner staminodes | | | | |
|   Presence | | Disposition | | |
| Stamens | | | | |
|   Colour of Filament Anther | | Disposition | Length relative to petals | |
| Stigmas | | | | |
|   Number | Form | Disposition | | |
| Ovary | | | | |
|   Shape above | | Cell shape in V.S. | Placentation | |
| Fruit | | | | |
|   Shape | | Type & dehiscence | | |
|   Cell roofs | | Cell tubercles | Expanding keels | |
| Valves | | | | |
|   Colour | Shape | Disposition when expanded | Marginal wings | |
| Seeds | | | | |
|   Colour | Shape | Surface | Number per cell | |
| Cytology | | Pollen | | |
|   Chromosome number | | % viability | | |

| Stems | O | | O = Glabrous |
|---|---|---|---|
| Branches | O | | gl = Glaucescent |
| Petioles | P | | Gl = Glaucous |
| Leaves, above | Gl | | F = Farinose |
| below | T, G | | p = Puberulent |
| Inflorescences | O | | P = Pubescent |
| Bracts | p, G | | Pa = Papillate |
| Pedicels | p | | T = Tomentose |
| Sepals | T | | V = Villous |
| | | | G = Glandular |

**Sample record sheet marked up**          **Key to abbreviations used**
**for distribution of indumentum**

Record sheets of this type can be made out for use on taxa at any level, from Orders and Families down to genera or single species, and for scoring either actual specimens or tabulating data from the literature in strictly standardized format.

The occasional hybrid can be treated in the same way as species, but if hybrids are to be made the subject of special study, as in a breeding programme, it would be better to design a separate score sheet with space for the pedigree.

If one sheet has been filled in for each individual plant studied, a collective sheet can then be drawn up to cover those considered to constitute one species. The hour of reckoning has come, and any plants lying outside the general range demand especial attention. Are they, perhaps, chance hybrids, and between what? Or has there been a mix-up of labels, or similar mishap? Or are the species limits wider than published descriptions lead us to believe?

Another use of score sheets is for placing unidentified specimens, by matching their characters against those of other, named, plants. And here we come up against a problem: visual matching from sheet to sheet is rather laborious, particularly when we want to investigate linkage groups—that is, sets of characters inherited as a group. There are various ways of presenting the same data so that comparisons can be made more readily.

Pictorial, graphical and statistical methods are much used by taxonomists in portraying patterns of variation. If the origin of the plants is known, each can be indicated on a map using dots of different colours or shapes or variously coded to indicate selected morphological features. Often this reveals that certain characters are shown only in certain areas, and strengthens the claim to recognize, for example, separate subspecies. Full details of these methods, which tend to be rather technical, can be found in Davis and Heywood (1963).

Another approach is to transfer the data to punched cards (or to start with these in the first place). Punched cards come in a range of shapes and sizes, and can even be printed to order to suit one project. The basis is a series of, perhaps, a hundred holes punched round the periphery and coded by number. The characters are first redefined in such a way that a simple yes/no answer is possible, and a hole is allotted to each pair of alternatives, as shown below.

Comparison of a record sheet (left) and punched card (right) for the same features of a leaf margin

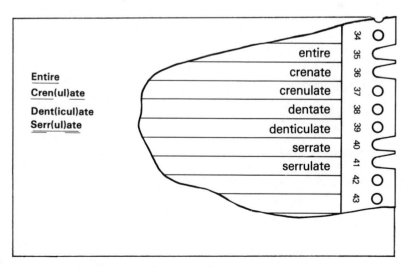

For each applicable character on the punched card, a V-shaped notch is clipped out using an ordinary ticket-collector's clippers. Reading either of the two examples given above, we learn that the leaf can be **entire**, **crenate**, **serrate** or **serrulate**. Where two character states are mutually exclusive, such as Plant dioecious/Plant monoecious, only a single hole is needed instead of two, but such instances are rare.

Each card is completed with the name and accession number written in, plus any other data you like, such as anomalous features and those uncertain in scoring. To sort out all those plants with denticulate leaves, you merely insert a knitting needle through hole 39, shake the pack gently, and it immediately separates into two groups. It is a matter of seconds to find out if all plants with denticulate leaves also have pink flowers, or are annual, or whatever you please. Punched cards are marvellously adaptable. They can be stored in any order, rejected, altered or added to at will, and serve as a permanent storehouse of information: the poor man's computer, if you like. They provide the simplest mechanical system for identification, and the ideal basis for constructing an identification key. Small wonder that their use extends to many fields of industry, police files, archives and data storage generally.

# CHAPTER 5

# Discovering a Novelty

'Wherever we are able rigidly to define, or assign limits to, our genera and species, surely it is because either we do not possess all the intermediate forms that actually exist, or else those forms have already ceased to be, through the action of the inevitable law of the Survival of the fittest.'

*(R. Spruce)*

What, then, should be your attitude if, on making a detailed study of any group of succulents, you find a plant that fits none of the published descriptions? The first question to ask concerns its origin: is it from the wild, or of garden ancestry? It may be a chance hybrid, even if the seed came from the wild. If you suspect this, what are the likely parents? Confirmation of hybridity is a little difficult and may involve specialist study: the nature of chromosome pairing at meiosis, and the percentage of viable pollen. If it is possible to self-pollinate the suspected hyrid and raise the next generation of seedlings, a high degree of diversity with near-reversions to the two parents is typical of an interspecific cross. But these are only generalizations: a hybrid with doubled chromosomes can behave like a true species! For further details, see Chapter 5 of Rowley (1978).

Our unidentifiable specimen may represent an extreme variation of an already named species. It is so easy to obtain a stereotyped image of what, say, *Echinocereus coccineus* looks like that on first encountering the spineless mutation of it we fail to associate the plant with that species at all. Yet this local variant grows mixed with normal spiny specimens with which it hybridizes to produce intermediates with weak spines, and there is scarcely justification for giving it separate taxonomic status even as a form. Thus novelties can be assessed only in the light of a full understanding of related taxa and their distribution in the field.

If you are convinced that the disputed plant merits a name, it is still worth erring on the side of caution if there is any doubt regarding its wild origin by giving it a cultivar name. Posterity will chide you less if the supposed novelty turns out to be not so novel as you at first thought. Even so, it is a waste of time to launch a new name unless you intend to launch plants to go with it, so propagation and wide distribution to nurseries and specialists should be a priority. The literature is already full of wasted names of cultivars that died along with the original plant.

## Naming a New Species (and why not to!)

The subject of names and naming has been covered in some detail here: first because so few other books venture to do so, and second because I feel it is vital that anyone feeling inspired to plunge into authorship of new names should be fully aware of what systematic botany involves. The foregoing will have made it clear that there is a lot more to it than rewriting the labels and distributing cuttings, and the subject should not be undertaken lightly. I am not aware of any rush to become amateur dentists or cut-price surgeons, offering instant appendectomies without queueing, yet every year appalling nomenclatural bungles are perpetrated by hopeful would-be taxonomists who often are not even aware that the naming of plants is governed by rules at all. One could dismiss the results with a laugh if it were not that, once in print, the names are there for all time, and someone has to come along later and clear up the mess. The editors of small-time journals are often as much to blame in not knowing their jobs and failing to have such papers refereed before rushing them into print.

Succulents have suffered more than most plants from a surfeit of tinkering and superfluous names. It is not difficult to see why. Professional botanists fight shy of succulents because they cannot be put through the traditional herbarium routine. It often takes years to find out enough about a particular plant to be able to say: 'This is a new species'. One needs living material—not just one plant from a dealer, but as many as possible, ideally from different localities that can be plotted on a map and related to the distribution of variability. One needs dissections and drawings or photographs of flowers and magnified views of seeds. A person unable to visit the habitat himself must depend upon the collector sending accurate data on localities and conditions under which the plants grow, and has to rely on his judgement concerning the populations he has studied. On top of all this he needs to compare the supposed new species against all previously described species with which it might possibly be related or identical. This involves much book-searching, photocopying and translating. All this before anything goes into print! Meanwhile, dealers will no doubt have been busy propagating the same plants and selling them off. Since labels merely stating '*Parodia* sp. nov.' or '*Parodia* XYZ/317' (the collector's initials and field number) are not considered to have much sales value, a new name will often have been dreamed up by the collector or nurseryman: the more, the merrier, to satisfy both seller and buyer. When the botanist finally comes up with the answer that the plants are all just a local variant of *Parodia microsperma*, the damage is done: nobody likes rewriting labels or confessing that they have bought the same plant twice!

Obviously there are not enough botanists around to keep up with the influx of new material, and those that are have their hands full trying to disentangle past muddles. Gradually, bit by bit, advances are made, and each monograph takes a dreadful toll of names, many of which fall into synonymy. Thus a recent (1973) well-researched revision of *Argyroderma* has reduced 60 'species' to 10, and large reductions have also been made in *Lithops*, *Haworthia*, *Crassula* and other genera.

New converts to collecting and growing succulents are apt to develop too great a faith in names. They read one book that says there are, say, 87 species of *Parodia*, so they set out spaces for 87 pots, reserve 87 labels and attempt to collect them all as one might collect stamps or spot aircraft. It naturally comes as a shock when they see other books that describe extra species, or alternatively reduce them all to a much smaller number. No two botanists will agree over the number, so it is useless to exaggerate its importance. Far better to collect only Status A, B and C plants of *Parodia* and focus interest on patterns of variation—perhaps within a single species or species complex. The plants are then labelled with accession numbers and any names treated as provisional.

# References (Part I)

BORROR, D. J. 1960 *Dictionary of Word Roots and Combining Forms* (California: Mayfield Publishing Co., Palo Alto).

BRIGGS, D. and WALTERS, S. M. 1969 *Plant Variation and Evolution* (London: World University Library).

DADE, H. A. 1949 *Colour Terminology in Biology* (Kew: Commonwealth Mycological Inst.).

DAVIS, P. H. and CULLEN, J. 1979 *The Identification of Flowering Plant Families*. 2nd Edn. (London: Cambridge U.P.).

DAVIS, P. H. and HEYWOOD, V. H. 1963 *Principles of Angiosperm Taxonomy* (Edinburgh and London: Oliver and Boyd).

*Handbook on Orchid Nomenclature and Registration* 1976 Eds. J. S. L. GILMOUR *et al.* 2nd Edn. (London: Royal Horticultural Society).

HEYWOOD, V. H. 1967 *Plant Taxonomy* (London: Arnold).

HUTCHINSON, J. 1967 *Key to the Families of the Flowering Plants of the World* (Oxford: Clarendon).

*Index Kewensis* 1895 Eds. J. D. HOOKER *et al.* 2 Vols. (Oxford: Clarendon Press) with supplements at mostly five-year intervals.

*Index Londinensis* 1929-31 Eds. O. STAPF *et al.* 6 Vols. (London: Oxford U.P.) with supplements in 2 Vols., 1941.

*Index Nominum Genericorum* 1980 Eds. E. R. FARR *et al.* in *Regnum Vegetabile* 100-102. 3 Vols. (The Hague).

*International Code of Botanical Nomenclature (ICBN)* 1978 Eds. F. A. STAFLEU *et al.* in *Regnum Vegetabile* 97 (Utrecht).

*International Code of Nomenclature of Cultivated Plants* 1969 Eds. J. S. L. GILMOUR *et al.* in *Regnum Vegetabile* 64 (Utrecht).

IVIMEY-COOK, R. B. 1974 *Succulents—A Glossary of Terms and Descriptions* (Oxford: National Cactus and Succulent Society).

JEFFREY, C. 1968 *An Introduction to Plant Taxonomy* (London: Churchill).

JEFFREY, C. 1973 *Biological Nomenclature* (London: Arnold).

KELSEY, H. P. and DAYTON, W. A. 1942 *Standardized Plant Names* 2nd Edn. (Harrisburg, U.S.A.: J. Horace McFarland & Co.).

LAWRENCE, G. H. M. 1955 *An Introduction to Plant Taxonomy* (New York: Macmillan).

LINNAEUS, C. 1753 *Species Plantarum* 1st Edn. (Facsimile by Ray Society, London, 1957, with introduction by W. T. STEARN).

LINNAEUS, C. 1754 *Genera Plantarum* 5th Edn. (Facsimile by Wheldon and Wesley, Codicote, Herts, with introduction by W. T. STEARN).

NEILSON-JONES, W. 1964 *Plant Chimaeras and Graft Hybrids* (London: Methuen).

PARKHURST, R. J. 1978 *Biological Identification* (London: Arnold).

RAY, J. in WILKINS, J. 1668 *Essay towards a Real Character and Philosophical Language* (London: Royal Society).

*Repertorium Plantarum Succulentarum 1951 et seq.*, annually. Eds. G. D. ROWLEY *et al.* (Richmond: I.O.S. British Section, 67 Gloucester Court, Kew Road).

R.H.S. 1966 *R.H.S. Colour Chart* (London: Royal Horticultural Society).

ROWLEY, G. D. 1978 *Illustrated Encyclopedia of Succulent Plants* (London: Salamander) Chaps. 2, 4, 5.

ROWLEY, G. D. 1979a *Cact. Succ. J.* (GB) 41, 7–9.

ROWLEY, G. D. 1979b *Nat. Cact. Succ. J.* 34, 63–64.

ROWLEY, G. D. and HUNT, D. R. 1975 *Register of Specialist Collectors of Succulent and Allied Plants in the UK* (Richmond: Cactus and Succulent Society of Great Britain).

SMITH, A. W. 1972 *A Gardener's Dictionary of Plant Names.* Revised and enlarged by W. T. STEARN (London: Cassell).

STAFLEU, F. A. 1967 Taxonomic Literature in *Regnum Vegetabile* 52 (Utrecht), 2nd Edn. in course of publication, 1967 *et seq.*

STEARN, W. T. 1966 *Botanical Latin* (London: Nelson).

WOODELL, S. R. J. 1973 *Xerophytes* in *Oxford Biology Reader No. 39.* (London: Oxford U.P.)

SOME VITAL STATISTICS

Succulents were first recognized as a group apart from all others by a Swiss botanist, Jean Bauhin, in 1619 (*Cact. Succ. J. Amer.* 48: 184-189, 1976).

The first attempt at a key was by the great English naturalist, John Ray, in 1668 (*Cact. Succ. J. Gt. Brit.* 28: 10-11, 1966).

In number of species, succulents make up perhaps 3-4% of all known flowering plants. There is no appreciable development of succulence in conifers, ferns and lower plants generally, nor are there any undisputed fossil remains (*Nat. Cact. Succ. J.* 33: 19, 1978).

The oldest pot plant in Europe is a veteran *Fockea crispa*, cultivated at Schönbrunn since 1799.

# PART TWO

## Systematics:
## The Families of Succulents

# CHAPTER 6

# Identification

'To interpret Nature, let us observe Nature.'
*(Allman)*

Most of us have played that popular guessing game at parties where one person thinks of the name of a well-known celebrity and the others can ask up to ten questions to try to find out the name. 'Is it a man or a woman?' says someone, then 'Alive or dead?', 'English or foreign?' and so on. Success comes largely from the careful choice of questions and the order in which they are put. Botanists play a similar game when trying to find out the identity of an unfamiliar plant. For them the pairs of questions are set out in a special format in what is called a key.

## Keys and Synopses

The essence of a **key** is a logical sequence of paired leads, the answer to each of which narrows down the field until finally all else is eliminated and the remaining name must apply to the plant in question. Such a key is called dichotomous if each step offers a choice between two alternative statements, but sometimes three or more alternatives may be offered—as in the number of stigmas in a flower. There are various ways in which the pairs of leads may be printed; the keys in the present volume (p. 72 *et seq.*) are called indented because they step down the page and the eye can follow the stages and back-track more easily if a mistake has been made.

It is important to make the distinction between a key and a classification. A key is a purely artificial aid to finding a name. Any characters may be used, and in any order, and so long as the name emerges at the end it does not matter how little the arrangement reflects any given system. A **synopsis**, on the other hand, sets out in telegram style the characters of groups in systematic order and presents a digest of a system of classification. It is a lot easier to make than a key, and in many reference works a synopsis is all that you will find. It can be an aid to identification, also, but you have to read through every entry in turn and hope that your plant fits one better than the others.

## How to Use a Key

Before anything else, take a good look at the plant you wish to identify. A ×8 or ×10 magnifier is ideal for unravelling the finer details, and no botanist or observant gardener should be without one. If the lead calls for hairs on a midrib, for instance, they could easily be missed by a superficial glance. Select several leaves from different parts of the plant, and inspect each midrib with the lens against the light, if possible flexing the leaf in such a way that the hairs—which may be very sparse or tiny—show up against a contrasting background. Make sure that you are interpreting the plant correctly, and not calling stems leaves (p. 5) or mistaking the compound flower heads of Compositae (p. 142) or Euphorbiaceae (p. 170) for single blooms.

Flowering time is the ideal opportunity for checking names of succulents. Although every effort has been made to base these keys on readily observable features, the only constant differences between genera very often lie in small details of the flowers, fruits and seeds, without which one can only make guesses.

Proceed as follows. Turn to p. 71 for the start of the Main Key to Families. The pairs of leads are here coded with letters; those in the generic keys with numbers. Notice that the leads are all arranged in pairs (rarely three or more together) and similarly lettered and indented so that the eye quickly runs down the page to pick out the second of a pair. Begin with lead A: 'Water storage in . . . leaves' for which the alternative, AA, is 'Water storage in . . . stems'. If the former applies, this takes us to 'Group I LEAF SUCCULENTS' and we can start at once on the key to Group I below. If the second alternative applies, you take the next step in and read the pair of leads B and BB, and again make the choice leading to Groups II or III.

Following the key for any of these groups leads to the name of the Family to which your plant belongs. Note that some Family names appear more than once in the key, and sometimes the name of the genus or even species can be given at once, so the quest is ended. But in any case, turn next to the account of the Family and check the plant against the description (and illustrations) to make sure you are on the right track. If the Family has more than one genus showing succulence, you will be presented with a further key to genera, beginning with a pair of leads cued 1 and stepping down the page in the same fashion as the Main Key. Finally, when you arrive at the name, check the description in the alphabetical list of genera.

It should be explained that the key characters used here apply only to genera of succulents included in this book; the keys cannot be expected to work for non-succulent plants of the same genera.

If you have never used a key before, start on something simple. Avoid cacti and try a known plant of the Crassulaceae: any *Kalanchoe* or *Sempervivum* you may have in flower, for example. By knowing the answer in advance you can check each step by looking ahead to see if you are going in the right direction, and stop if an error has been made.

## Hints and Pointers

Read both leads—not just one—carefully. The wording is brief but precise, and hasty reading may miss a vital point. If uncertain over a technical term, consult the glossary.

If your plant answers equally to both alternative leads, or seems to fall midway between them, try both in turn. The answer should turn up under either. If you come to an impasse, where neither alternative makes sense, retrace your steps to see if a slip has been made. The same applies if the final name turns out to be wrong. If the impasse is due to lack of material—flower colour, say, when the petals have fallen—try each lead in turn and check to see which gives the right answer.

It should be borne in mind that dimensions, colours and shapes used in these keys are drawn from typical, well-grown, adult plants in cultivation. The purist might object that the plant as found in nature should supply the model, but who ever sees succulent euphorbias 20 m (67 feet) high in Europe, or spines as sturdy or colours as vivid as those burnished by the Mexican sun? In any case, field floras are more suited to those fortunate enough to encounter succulents in habitat.

Adult plants of succulents may differ in many ways from juveniles. The first leaves of a seedling may be quite unlike those of mature specimens, spiralled tubercles may be replaced by straight ribs or vice versa, spheres may grow into columns, and so on. Where a plant has a characteristic type of swollen rootstock or tubers, these may take years to develop when the plant is propagated by cuttings, or develop uncharacteristically. Extreme differences between juvenile and adult foliage can be seen in *Gasteria*. It is asking the impossible to make a key for distinguishing seedlings, although experienced growers and nurserymen develop extraordinary skill at recognizing them. But their knowledge, alas, cannot be expressed on paper.

Fasciation causes further problems for plant identifiers: the abnormal pattern of growth in which globose or cylindrical shoots grow out as fans or brainlike masses, with consequent upset to ribs, tubercles and symmetry generally. The result can be so unlike the parent plant that the only hope of identification, if the label is lost, is to wait for a reversion and grow it on to flowering.

## Checking against Descriptions

The descriptions of genera provided here are made as compact as possible, avoiding repetition and concentrating on diagnostic features for distinguishing the genus in question from others that might easily be confused with it. Characters used in the key, or common to the whole Family, are not in general repeated, and extra information on the genus can be extracted from these sources. Thus, for example, to the brief description of *Khadia* (p. 208) one can add that the flowers would have a large number of linear petals and stamens (Family description on p. 189) and, by working backwards up the key from lead 59, that it has a thick and tuberous root (lead 55), an annular nectary (46), leaves at least three quarters free at the base (43) and so on. The reference to the description of *Nananthus* builds up the picture further.

The references cited after each Family and genus are limited to those concerned with names and identities, especially those having keys to species or useful synopses. Cultivation is abundantly covered by other books. No keys to species are included in the present volume, much as I would have liked to do so. But in the present climate of controversy over names and identities it is difficult to see how this could be done. For many of the larger genera there are no published keys to species—at least, none recent enough to have any relevance today. Identifying the species can be a major task for botanists, involving long searching in herbaria and libraries and sifting through original descriptions.

Attention is particularly drawn, however, to the list of general references following the description of each Family. These may include monographs with keys to genera and species that are not cited separately under each genus entry.

At the head of each generic description the place of first publication is cited, together with the name of the type species, taken mostly from the *Index Nominum Genericorum*. Where the genus was monotypic when published, typification is automatic. When a later lectotype has to be selected, there may be two or more names from which to choose. In critical work, as in dividing a genus or deciding which subgenus and section bear the same name as the genus (pp. 29–32) the original sources should be consulted.

## Cherish your Labels

It will be evident that finding the correct name of even the genus of a succulent can involve much time and trouble. All the more reason, therefore, to make sure that the labelling on plants in cultivation is maintained, and that labels are replaced as soon as they begin to become illegible. Ideally, each plant should bear an accession number which remains permanently associated with it regardless of changes of name, and refers to a register or card index where full details are recorded. A name once lost can be replaced often only with difficulty, if at all. The conservation-minded will need no second prompting to preserve the label as much as the plant, and to avoid the spread of false names.

## References to Chapter 6

DAVIS, P. H. and CULLEN, J. 1979 *The Identification of Flowering Plant Families* 2nd Edn. (London: Cambridge U.P.).

HUTCHINSON, J. 1967 *Key to the Families of Flowering Plants of the World* (Oxford: Clarendon Press).

*Index Nominum Genericorum* 1980 Eds. E. R. Farr, J. A. Leussink & F. A. Stafleu in *Regnum Vegetabile* 100-102. 3 Vols. (The Hague).

PANKHURST, R. J. 1978 *Biological Identification* (London: E. Arnold).

**Figs. 7.1-7.14**
**Group I: Leaf succulents**

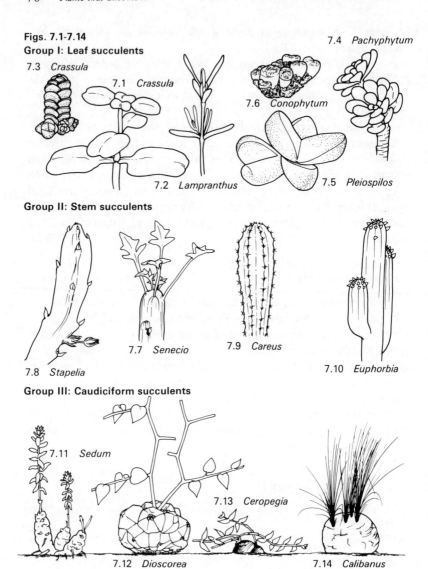

7.3   *Crassula*

7.1   *Crassula*

7.4   *Pachyphytum*

7.6   *Conophytum*

7.2   *Lampranthus*

7.5   *Pleiospilos*

**Group II: Stem succulents**

7.7   *Senecio*

7.9   *Careus*

7.8   *Stapelia*

7.10   *Euphorbia*

**Group III: Caudiciform succulents**

7.11   *Sedum*

7.13   *Ceropegia*

7.12   *Dioscorea*

7.14   *Calibanus*

# CHAPTER 7

# Key to the Families and Isolated Genera

For guidance on how to use a key, see p. 66.

If you get stuck, see p. 233.

'Unc.' signifies uncultivated, or for various reasons rarely to be seen outside of a few specialist collections.

A    Water storage in fat, fleshy, ± persistent leaves[1] which are at least more succulent than the stems (Figs. 7.1–6).      Group I    LEAF SUCCULENTS

AA   Water storage in fat, fleshy stems; leaves less fleshy and commonly deciduous, reduced or absent.      B

     B    Plants of cactiform or cereiform habit, without a conspicuously swollen base or, if so (*Pachypodium* spp.), then lacking thin deciduous shoots; stems commonly jointed, ribbed or tuberculate (Figs. 7.7–10).      Group II    STEM SUCCULENTS

     BB   Plants broadest below, with a swollen, fleshy, basal, ± amorphous caudex which is not jointed, ribbed or tuberculate[2], bearing either deciduous leaves direct from the crown or tapered gradually or abruptly into slender, scarcely succulent branches; leaves (if present) and sometimes also the branches deciduous (Figs. 7.11–14).      Group III    CAUDICIFORM SUCCULENTS

---

[1] Not to be confused with flattened, leaf-like stems (phylloclades).

[2] Except: *Adenia globosa, Dioscorea, Neoalsomitra*, q.v.

# KEY TO GENERA INCLUDING SUCCULENTS

## Group I—Leaf Succulents

1 Leaves tough, fibrous, not snapping cleanly, over 10 cm long or, if less, then
  spine-tipped or prickle-edged    **Agavaceae**
1 Leaves scarcely fibrous, snapping cleanly or, if not so, then less than 10 cm long
  and entire, without an apical spine
  2 Stems square in cross-section; flowers blue    **Labiatae**
  2 Stems, if developed, not square; flowers not blue*
    3 Leaves trifoliate, clover-like, with a long petiole, the leaflets drooping in the
      dark or in cold weather but widely expanded in sunshine    **Oxalidaceae**
    3 Leaves not so
      4 Individual flowers large or, if small, then in inflorescences other than
        spikes or capitula
        5 Flowers isomerous
          6 Flower parts uniformly in threes; carpels united into an ovary
            7 Perianth of 6 similar tepals, none wholly green    **Liliaceae**
            7 Perianth of 3 green sepals and 3 coloured petals    **Commelinaceae**
            *(Tradescantia)*
          6 Flower parts in fours or higher numbers; carpels ± free **Crassulaceae**
        5 Flowers not isomerous; carpels united into an ovary
          8 Petals 3–6; sepals 2; ovary usually superior; stipules mostly present,
            often as hairs    **Portulacaceae**
          8 Petals and stamens more numerous; sepals 5–8; ovary inferior;
            stipules absent    **Mesembryanthemaceae**
      4 Individual flowers small, massed into spikes or capitula
        9 Flowers in spikes, without bracts    **Peperomiaceae**
        *(Peperomia)*
        9 Flowers in capitula, surrounded by a common involucre of bracts
          **Compositae**

## Group II—Stem Succulents

1 Stems with felted areoles often bearing clusters of spines or bristles, or leafless
  epiphytes (Rhipsalinae) or with copious felt in the axils of tubercles *(Ariocarpus)*
  **Cactaceae**

---

*Except *Sedum coeruleum*.

1 Stems without felted areoles, although spines may be present and even clustered
  on horny shields (*Didierea, Euphorbia* p.p.); not leafless epiphytes or with felt
  in axils of tubercles
  2 Sap not milky
    3 Plants bearing spines or prickles as well as leaves (at least during the growing
      season)
      4 Spines 4 or more together                             **Didiereaceae**
        *(Didierea)*
      4 Spines 3 or fewer together
        5 Spines in threes                                    **Apocynaceae**
          *(Pachypodium)*
        5 Spines in twos or solitary
          6 Branch system zigzag                         **Didiereaceae**
            *(Decaryia)*
          6 Branch system not zigzag
            7 Midrib inconspicuous                     **Didiereaceae**
              *(Alluaudia, Alluaudiopsis)*
            7 Midrib conspicuous                      **Apocynaceae**
              *(Pachypodium)*
    3 Plants never with both spines or prickles and leaves
      8 Stems weak and trailing or climbing, with long internodes and usually
        petiolate leaves
        9 Tendrils present on adult shoots                  **Vitaceae**
          *(Cissus)*
        9 Tendrils never present
          10 Leaves lobed or incised                    **Geraniaceae**
            *(Pelargonium)*
          10 Leaves entire or undeveloped             **Asclepiadaceae**
            *(Ceropegia)*
      8 Stems not weak and long; internodes short; leaves when present sessile
        11 Leaves opposite or undeveloped
          12 Small-leaved, much-branched shrubs         **Portulacaceae**
          12 Solitary or dwarf clumping succulents; if shrubby, then leafless and
            ± cactiform                              **Asclepiadaceae**
        11 Leaves alternate
          13 Individual flowers small, massed into capitula with a common
            involucre                                 **Compositae**
          13 Individual flowers large and showy, solitary or few together
            **Apocynaceae**
            *(Adenium)*
  2 Sap milky
    14 Flowers in umbels, with a 5-pointed, starlike corolla; leafless, trailing or
      ascending shrubs with rodlike grey shoots        **Asclepiadaceae**
        *(Sarcostemma)*
    14 Flowers in cyathia, individually minute and surrounded by an involucre
      and paired bracts; habit various               **Euphorbiaceae**

## Group III—Caudiciform Succulents

1  Caudex a bulb with thick fleshy scales that become green when exposed to light
   **Liliaceae**
   *(Bowiea)*
NOTE: Many other South African bulbous genera such as *Haemanthus* and *Ornithogalum*, sometimes added to collections, are not included here.
1  Caudex not a green, fleshy bulb
   2  Leaves minute, hidden from view beneath white, papery stipules and borne on many short, thread-like branches covering the flat top of the caudex
      **Portulacaceae**
      *(Anacampseros alstonii)*
   2  Leaves not covered by white papery stipules
      3  At least some leaves opposite or whorled
         4  Leaves 1–4 pairs only, crowded rosette-like at the top of the bare flowering axis
            5  Leaves glabrous; flower star-like, white    **Crassulaceae**
               *(Crassula* p.p.*)*
            5  Leaves sericeous; flowers tubular, pinkish-orange    **Gesneriaceae**
               *(Rechsteineria leucotricha)*
         4  Leaves more numerous, in pairs spaced out along the branches
            6  Plant spiny or, if unarmed, resinous
               7  Leaves clustered in the spine axils; flowers long-tubed, with united petals    **Pedaliaceae**
                  *(Sesamothamnus)*
               7  Leaves not clustered in the spine axils; flowers flat to saucer-shaped; petals free    **Geraniaceae**
                  *(Sarcocaulon)*
            6  Plant unarmed, not resinous
               8  Fruit a pair of follicles; seeds many, plumed    **Asclepiadaceae**
               8  Fruit indehiscent, 4-winged; seeds 2–4    **Pedaliaceae**
                  *(Pterodiscus)*
      3  No leaves opposite or whorled
         9  Adult leaves entire and undivided, or at most crisped at the margins (shallowly 3-lobed in *Adenia,* q.v.)
            10  Plant dying right back to the caudex at or near ground level during the dormant season (Hemichamaephytes and Geophytes)
               11  Leaves radical; no aerial stems (apart from inflorescences)
                  12  Leaves flat or flattish; sap milky    **Euphorbiaceae**
                     *(Euphorbia* p.p.*)*
                  12  Leaves terete or almost as thick as wide; sap not milky
                     13  Flowers solitary, many-petalled    **Mesembryanthemaceae**
                        *(Sphalmanthus)*
                     13  Flowers several in a raceme, with 6 petals    **Liliaceae**
                        *(Bulbine)*

11 Some aerial branches at least, other than inflorescences, produced
  14 Leaf base wedge-shaped or broad and partly embracing stem; petiole undeveloped
    15 Caudex scaly; plants dioecious                **Crassulaceae**
                                             *(Sedum rosea)*

    15 Caudex not scaly; plants bisexual
      16 Leaves flat, green, scarcely succulent       **Portulacaceae**
      16 Leaves thick, splashed with purple, succulent    **Euphorbiaceae**
                                    *(Monadenium* p.p.*)*
  14 Leaf petiolate or abruptly narrowed at base
    17 Leaves arising direct from the thick caudex; no slender annual shoots
                                      **Moraceae**
                                       *(Dorstenia)*

    17 Leaves borne on slender, scarcely succulent aerial shoots
      18 Stipules present, usually branching and glandular     **Euphorbiaceae**
                                       *(Jatropha)*

      18 Stipules absent
        19 Caudex ± tessellate from large, polygonal, corky tubercles; tepals 6, free             **Dioscoreaceae**
                                     *(Dioscorea* p.p.*)*
        19 Caudex not tuberculate; sepals 5, petals 5, united into a bell
                                   **Convolvulaceae**
                                     *(Ipomoea)*
10 Plant with at least some perennial shoots above ground from which growth is resumed after dormancy (Chamaephytes and Phanerophytes)
  20 Plant unarmed or at most with twiggy dried inflorescences
    21 Leaves linear, from a sheathing base, never wholly deciduous    **Agavaceae**
    21 Leaves without a sheathing base
      22 Leaves scale-like, on thick, fleshy, radiating branches crowning the caudex                 **Euphorbiaceae**
                         *(Medusa-head euphorbias)*
      22 Leaves not reduced to scales; habit not medusiform
        23 Leaves distinctly petiolate
          24 Stipules present                   **Euphorbiaceae**
                                 *(Jatropha)*
          24 Stipules absent                    **Moraceae**
        23 Leaves not distinctly petiolate
          25 Flowers of one type, not capitulate      **Crassulaceae**
          25 Flowers of two types, rayed and rayless, in daisy-like capitula
                                   **Compositae**
                                   *(Othonna)*
20 Plant armed with sharp spines, prickles or thorns
  26 Plant with branching thorns               **Compositae**
                       *(Othonna euphorbioides)*

  26 Plant with unbranched armature

27  Armature solitary
    28  Armature petiolar, derived from persistent leaf stalks
                    **Fouquieriaceae**
    28  Armature not petiolar, never with a leaf blade at the tip
                      **Passifloraceae**
                      *(Adenia)*
27  Armature paired, often with a third smaller spine between 2 large
    ones                    **Apocynaceae**
                      *(Pachypodium* p.p.*)*
9  Adult leaves lobed, incised or compound
  29  Leaves lobed or incised but never with separate leaflets
    30  Vining plants with long, slender, non-succulent climbing stems
      31  Caudex squat, ± abruptly passing over into annual branches
        32  Flowers showy, purple, borne low down on the stems  **Convolvulaceae**
                      *(Ipomoea)*
        32  Flowers small, yellow, unisexual, borne distally  **Cucurbitaceae**
      31  Caudex long-tapering, gradually passing over into thin branches
        33  Tendrils absent or axillary        **Passifloraceae**
                      *(Adenia)*
        33  Tendrils present, opposed to leaf base    **Vitaceae**
                      *(Cissus* p.p.*)*
    30  Plants without climbing stems
      34  Leaves without a petiole, borne on slim annual shoots  **Crassulaceae**
                      *(Sedum rosea)*
      34  Leaves petiolate, borne direct on the thick stems
        35  Caudex silvery green with a white bark that peels off like thin paper;
           leaf lobes 10 cm or more long      **Vitaceae**
                      *(Cyphostemma)*
        35  Caudex without white papery peeling bark; leaf lobes less than
           10 cm long
          36  Leaves glabrous              **Compositae**
                      *(Othonna* p.p.*)*
          36  Leaves rough with bristles    **Cucurbitaceae**
                      *(Dendrosicyos)*
  29  Leaves compound, with distinct leaflets
    37  Leaves digitate              **Bombacaceae**
NOTE: Borderline succulents, keying out here, are *Cochlospermum* and *Cussonia*
(unc.)
    37  Leaves pinnate or pinnatisect
      38  Leaves simply pinnate with ± broad lobes
        39  Sap milky; ovary 1-celled; fruit utricular    **Anacardiaceae**
                      *(Pachycormus)*
        39  Sap not milky; ovary 3–4-celled; fruit drupaceous, splitting with
           2–3 leathery valves      **Burseraceae**
      38  Leaves pinnatisect or bipinnate    **Geraniaceae**
                      *(Pelargonium)*

NOTE: *Moringa* (unc.) has large bipinnate leaves.

## Sizes of Families and Genera

The size of a Family, as measured by the number of included genera, or of a genus in terms of its species, varies from one classifier to another by a factor of as much as three or even more. Thus, although collectors press for an exact figure, such estimates have little value when the units involved are so subjective.

The adjectives used here, which attempt to reflect an average or middle course, can be approximately translated as follows:

| | |
|---|---|
| Monotypic | 1 |
| Very small | 2–6 |
| Small | 7–20 |
| Medium-sized | 21–60 |
| Large | 61–200 |
| Very large | Over 200. |

All generic names likely to be encountered in gardens and current reference books are traceable through the index. Those not accepted by the author are referred to synonymy under the appropriate genus. Those accepted but rare or unrepresented in cultivation are not separately described, but will be found noted in the keys in the appropriate places. Hybrid generic names with an asterisk are published here for the first time.

There now follow in Chapters 8–35 keys to the genera including succulents in each of these families.

# CHAPTER 8

# Agavaceae

A small Family recognized as recently as 1934, this comprises genera once classified under Liliaceae and Amaryllidaceae. The limits are still undecided, but the core is made up of xerophytic, sometimes tree-like genera with robust rosettes of usually large, tough, fibrous leaves and a rhizome or offsetting habit. The karyotype is also distinctive: 5 large and 25 small chromosomes in *Agave* and *Yucca*, and other numbers and characteristic sizes in the remaining genera.

The flowers are trimerous and the fruits capsular or berrylike as in the two Families mentioned above. The obvious distinction is the absence of bulbs and the general life-form.

The distribution is wide but confined to the drier regions of the tropics and subtropics of both hemispheres.

In addition to the leaf- and caudiciform succulents keyed out below, others could arguably be called stem-succulent. *Yucca, Cordyline* and *Dracaena,* for example, mostly have thick, soft, fibrous to fleshy trunks recalling palms. Some yuccas are hardy and blend well with tender succulents put out for summer bedding. Other borderline genera sometimes favoured by collectors are *Beschorneria, Dasylirion, Furcraea* and *Hesperaloe.*

Young potted agaves look much like bromeliads and aloes, and in the absence of flowers experience is needed to separate them. Broadly speaking, bromeliads have thinner leaves, and aloes have juicier, less fibrous foliage which snaps in half cleanly, whereas an agave is so fibrous that one has to twist and wrench the leaf to part it. Also, these lack the stout terminal spine which is so characteristic of *Agave.*

## General References

HUTCHINSON, J. 1959 Agavaceae in *The Families of Flowering Plants* 2nd Edn. (Oxford), 662–665. Key to 19 genera.
GENTRY, H. S. 1972 *The Agave Family in Sonora* (Washington). Key to 7 genera and all species of Sonora only.

## KEY TO GENERA INCLUDING SUCCULENTS

1 Leaf succulents with rhizomes or ± stemless rosettes
  2 Leaves many, often large, commonly saw-edged and with a terminal spine, in solitary or clumped spiral rosettes     **Agave**
  2 Leaves few, entire and without a spiny tip, in spiral rosettes or distichous, sometimes on short stems     **Sansevieria**
1 Caudiciform succulents with rosettes of fibrous, linear leaves borne direct from the caudex
  3 Leaves flat, channelled, green, in a single terminal rosette; fruit with 3 angles, thin walled     **Nolina**
  3 Leaves filiform, grey, in several rosettes from one caudex; fruit not angled; globose, woody and thick-walled     **Calibanus**

## AGAVE

L. *Sp. Pl. Edn.* 1: 323, 1753; *Gen. Pl. Edn.* 5: 150, 1754.
Typ. *A. americana* L.
SYN. *Manfreda.*

Large, central American genus with often very large, stemless, monocarpic rosettes. Leaves up to 2 m (6½ ft.) long and up to ½ m (20 in.) thick at base. Inflorescence terminal, up to 6 m (20 ft.) or even more tall. Some species are of economic value for the leaf fibres (sisal) and for the intoxicating drinks fermented from the copious sugary sap.

BERGER, A. *Die Agaven.* Jena 1915. Key to all species (in German).
BREITUNG, A. J. *The Agaves.* California 1968. Species of S.W. U.S.A. only.
JACOBSEN. *Lexicon.* Synopsis.

## CALIBANUS

Rose in *Contr. U.S. Nat. Herb.* 10: 90, 1906.
Typ. *C. hookeri* Trel.
Monotypic genus from Tamaulipas, Mexico, of bizarre habit from the low, massive, lumpish caudex covered in what look like tufts of grass (Fig. 7.14).

## NOLINA ——————————————————————————————————

Michaux *Fl. Bor.-Am.* 1: 207, 1803 ('Nolinea').

Typ. *N. georgiana* Michx.

SYN. *Beaucarnea.*

Small genus from Mexico and the southern U.S.A. of which the most popular with collectors are *N. recurvata* and allies with a bottle- or flask-shaped trunk and crown of numerous, thin, sheathing leaves.

## SANSEVIERIA ——————————————————————————————

Thunberg *Prodr. Pl. Cap* 5; 65, 1794, Nom. cons.

Typ. *S. hyacinthoides* (L.) Druce.

Medium to large genus from Africa to India including many ± succulent species familiar as tough, long-lived house plants. Leaves flat, channelled, semiterete or terete. Flowers mostly whitish, tubular, often scented, with copious nectar. Like *Agave,* some species are grown commercially for fibre.

BROWN, N. E. in *Kew Bull.* 1914: 273–279; 1915: 185–261. **Key** to 54 species.

GRAF, A. B. *Exotica III,* pp. 1710–1711; Ills. 1105–1110. Rutherford 1957.

GRAF, A. B. *Tropica,* pp. 1074–1075; Ills. 596, 607–612. Rutherford 1978.

MORGENSTERN, K. D. *Sansevierias.* Kempten 1979.

PFENNIG, H. in *Cact. Succ. J. Gt. Brit.* 41 (3): 56 *et seq.,* 1979.

# CHAPTER 9

# Anacardiaceae

This medium-sized, mainly tropical Family includes economic plants like the mango, *Mangifera,* and ornamental shrubs some of which, as the sumach, *Rhus*, are hardy and grown in temperate gardens.

One genus of bizarre pachycaul habit has caught the attention of lovers of bonsai and unusual succulents. Its habitat overlaps that of *Bursera microphylla* which looks rather similar (see p. 100), from which, in the absence of flowers, it is most readily distinguished by having a white, milky latex.

Genus including Succulents: *PACHYCORMUS* only.

## PACHYCORMUS ————————————————————————

Coville ex Standley in *Contr. U.S. Nat. Herb.* 23: 671, 1923.
Typ. *P. discolor* (Benth.) Cov. ex Standl.

The sole species of this monotypic genus, *P. discolor,* is endemic to Baja California where it gives an extraordinary, unworldly look to the landscape with its massive lumpish trunk and gnarled branches. The tiny pinnate leaves drop in the dormant season. Small plants are in short supply but not difficult to grow and much in demand by collectors.

**Figs. 10.1-10.7  Apocynaceae: *Adenium obesum***

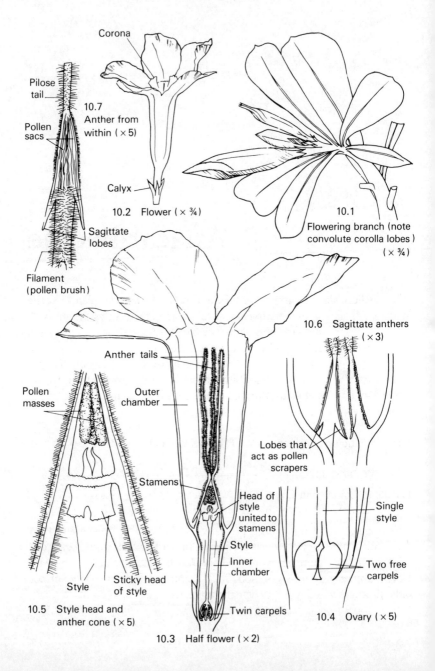

Corona

Pilose
tail

Pollen
sacs

10.7
Anther from
within ( × 5)

Calyx

Sagittate
lobes

Filament
(pollen brush)

10.2   Flower ( × ¾)

10.1
Flowering branch (note
convolute corolla lobes )
( × ¾)

Anther tails

10.6   Sagittate anthers
( × 3)

Pollen
masses

Outer
chamber

Stamens

Lobes that
act as pollen
scrapers

Head of
style
united to
stamens

Single
style

Style

Inner
chamber

Two free
carpels

Style

Sticky head
of style

10.5   Style head and
anther cone ( × 5)

Twin carpels

10.4   Ovary ( × 5)

10.3   Half flower ( × 2)

# CHAPTER 10

# Apocynaceae

This large, predominantly tropical Family is made up in the main of creepers and twiners, including a few that are hardy, such as the periwinkles (*Vinca* spp.) of European gardens. Some have large and showy flowers, as for example *Allamanda*, favoured as a glasshouse climber. *Nerium* is the oleander and *Plumeria* frangipani, extensively planted in tropical gardens for their scented blooms. The more than usually thick shoots of the latter led Jacobsen to list it as a succulent.

Apocynaceae have flower parts basically in fives, but with only two free carpels that ripen into a pair of long horn-like follicles packed with plumed seeds. In these respects they show affinities with the Asclepiadaceae, and have an equally sophisticated mechanism that ensures cross-pollination. The often large and showy flowers of the two succulent genera detailed below have a tubular corolla divided into an outer and an inner chamber by the cone of five stamens, whose anthers are sagittate and block the entry to the inner chamber, except for narrow slits through which a long proboscis can penetrate to seek nectar at the bottom of the tube. *Adenium* also has long whiskery tails to the tops of the anthers that act as nectar guides for insects entering the tube (they could be easily confused for stigmas by the uninitiated). The two free carpels have the styles united above and further joined to the stamens at the top forming a rigid dome. The enlarged head of the style secretes a viscid gum. Pollen is shed inside the apex of the anther cone and at first sight would seem destined to self-pollinate the stigmas below. However, even if any drops down of its own accord, no seed is set since the plants appear to be self-incompatible.

An insect probing for nectar feels its way down the wall of the tube, carrying pollen from a previous visitation stuck part way up the proboscis. On retreating, this pollen is drawn off against the stigma by the curious pointed lower lobes of the anthers, which act as scrapers. The copious hair on the filaments also acts as a brush. At the same time the proboscis is freshly gummed by contact with the style head and draws off a mass of new pollen from directly above it.

The corolla lobes are convolute in the bud, and are linked together at the mouth of the tube by small outgrowths forming a low corona. Apocynaceae typically have a white milky sap containing alkaloids that protect the plants against grazing animals. In the succulent representatives the sap is quite thick and not white. In view of its poisonous nature, they are best handled with the same care as euphorbias.

## General Reference

ROWLEY, G. D. 1974 *Cact. Succ. J. Amer.* 46, 160–165. **Key** to genera and species.
ROWLEY, G. D. *Pachypodium and Adenium Handbook.* Nat. Cact. & Succ. Society (in press).

## KEY TO GENERA INCLUDING SUCCULENTS

1 Plant unarmed; anthers long-tailed above; seed with a deciduous tuft of hairs at
   each end                                                        **Adenium**
1 Plant spiny (spines minute and deciduous in *P. decaryi*); anthers not tailed above;
   seed with a deciduous tuft of hairs at one end only               **Pachypodium**

## ADENIUM ――――――――――――――――――――――――――――――

Roemer & Schultes *Syst.* 4: 411, 1819.

Typ. *A. obesum* (Forsk.) Roem. & Sch.

Monotypic genus ranging from S.W. Africa to Arabia, with smooth fleshy branches from a thick, tapered, variously branched caudex. Leaves ± crowded in terminal rosettes, spiralled, flat, laurel-like, ± deciduous. Flowers showy, with a tube 4 cm (1½ in.) or more long, red or pink (Figs. 10.1–7).

JACOBSEN: **Key** to species (here regarded as subspecies), p. 665.

## PACHYPODIUM ――――――――――――――――――――――――――

Lindley in *Bot. Reg.* 16: 1321, 1830 non Webb & Berth. 1836 nec. Nuttall 1838.

Typ. *P. succulentum* (Thunb.) DC.

Small genus from S. Africa and Madagascar with a range of very succulent life forms from underground caudex to tree-like, typically armed with spines in pairs or threes. Leaves flat, ± deciduous. Flowers white or flushed in drab purple, yellow or red.

JACOBSEN: Synopsis and **key** to species, pp. 310–311.

RAUH, W. in *Cact. Succ. J. Amer.*, 44: 7–31, 1972; in *Ashingtonia* 2 (7): 129, 131–134, 1976.

---

## TECHNICAL TERMS

Having trouble with unfamiliar words?

You are reminded that all botanical terms used in text are defined, and many illustrated as well, in the Glossary, pp. 235–253.

**Figs. 11.1-11.5   Asclepiadaceae: *Orbea variegata***

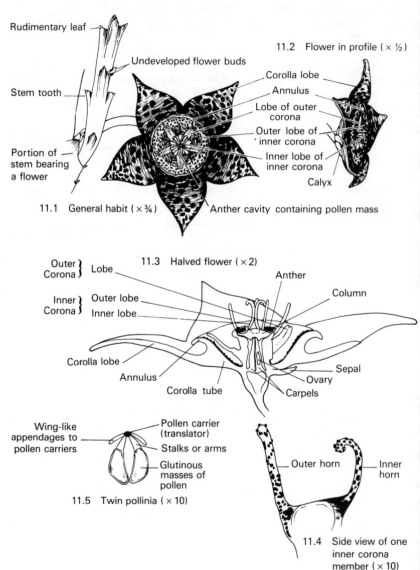

Rudimentary leaf

Undeveloped flower buds

11.2   Flower in profile ( × ½ )

Corolla lobe

Annulus

Stem tooth

Lobe of outer corona

Outer lobe of inner corona

Portion of stem bearing a flower

Inner lobe of inner corona

Calyx

11.1   General habit ( × ¾ )

Anther cavity containing pollen mass

Outer } Corona }   Lobe

11.3   Halved flower ( × 2)

Anther

Column

Inner } Corona }   Outer lobe

Inner lobe

Corolla lobe

Annulus

Corolla tube

Sepal

Ovary

Carpels

Wing-like appendages to pollen carriers

Pollen carrier (translator)

Stalks or arms

Glutinous masses of pollen

11.5   Twin pollinia ( × 10)

Outer horn

Inner horn

11.4   Side view of one inner corona member ( × 10)

# CHAPTER 11

# Asclepiadaceae

The large milkweed Family is centred in Africa but extends throughout the tropics. It is closely related to the Apocynaceae and, like that Family, made up mostly of climbers, but there are some shrubs and herbs. The leaves are opposite, simple and entire, but reduced or absent in the xerophytes, and certain genera have a white milky latex. The outstanding feature that makes the Family at once recognizable is the complex structure of the five-parted flower, which at first glance appears to have no obvious stamens, pollen, carpels or stigmas. Taking *Orbea* as an example (Figs. 11.1–5), we find five small sepals on the outside, surrounding a corolla made up of 5 more or less united petals which form a saucer- or cup-shaped tube at the base. Compared with other flowers, the petals are thick and leathery, and the colours mostly sombre. Moving inwards, one meets next a series of outgrowths that are related to the attraction of certain insects that effect pollination and the exclusion of others. First there is the **annulus**; then two **coronas** ('little crowns'), each made up of 5 members, the corona nearer the centre having two lobes, an inner and an outer. These are elevated on a central column that completely overtops the two free carpels.

The five stamens are visible as humps at the top of the column. Each sessile anther contains two pollen masses which never break up to release single pollen grains but are transferred as a whole, linked together by a yoke. Each pollen mass is called a **pollinium**, and the whole has a parallel in the unrelated orchid Family. In *Ceropegia* (Fig. 2.18) there is a further complication in the extension of the corolla into a tube surmounted by various appendages at the open mouth, suggesting a Japanese lantern. These act as insect traps, tiny flies being confined in the belly of the tube for long enough to pick up pollinia before escaping to enter another flower and pollinate it. Pollination requires that the leg or proboscis brushes against an anther, whereupon the carrier becomes firmly hooked on the bristles and is torn away. The receptive stigma is situated in a cleft beneath the stamen, overhung by a rim that acts as scraper and detaches the pollinia on arrival. Flowers of the Asclepiadaceae are very selective, each species having only one pollinator, as in orchids. In the rank-smelling flowers of Stapelieae, which often look remarkably like carrion, this is typically a species of blow-fly. Pollination is difficult to carry out by hand, and growers are rarely successful, although fruits often set in collections as a result of random visitations by insects. The progeny from seed, however, often turn out to be hybrid.

The fruit in Asclepiadaceae is a pair of follicles, often several inches long, which splits to release a cloud of black seeds, each with a silky white parachute.

The Family is divided into six overlapping Tribes, in all but one of which some form of succulence has evolved, although in the most marked degree in Tribe VI Stapelieae, where all the species are succulent. Structure of the corona has been much emphasized in segregating the genera here, and it is hence not possible to make a key based solely on vegetative characters since some of the plants are indistinguishable until they flower.

The prevalence of intergeneric hybrids, mostly of wild origin, will be noted. It suggests that, despite the specialized and unique character individualizing each flower, flies sometimes make mistakes, and second, it throws further doubt on the wisdom of recognizing so many separate genera.

In addition to the genera keyed out below, Jacobsen includes *Dischidia* and *Hoya*, some of whose species have thick, semi-fleshy leaves, and certain Madagascan rarities with white-felted or oddly pustulate stems (*Seyrigia, Karimbolea*). I am indebted to Larry Leach and Colin Walker for helpful criticisms of this difficult and still imperfect key.

## General References

BRACK, S. 1973 *Bull. Afr. Succ. Pl. Soc.* 7, 230–233. Key to the succulent Asclepiadaceae.

BROWN, N. E. 1907–09 Asclepiadaceae in *Fl. Capensis* 4, 518–1036; and in 1906 *Fl. Trop. Africa* 4, 213–503. Synopses of genera and keys to species.

DYER, R. A. 1975 *The Genera of Southern African Flowering Plants* Vol. I. (Pretoria). Key to S. African genera.

KELLER, F. 1971 *Cact. Succ. J. Amer.* 43: 163–167. *Checklist of Stapeliads published since The Stapelieae* (1937–1971).

LUCKHOFF, C. A. 1952 *The Stapelieae of Southern Africa* (Cape Town). **Key** to genera.

STRONG, R. and BENCE, T. A. 1976 *Asclepiadaceae* 9, 10–11. New names in Stapelieae published since Fred Keller's Checklist.

WHITE, A. and SLOANE, B. L. 1937 *The Stapelieae* 2nd Edn. 3 Vols. (Pasadena). Stapelieae alone; **keys** to all genera and species.

## KEY TO GENERA INCLUDING SUCCULENTS

1 Stem succulents
  2 Stems soft and very fleshy, with short internodes, often cactiform
    3 Corolla lobes eventually free at the tips
      4 Corolla with intermediate lobes or points at the sinuses between the lobes; tubercles usually not bristle-tipped (exc. *S. pilosus*)
        5 Outer corona arising from the staminal column in an erect to diverging crown     **Stapelianthus**
        5 Outer corona sessile or adnate to the base of the corolla or absent     **Huernia**
      4 Intermediate lobes absent or, if present, then tubercles bristle-tipped (*Hoodia*) or outer corona reduced to a pair of teeth (*Huerniopsis*)
        6 Flower with a long narrow tube 2–4 cm long and 3–4 mm wide midway, ending in linear corolla lobes     **Ceropegia** p.p.
        6 Flower without a long narrow tube; if tubular, then corolla lobes not linear
          7 Stems acute- or obtusely-ribbed; tubercles, if developed, not bristle-tipped although sometimes sharply acute
            8 Ribs 4–6, not regularly hexagonal-tuberculate or, if so, then flowers 15 mm or more in ∅
              9 Corona simple, of 5 lobes
                10 Sepals small; corolla lobes free for more than half their length; corona lobes with a dorsal or transverse crest at base     **Piaranthus**
                10 Sepals large; corolla lobes united at least up to halfway; corona lobes thick, without a dorsal crest, produced above the column into subulate points     **Huerniopsis**
              9 Corona double or triple
                11 Outer corona lobes free to the base, spreading
                  12 Stems mostly pubescent, with tiny, erect, deciduous scale leaves and small, ± erect, tubercular teeth; flowers mostly hairy     **Stapelia**
                  12 Stems glabrous, leafless, with wide-spreading, prominent, tubercular teeth; flowers almost or quite glabrous or ciliate
                    13 Stems ± erect; tubercle teeth large, prominent, usually with two smaller lateral teeth below the apex; corolla mostly ciliate; corona glabrous

14  Flowers rotate, more than 3 cm ∅
   15  Flowers opening successively in a cyme; annulus present **Orbea**
   15  Flowers opening ± simultaneously in an umbel; annulus absent **Orbeopsis**
14  Flowers campanulate, less than 3 cm ∅, stiff, fleshy, in lateral fascicles **Pachycymbium**
  13  Stems trailing, rooting adventitiously, with small tubercle teeth but no lateral teeth; corolla glabrous; corona hairy **Orbeanthus**
11  Outer corona lobes ± united below into a tube or disc, or short, forming pouches
   16  Tips of inner corona lobes dilated **Edithcolea**
   16  Tips of inner corona lobes not dilated
     17  Outer corona a solid disc **Duvalia**
     17  Outer corona long tubular, with short incurved lobes **Stapeliopsis**
     17  Outer corona various, but not as above **Caralluma**

NOTE: *Whitesloanea* (unc.) has bifid outer corona lobes free almost to the base; *Rhytidocaulon* (unc.) differs from *Caralluma* only in the irregularly rugose-papillate, tessellate stem.

  8  Ribs 6–13(–20), regularly divided into elongated hexagonal tubercles; flowers 4–10(–25) mm ∅ **Echidnopsis**
7  Stems tessellate with flat, ± polygonal tubercles arranged ± randomly, or stems with rows of tubercles each tipped with 1 or 3 bristles
  18  Each tubercle tipped with 3 stiff bristles **Tavaresia**
  18  Tubercles not tipped with 3 bristles
   19  Flowers 2.5–20(–25) mm ∅, clustered
    20  Flowers borne in usually lateral umbels; corolla with a cup-shaped tube **Pseudolithos**
    20  Flowers not umbellate, scattered near the crown of the plant; corolla flat or saucer-shaped **Trichocaulon**
   19  Flowers 22–200 mm ∅, solitary **Hoodia**
3  Corolla lobes remaining united at the tips, or, if free, then inner corona lobes incurved and often connivent over anthers (*Pectinaria*)
  21  Flowers usually solitary, lateral on the main stems
   22  Corolla lobes inflexed, the flower looking like a miniature green apple **Pseudopectinaria**
   22  Corolla lobes not inflexed **Pectinaria**
  21  Flowers borne on slender, elongated, terminal inflorescences **Ceropegia** p.p.
2  Climbers, creepers or shrubs with terete, sparingly succulent stems with long internodes
  23  Corolla tubular **Ceropegia** p.p.
  23  Corolla ± flat, rotate; petals shortly united at the base

    24  Corona usually double, below the level of the stamens    **Sarcostemma**
    24  Corona single, equal to or exceeding the stamens    **Cynanchum**
1  Caudiciform succulents
    25  Corolla tubular, with the lobes united again at the tips    **Ceropegia** p.p.
    25  Corolla ± flat, rotate; petals shortly united at the base and free at the tips
        (united at first in *Brachystelma barberae*)
      26  Filaments free; pollen granular    **Raphionacme**
      26  Filaments united or stamens sessile; pollen massed into pollinia
        27  Anthers tipped with a large, inflated, membranous appendage    **Fockea**
        27  Anthers not so    **Brachystelma**

## × BRACHYPELIA*

Rowl.

= *Brachystelma* × *Stapelia.*

1 cultivar.

## BRACHYSTELMA

R. Brown in *Curtis Bot. Mag.* 1822 t. 2343.

Typ. *B. tuberosum* (Meerb.) R. Br.

Medium-sized African genus of dwarf succulents that parallel in habit the tuberous ceropegias and are distinguished only by the flat, saucer- or rarely cup-shaped flower with petals united for halfway or less and with the tips usually free.

Intergeneric hybrid: × *Brachypelia.*

DYER, R. A. in *Fl. Southern Africa* 27(4): 1–41, 1980. Key to S. African species.

## × CARALLITHOS*

Rowl.

(*Caralluma* × *Pseudolithos*).

One cultivar.

## CARALLUMA

R. Brown in *Mem. Wern. Soc.* 1: 25, 1809.

Typ. *C. adscendens* (Roxb.) Haw.

SYN. *Boucerosia, Frerea.*

Large, heterogeneous assemblage of stapelia-like stem succulents from Africa, the Canary Isles, Arabia, Socotra and eastern India. It is a 'dustbin genus', including all species not already segregated on corona structure, and as such is in urgent need of revision.

JACOBSEN: Synopsis.

Intergeneric hybrids: × *Carallithos*, × *Carapelia*, × *Hoodialluma.*

## × CARAPELIA

Rowl. in *Rep. Pl. Succ.* 23:6, 1972.
= *Caralluma* × *Stapelia.*
Few wild hybrids.

## CEROPEGIA

L. *Sp. Pl.* Edn. I: 211, 1753; *Gen. Pl.* Edn. V: 100, 1754.
Typ. *C. candelabrum* L.

Large genus of mostly weak-stemmed creepers, climbers or rarely shrubs, sometimes with fleshy roots or a caudex (Fig. 7.13). Leaves ± fleshy and simple or reduced to scales; a few species are stem succulent and almost like stapelias in habit. The peculiar flytrap flowers (Fig. 1.17,18) have a ± long corolla tube with 5 free lobes which, at least at first, remain united by the tips to form a lantern- or umbrella-like canopy; corona double.

HUBER, H. in *Mem. Soc. Brot.* 12: 1–214, 1957. Key to species (in Latin).
DYER, R. A. in *Fl. Southern Africa* 27(4): 43–82, 1980. Key to S. African species.
JACOBSEN: Synopsis and key to species.

## CYNANCHUM

L. *Sp. Pl.* Edn. I: 212, 1753; *Gen. Pl.* Edn. V: 101, 1754.
Typ. *C. acutum* L.

Large genus, widespread in the tropics and subtropics, including a few fleshy-stemmed climbers or small shrubs without leaves that have infiltrated succulent collections. In some species the stem surface is curiously and irregularly pustulate.

## DUVALIA

Haworth *Syn. Pl. Succ.* 44, 1812.
Typ. *D. elegans* (Mass.) Haw.

Small genus from S.W. and E. Africa and Arabia. Stems typically short, fat and often like small potatoes, with 4–6 low angles. Flowers small, with 5 usually narrow corolla lobes reflexed at the margins and with a raised centre; the disc-like outer corona is the main diagnostic feature.

From *Huernia* it is distinguished by having the corolla lobes usually ciliate and folded back at the margins, tiny teeth at the base of the scale leaves, and a stalked corona with dorsal prolongation of the inner lobes.
Intergeneric hybrid: × *Duvaliaranthus.*

## × DUVALIARANTHUS

Bruyns in *J. S. Afr. Bot.* 42: 365, 1976.
= *Duvalia* × *Piaranthus.*
1 wild hybrid.

## ECHIDNOPSIS

Hook. F. in *Curtis Bot. Mag.* 1871 t. 5930.
Typ. *E. cereiformis* Hook. f.
Medium-sized genus from the hotter parts of Africa, Arabia, Socotra and S. Africa, recognizable by the tessellated appearance of the stems with 6–13 or more regular rows of ± hexagonal, low, flat tubercles, and minute flowers.

## EDITHCOLEA

N. E. Brown in *Kew Bull.* 1895: 220.
Typ. *E. grandis* N. E. Br.
Monotypic genus related to *Caralluma* from E. Africa and Socotra, notable for the large and showy flowers but infrequently seen on account of difficulties of cultivation. The short-jointed stems have sharp-pointed tubercles in 4 or 5 rows.

## FOCKEA

Endlicher *Icon. Gen. Pl.* t. 91, 1838.
Typ. *F. capensis* Endl.
Small African genus of dioecious xerophytes with large ± underground caudices and long, slender, erect or twining, annual branches with opposite, simple leaves. Flowers not often produced in cultivation.

## HOODIA

Sweet in DC *Prodr.* 8: 664, 1844.
Typ. *H. gordonii* (Mass.) DC.
Small genus from S. and S.W. Africa forming grey-skinned, cereiform shrubs up to 1 m (40 in.) tall with the branches covered in conical tubercles each tipped with a stiff, sharp prickle. The large, flat, dish-like flowers at once distinguish it from any other genus.
Intergeneric hybrids: × *Hoodialluma,* × *Hoodiapelia.*

## × HOODIALLUMA

Rowl. in *Rep. Pl. Succ.* 27: 4, 1979.
SYN. *Hoodiopsis* Luckh.
= *Hoodia* × *Caralluma.*
1 wild hybrid.

## × HOODIAPELIA

Rowl. in *Rep. Pl. Succ.* 27: 4, 1979.
SYN. *Luckhoffia* W. & S.
= *Hoodia* × *Stapelia.*
1 wild hybrid.

## HUERNIA

R. Brown in *Mem. Wern. Soc.* 1: 22, 1809.
Typ. *H. campanulata* (Mass.) Haw.

Large genus from S. Africa to E. Africa and Arabia; very dwarf, with 4–7-angled stems or, rarely, spiralled tubercles. The extra lobes between the five main petals are the best spot character, but tiny lobes also appear in *Huerniopsis* and other genera, so the separation is weak.

From *Duvalia*, further distinctive features are the glabrous corolla lobes only slightly folded back at the margins, and the 5 simple, knobbed or ridged inner corona lobes without a dorsal prolongation.
JACOBSEN: Synopsis.

## HUERNIOPSIS

N. E. Brown in *J. Linn. Soc. Bot.* 17: 171, 1878.
Typ. *H. decipiens* N. E. Br.

Very small genus from S. and S. W. Africa and Botswana, doubtfully distinct from *Huernia* by the reduction of the outer corona to a pair of teeth.

## ORBEA

Haworth *Syn. Pl. Succ.* 37, 1812.
Typ. *O. variegata* (L.) Haw.
SYN. *Diplocyatha, Stultitia.*

Small S. African genus with outliers in tropical and E. Africa, segregated from *Stapelia* by minor vegetative differences and by the presence of a ring-like annulus (Figs. 11.1–5).

Intergeneric hybrid: × *Orbelia.*
LEACH, L. C. in *Excelsa Taxonomic Series* No. 1, 1978. **Key** to species.


## ORBEANTHUS

Leach in *Excelsa Taxonomic Series* No. 1: 71–74, 1978.
Typ. *O. conjunctus* (W. & S.) Leach.
Very small genus from the Transvaal, formerly included under *Stultitia* and removed by virtue of small differences in flower structure.
LEACH, L. C. in *l.c.* **Key** to species.


## × ORBELIA *

Rowl.
= *Orbea* × *Stapelia.*
Few wild hybrids.


## × ORBEOPELIA *

Rowl.
= *Orbeopsis* × *Stapelia.*
Few wild hybrids.


## ORBEOPSIS

Leach in *Excelsa Taxonomic Series* No. 1: 61–69, 1978.
Typ. *O lutea* (N. E. Br.) Leach.
Small S. African genus segregated from *Caralluma* from which it differs in minor floral characters.
Intergeneric hybrid: × *Orbeopelia.*
LEACH, L. C. in *l.c.* **Key** to species.


## PACHYCYMBIUM

Leach in *Excelsa Taxonomic Series* No. 1: 69–71, 1978.
Typ. *P. keithii* (Dyer) Leach.
Very small genus from S. Africa, segregated from *Caralluma* by minor features of the flower.
LEACH, L. C. in *l.c.* **Key** to species.

## PECTINARIA————————————————————

Haworth *Suppl. Pl. Succ.* 14, 1819, Nom. cons.

Typ. *P. articulata* Haw.

Small genus from the Cape with 4–6-angled tuberculate stems, easily recognizable when in flower by the diverging corolla lobes which unite at the tips to form a canopy rather like that of *Ceropegia* (*q.v.*) or by the semi-subterranean habit and inner corona lobes incurving and often connivent over the anthers.

## PIARANTHUS ————————————————————

R. Brown in *Mem. Wern. Soc.* 1: 23, 1809.

Typ. *P. punctatus* (Mass.) Schult.

Small S. and S.W. African genus of dwarf species with ± short joints, often like small potatoes, with *c.* 4 low angles; flowers notable for the absence of an outer corona.

Intergeneric hybrid: × *Duvaliaranthus.*

## PSEUDOLITHOS ————————————————————

Bally in *Candollea* 20; 41, 1965.

Typ. *P. migiurtinus* (Chiov.) Bally.

SYN. *Lithocaulon.*

Very small genus of rare and tender highly succulent species from Somalia with mostly simple, spherical or squarish, very soft stems covered in flat polygonal tubercles. Flowers minute, in umbels.

JACOBSEN: **Key** to 4 species pp. 680–681.

Intergeneric hybrid: × *Carallithos.*

## PSEUDOPECTINARIA ————————————————————

Lavranos in *Cact. Succ. J. Amer.* 43: 9, 1971.

Typ. *P. malum* Lavr.

Monotypic genus from Somalia distinguishable from all other Stapelieae by the small, urn-shaped flower which has the corolla lobes turned inwards and united at the centre, leaving five slits for insect entry.

## RAPHIONACME

Harvey in *London J. Bot.* 1: 22, 1842.
Typ. *R. divaricata* Harv.

Small African genus of which a few caudiciform species may occasionally be encountered in specialist collections, but are of botanical interest only. The tiny star-like flowers are green or purplish and borne in cymes; habit as for *Fockea*.

## SARCOSTEMMA

R. Brown in *Mem. Wern. Soc.* 1: 50, 1809.
Typ. *S. viminale* (L.) R. Br.

Small genus widespread in the tropics and subtropics, consisting of leafless, twiggy, sprawling or suberect or liana-like and slightly succulent shrubs. Flowers infrequently seen in cultivation; white, usually scented, in umbels.

## STAPELIA

L. *Sp. Pl.* Edn. I: 217, 1753; *Gen. Pl.* Edn. V: 102, 1754.
Typ. *S. hirsuta* L.

Large genus of mainly African stem succulents extending through Tanzania and Kenya to E. India, and scarcely to be distinguished from *Caralluma* (Fig. 7.8). Stems ± square in cross-section and flowers rarely small, sometimes very large, often hairy and simulating carrion in colour, texture and smell. JACOBSEN: Synopsis.

Intergeneric hybrids:  × *Brachypelia,*  × *Carapelia,*  × *Hoodiapelia,* × *Orbelia,* × *Orpeopelia,* × *Trichopelia.*

## STAPELIANTHUS

Choux ex White & Sloane *Stapelieae* Edn. I: 71, 1933.
Typ. *S. madagascariensis* Choux.

Small, rather diverse, genus from S. and S.W. Madagascar doubtfully separable from *Huernia* on minor characters of the flower.

## STAPELIOPSIS

Pillans in *S. Afr. Gard. & Country Life* 18: 32, 1928, non Choux 1931 nec Phillips 1932.

Typ. *S. neronis* Pill.

Very small genus from S. and S.W. Africa resembling *Stapelia* but segregated on account of the unique form of the outer corona.

## TAVARESIA

Welwitsch in *Bol. Ann. Cons. Ultr.* No. 7: 79, 1854.

Typ. *T. angolensis* Welw.

SYN. *Decabelone.*

Very small (monotypic?) genus of cereiform appearance, widespread from S.W. and S. Africa to Zimbabwe. 6–12 ribs are divided into conical tubercles, each tipped with 3 small, diverging bristles which make the genus instantly recognizable. Equally distinctive are the large tubular flowers and caudate outer corona lobes.

JACOBSEN: **Key** to 3 species p. 682.

## × TRICHOCAULON

N. E. Brown in *J. Linn. Soc. Bot.* 17: 164, 1878.

Typ. *T. piliferum* (L.f.) N. E. Br.

Small genus from S. and S.W. Africa with very fleshy cereiform or cactiform stems covered in polygonal tubercles which are flat or conical and bristle-tipped as in *Hoodia*, from which genus the tiny flowers at once distinguish it. Intergeneric hybrid: × *Trichopelia.*

## × TRICHOPELIA *

Rowl.

= *Trichocaulon* × *Stapelia.*

One wild hybrid.

# CHAPTER 12

# Bombacaceae

This small Family of tropical trees is notable for the pachycaul habit: that is, the expansion of trunk and sometimes main branches also with soft, spongy, water-storing tissues giving an often gigantic and grotesque appearance, of which the giant baobab, *Adansonia*, is a classic example. Whether one calls them all succulents or not has been much argued, although they look out of place in a glasshouse collection of succulents and require to grow large before the trunk starts to thicken. The flowers, which are often large and spectacular, are also unlikely to be seen. *Adansonia, Cavanillesia* and *Chorisia* (with a spiny trunk) are listed by Jacobsen in addition to the genus mentioned below. Choice of which to include is arbitrary here as none of the genera is commonly cultivated and the merits and demerits of each are much the same.

Genus including Succulents: *BOMBAX* only.

## BOMBAX

L. *Sp. Pl.* Edn. I: 511, 1753; *Gen. Pl.* Edn. V: 227, 1754.
Typ. *B. ceiba* L.

A small genus from tropical Africa and Asia of which *B. ellipticum*, which rapidly forms a swollen caudex from seed, is perhaps the most frequently offered to collectors.

# CHAPTER 13

# Burseraceae

A small Family of tropical trees and shrubs, Burseraceae are noteworthy in containing aromatic resins and balsams, many of them of economic importance. The leaves are alternate and usually compound. The two similar-looking genera keyed out below appeal to lovers of bonsai because of their thick, gnarled trunks.

*Bursera* is American; *Commiphora* ranges from Africa to India. For distinctions from the superficially similar *Pachycormus,* see p. 81.

## General References

ENGLER, A. 1897 *Die Natürl. Pflanzenfam.* III. iv 231–257. Burseraceae.

GILLETT, J. B. 1979. Kew Bull. 34(3): 569–587. *Commiphora* Jacq. (Burseraceae) in South America and its relationship to *Bursera*.

## KEY TO GENERA INCLUDING SUCCULENTS

1  Plant ± unarmed; petiole often winged; sepals ± free and erect or spreading in bud revealing the corolla within     **Bursera**
1  Plant usually armed; petiole very rarely winged; sepals ± united into a tube and covering the bud so that the corolla is hidden     **Commiphora**

## BURSERA

Jacquin ex L. *Sp. Pl.* Edn. II: 471, 1762, Nom. cons.

Typ. *B. simaruba* (L.) Sarg.

Large genus of xerophytic shrubs from the warmer, drier parts of the New World. The species most likely to be seen in cultivation are recognizable from other caudiciforms by the pinnately compound leaves.

## COMMIPHORA

Jacquin *Hort. Schoenbr.* 2: 66, 1797, Nom. cons.
Typ. *C. madagascariensis* Jacquin.

Large genus, the counterpart of *Bursera* in the Old World and distinguishable from it only when in flower. It is a matter of taste how many pachycaul Burseraceae are regarded as worthy of inclusion in a succulent collection.

PALMER, E. *A Field Guide to the Trees of Southern Africa,* 159–165, 1977.
**Key** to species.

---

### USING THE KEYS

If you cannot follow the keys, re-read the guidance given on p. 66.
If you can follow them, but do not get results, consult 'In Case of Failure' on p. 233.

**Figs. 14.1-14.4  Cactaceae: 14.1-14.3 *Echinopsis* sp.; 14.4 *Opuntia* sp.**

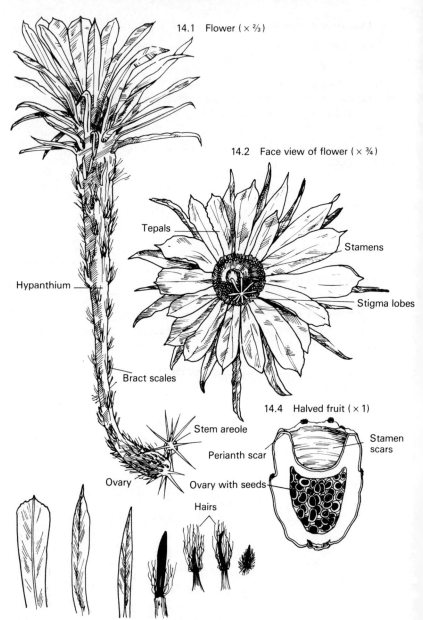

14.1    Flower ( × ⅔ )

14.2    Face view of flower ( × ¾ )

Tepals

Stamens

Hypanthium

Stigma lobes

Bract scales

14.4    Halved fruit ( × 1 )

Stem areole

Perianth scar

Stamen scars

Ovary

Ovary with seeds

Hairs

14.3    Transitional series down the receptacle tube from petals (left)
through sepals to scaly bracts (right). Note axillary hairs. ( × 1)

# CHAPTER 14

# Cactaceae

The large cactus Family is indigenous to the New World, where it extends from Canada and the northern United States in the north to Patagonia in the South (*Opuntia*), but attains maximum diversity in the dry mountainous regions on either side of the Equator. A few (or one) species of *Rhipsalis* extend to parts of Africa, Madagascar and Sri Lanka and may be native there. The plants are all perennial, ranging in size from the tiny button-sized *Blossfeldia* to giant candelabra *Pachycereus* and *Carnegiea*, as well as forest trees of *Pereskia*, tallest of all, up to 24 m (80 ft.). *Pereskia* stands apart from the rest and is regarded as a primitive 'missing link': the stems are sparingly succulent and bear large flat leaves, and the flowers and fruits are also simpler in form. The remaining genera all have reduced or undeveloped leaves, whose function is transferred to the green fleshy stems, which are commonly ribbed, angled or winged or covered in tubercles in spiral rows. Spines are commonly present, but not always; they are interpreted as reduced leaves (Figs. 4.2–15). In the more humid tropical regions the habit is less extremely modified, and cacti are represented by epiphytes with long winged or leaflike stems bearing aerial roots.

The most characteristic feature of the plant body is the presence of felted cushions, called **areoles**, each subtended by a leaf and from which arise spines, new branches and flowers. Exceptions to this arrangement are the genus *Mammillaria*, where the flower arises in the axil of the spine-bearing tubercles, and *Coryphantha* and its allies, where it springs from the base of a groove running from the areole down the upper face of the tubercle. The areole is considered to result from the telescoping of a short lateral branch (spur shoot).

A white milky latex is present in some species of *Mammillaria*.

*Pereskia* has stalked flowers, but elsewhere the flowers are sessile and typically tubular, made up of a continuous spiral series beginning with numerous petals which pass into sepals and these into scaly bracts. The inferior ovary often bears areoles and sometimes spines as well, suggesting that it has become immersed in a modified shoot. Much weight has been given to the exact nature of the vesture of the receptacle tube in differentiating genera: criteria neither clear cut nor all that easy to observe. The stamens are also numerous and spiralled, arising at one or more levels up the inside of the tube, and they surround a central long style. Flowers are white or any colour except blue (but see *Disocactus*), usually short-lived and actinomorphic, rarely oblique to zygomorphic. The fruit is typically a juicy 'berry', with transitions to a dry capsule which splits open irregularly. The seeds are mostly black and have a curved embryo.

The Cactaceae are not closely related to any other living Family, but are grouped into one Order, Caryophyllales, along with the Mesembryanthemaceae, Portulacaceae, Didiereaceae and others on grounds of morphological similarities in flower and seed structure, embryology and a biochemical link—possession of the purple pigment betacyanin.

A glance at the pictures here of flowers of cacti (Figs. 15.1–4) and euphorbias (Figs. 23.1–4) will immediately dispel any likelihood of confusing the two even when the plant bodies are similar. In absence of flowers, the presence of felted (not scaly) areoles in Cactaceae is the surest guide.

## General References

BACKEBERG, C. 1958–62 *Die Cactaceae* 6 Vols. (Jena). **Keys** to genera and species in German.

BACKEBERG, C. 1978 *Cactus Lexicon* (Poole). **Key** to genera.

BORG, J. 1937 and later editions. *Cacti* (London).

BRITTON, N. L. and ROSE, J. N. 1919–23 *The Cactaceae* 4 Vols. (Washington). **Keys** to genera and species.

BYLES, R. S. 1957 *A Dictionary of Genera and Subgenera of Cactaceae* (Sherwood: Nat. Cact. & Succ. Soc.).

HUNT, D. R. in HUTCHINSON, J. 1967 *The Genera of Flowering Plants* II, pp. 427–467. Reprinted 1979. **Key** to genera.

MARSHALL, W. T. and BOCK, T. M. 1941 *Cactaceae* (Pasadena). Illustrated **key** to genera.

RAUH, W. 1979 *Kakteen an ihren Standorten* (Berlin and Hamburg). **Key** to genera in German.

QUICK SPOTS

Certain cactus genera or groups of genera are immediately recognizable by spot characters, saving the time of working through the full key. A selection of these follows:

White floccose scales covering plant: *Astrophytum, Uebelmannia*
Ribs thin and plate-like: *Echinofossulocactus*
Ribs horizontally creased: *Aztekium*
Tubercles long and finger-like: *Leuchtenbergia*
Glochids present: *Opuntia*
Cephalium present: *Cephalocereus, Discocactus, Espostoa, Melocactus*
Flowers from the axils of tubercles: *Mammillaria*
Flower breaking out from a green, stem-like 'bud': *Calymmanthium*
Flower zygomorphic: *Aporocactus, Borzicactus, Rathbunia, Schlumbergera* p.p. and *Mammillaria* Subg. *Cochemiea*
Flower cleistogamous: *Frailea.*

The Cactaceae are among the most difficult of all families of flowering plants to key, because the plants seem to be in a state of active evolution, without sharp lines of discontinuity separating the species or genera. This is especially true of the most popular group in cultivation, the dwarf, free-flowering South American cacti. The problem has been aggravated by the creating of a large number of worthless names based on imaginary distinctions which field work shows to have no factual basis. To this state of uncertainty, the present key cannot hope to add a solution, and the inclusion of microscopic characters such as seed structure is only a partial remedy, and inconvenient for the practical user. The treatment of genera is closer to the conservative system of Hunt (1967, 84 genera) than the radical subdivisions of Backeberg (1958–62, 1978, over 230 genera). For a model pictorial presentation of the system of Britton and Rose (1919–23), see Marshall & Bock (1941).

## KEY TO GENERA

1 Plants with leaves, which may be reduced to small conical green scales on the new
growth only; flowers mostly rotate
  2 Leaves flat
    3 Glochids absent; seeds smooth and glossy, not arillate         **Pereskia**
    3 Glochids present; seeds arillate or hairy
      4 Seeds enveloped in a bony white aril         **Quiabentia**
      4 Seeds enveloped in matted hairs         **Pereskiopsis**
  2 Leaves terete
    5 Seeds winged         **Pterocactus**
    5 Seeds not winged
      6 Tepals rolling back, with a ring of hairs between them and the stamens,
which are exserted         **Tacinga**
      6 No hairs between tepals and stamens, which are shorter than the tepals
        7 Glochids absent; seeds small, black and glossy     **Maihuenia**
        7 Glochids almost always present; seeds large, encased in a bony white
aril         **Opuntia**
1 Plants without leaves or glochids; flowers mostly with a tube
  8 Cereiform plants with elongated stems composed usually of more than one joint
and flat, angled or ribbed
    9 Epiphytes with long, weak, trailing or hanging stems producing aerial roots;
ribs commonly few; spines absent or rarely up to 1 cm long
      10 Flowers 3 cm or less in $\varnothing$; tepals spreading, almost or quite free at base
        **Rhipsalis**
      10 Flowers larger, funnelform to salverform; tepals united into a
tube
        11 Plant composed of chains of flat joints up to 6 cm long like
leaves or miniature prickly pear pads; stamens inserted at
two levels up the tube     **Schlumbergera**
        11 Habit otherwise; stamens not at two separate levels
          12 Ultimate branches flat or rarely 3-winged, almost or quite
unarmed (Epicacti key out here: see p. 122)
            13 Flowers white, mostly nocturnal
              14 Flowers 10–30 cm long; tube longer than limb   **Epiphyllum**
              14 Flowers 6–7 cm long; tube shorter than limb   **Weberocereus**
            13 Flowers pink, orange or red or even blue, diurnal, or if white
then less than 6 cm long
              15 Tepals few, lax or disposed in a narrow funnel   **Disocactus**
              15 Tepals numerous; perianth broad funnelform   **Nopalxochia**
          12 Stems and branches with 3 or more ribs, armed with spines or
bristles
            16 Stems with 3–6 angles
              17 Tube and fruit bearing broad foliaceous scales   **Hylocereus**
              17 Tube and fruit bearing minute scales

18 Flowers white, greenish white or pink, nocturnal
   19 Flowers up to 10 cm long              **Weberocereus**
   19 Flowers 12 cm long or longer        **Selenicereus**
18 Flowers red (white in 1 variety of *H. speciosus*), diurnal
                                           **Heliocereus**
  16 Stems with 7–12 angles
    20 Flowers 15 cm or more long, white, nocturnal    **Selenicereus**
    20 Flowers up to 10 cm long, red, diurnal
      21 Limb oblique; seeds reddish brown     **Aporocactus**
      21 Limb regular; seeds black          **Morangaya**
9 Terrestrial plants, erect or procumbent, rarely producing aerial roots; spines usually well in evidence
  22 Dwarf, solitary or clump-forming cacti with stems up to 50 cm long
    23 Flower tube longer than limb
      24 Flowers orange to scarlet, diurnal, oblique-limbed, with a well-developed nectar chamber              **Borzicactus**
      24 Flowers white (rarely pink, red or yellow), nocturnal, regular; nectar chamber undeveloped
        25 Stems short-jointed            **Arthrocereus**
        25 Stems not jointed              **Echinopsis**
    23 Flower tube shorter than limb; flowers diurnal
      26 Flowers small, yellow; stigmas not green; ovary spineless    **Mila**
      26 Flowers large, pink, purple, greenish or rarely yellow; stigmas green; ovary spiny      **Echinocereus**
  22 Tall-growing plants with stems over 50 cm long
    27 Trees or self-supporting shrubs with at least some stiffly erect vertical stems
      28 Areoles very large, the flowering ones proliferous, with much brown wool and bearing more than 1 flower    **Neoraimondia**
      28 Areoles not as above, bearing 1 flower only (more than 1 in *Myrtillocactus*)
        29 Flower bud enclosed within a green shoot which splits open to reveal the perianth       **Calymmanthium**
        29 Flower buds not enclosed
          30 Fruit covered in persistent spines like a chestnut burr
            31 Stems 3–6 cm thick, covered in golden spines; flowers yellow; fruit juicy      **Bergerocactus**
            31 Stems stouter, not covered in golden spines; flowers not yellow; fruit dry      **Pachycereus**
          30 Fruit not as above
            32 Receptacle tube spiny or bristly
              33 Flowers broadly campanulate to broadly funnelform, diurnal, small, 2–7.5 (–10) cm long
                34 Thicket-forming plants with red, orange or yellow flowers and some spines on fruits    **Corryocactus**

34 Shrubs or trees with white or pink flowers and ± naked, non-spiny
    fruits        **Eulychnia**
33 Flowers narrowly campanulate or narrow funnel-form to tubular, mostly
    nocturnal, 4–20 cm long
NOTE: *Brachycereus* (unc.) forms clumps of short stems with 12–18 ribs com-
    pletely covered in spines; *Leocereus* (unc.) is slender-stemmed with
    12–16 ribs and small white flowers; *Leptocereus* (unc.) has 3–8 ribs and
    tubular-campanulate flowers.
  35 Slim, weak-stemmed shrubs with large funnel-form flowers without a
    separate nectar chamber        **Nyctocereus**
NOTE: *Rathbunia* (unc.) has narrow tubular flowers with an oblique limb and
    exserted stamens.
  35 Stout shrubs, trees or thicket-forming with small, shortly funnelform to
    campanulate flowers (large in *S. eruca* and *gummosus*); lowest stamens
    usually incurved to roof a nectar chamber    **Stenocereus**
NOTE: *Armatocereus* (unc.) with narrow funnelform flowers keys out here.
32 Receptacle tube naked or with scales or hairs but no spines
  36 Flowering areoles different from the non-flowering, ± confluent and with
    copious wool or fine bristles but weaker spines
    37 Giant, thick, columnar cacti with broad-tubed diurnal flowers *c.* 12 cm
      long        **Carnegiea**
NOTE: *Neoabbottia* (unc.) has occasional bristles on the receptacle tube and 4–6-
    ribbed joints as compared with 12–24 ribs in *Carnegiea*.
    37 Trees or shrubs with narrow-tubed nocturnal flowers 10 cm long or less
      38 Flowers 1, 2 or more per areole; flowering areoles more bristly than
        woolly; no separate nectar chamber developed    **Lophocereus**
      38 Flowers only 1 per areole; flowering areoles more woolly than bristly;
        nectar chamber roofed by lowermost stamens
        39 Receptacle tube felted    **Espostoa**
        39 Receptacle tube naked or with a few hairs    **Cephalocereus**
  36 Flowering and non-flowering areoles similar (the former longer-spined in
    *Denmoza*)
    40 Flowers tubular, the tepals not opening; limb erect
      41 Nectar chamber plugged with staminodial hairs    **Denmoza**
NOTE: The shrubby *Zehntnerella* (unc.) has a straight, not bent, perianth tube
    with included stamens and style.
      41 Nectar chamber not plugged with hairs
        42 Style exserted; fruit naked or slightly hairy    **Cleistocactus**
NOTE: *Dendrocereus* (unc.) is a small tree with stout, woody trunk and domed
    head of 3–5-angled branches
        42 Style included; fruit covered in broad scales    **Escontria**
    40 Flowers narrow to broad funnelform or campanulate, opening normally
      43 Flowers very small, up to 2.5 cm long, rotate, commonly more than 1
        per areole    **Myrtillocactus**

43 Flowers larger, only 1 per areole
  44 Receptacle tube naked below or with scales only, without hair
    45 Ribs 12–30            **Browningia**
    45 Ribs 3–10
      46 Fruit covered in broad, persistent scales; seeds brown      **Stetsonia**
      46 Fruit naked or nearly so; seeds black
        47 Stout, erect, columnar cacti; perianth falling from fruit but style persisting      **Cereus**
        47 Slender, weak-stemmed shrubs or thicket-forming; perianth persistent      **Monvillea**
  44 Receptacle tube scaly and hairy
    48 Flowers ± oblique-limbed, with exserted stamens and style      **Borzicactus**
    48 Flowers regular, with at least the stamens included
      49 Flowers 5–12 cm long; tube short and thick
        50 Flowers nocturnal; perianth persistent on fruit      **Haageocereus**
        50 Flowers mostly diurnal; perianth not persistent on fruit      **Stenocereus**
      49 Flowers larger; tube slender, longer than limb

NOTE: *Jasminocereus* (unc.) has a trunk and crown of vertical branches, 15–18 ribs and branches *c.* 14 cm ⌀.

        51 Stout erect shrubs or trees with usually numerous ribs on stems (4–) 10–30 cm ⌀      **Echinopsis**
        51 Slender-stemmed arching or vining bushes with 3–12 ribs on stems 1.2–6 (–8) cm ⌀      **Harrisia**
27 Climbers, scramblers or lax shrubs with relatively slender, long-jointed stems relying on support, or pendulous
  52 Flowering areoles different from non-flowering, ± confluent into a cephalium and with copious wool and fine bristles but weaker spines      **Cephalocereus**
  52 Flowering and non-flowering areoles similar
    53 Plants with very slim, woody branches from massively thickened roots
      54 Root a single, massive 'turnip'; flowers salverform, 15–20 cm long, with a long narrow tube      **Peniocereus**
      54 Roots a cluster of dahlia-like tubers; flowers funnelform to campanulate, 3–12 cm long      **Wilcoxia**

53  Roots not massively thickened
   55  Flowers diurnal, red, orange or yellow, small or rarely up to 20 cm long
NOTE: The small-flowered *Leocereus* (unc.) has 12–16 ribs, and *Leptocereus* (unc.) has 3–8 ribs and tubular campanulate flowers.
      56  Perianth limb ± oblique; stamens and style exserted; withered perianth persistent on fruit
         57  Ribs 8–20 or more; fruit smooth, hairy or minutely bristly **Borzicactus**
         57  Ribs 4–8; fruit spiny, at least at first **Rathbunia**
      56  Perianth limb regular; stamens and style included; perianth not persistent **Stenocereus**
   55  Flowers nocturnal, white to pink, large
      58  Receptacle tube spiny or bristly
         59  Joints angled; withered perianth persistent on fruit **Acanthocereus**
         59  Joints ribbed; perianth not persistent
            60  Flowers short-funnelform to campanulate, with limb longer than tube **Stenocereus**
            60  Flowers funnelform, with tube longer than limb **Nyctocereus**
      58  Receptacle tube not spiny or bristly
         61  Scales on receptacle tube without axillary hairs **Monvillea**
         61  Scales on receptacle tube with hairs in axils **Harrisia**
NOTE: A few slender-stemmed species of *Echinopsis* may key out here.
8  Cactiform plants with ± globose or short columnar stems, usually of 1 joint only and ribbed or tuberculate
   62  Flowers arising from a central cephalium of copious spines and wool; flowers never yellow
      63  Flowers more than 4 cm long, white, nocturnal **Discocactus**
      63  Flowers less than 4 cm long and mainly hidden within the cephalium, coloured, diurnal **Melocactus**
   62  Cephalium not developed although the stem apex may be woolly (*Notocactus* p.p.) in which case the flowers are yellow
      64  Flowers borne laterally
         65  Ovary and fruit spiny; stems soft; stigmas green **Echinocereus**
         65  Ovary and fruit not spiny; stems firm; stigmas not green
            66  Miniature, tuberculate cacti without ribs, flowering basally; receptacle tube slender, naked or sparsely hairy **Rebutia**
            66  Ribs ± developed; flowers distal to subbasal; receptacle tube moderately thick and ± felted
               67  Flowers large, 15–20 cm long, white or rarely pink, nocturnal, with tube longer than limb **Echinopsis**
               67  Flowers small to medium-sized, 2½–14 cm long, coloured, diurnal, with tube usually equal to or shorter than limb **Lobivia**

64 Flowers borne centrally in the crown
  68 Perianth bent ± like an S; stamens and style exserted
    69 Ribbed plants with straight spines and flowers borne at spiniferous areoles
      70 Perianth tubular; limb not opening           **Denmoza**
      70 Perianth narrow funnelform, limb opening and usually oblique
                                        **Borzicactus**
    69 Tuberculate plants with hooked centrals (exc. *M. halei*) and flowers borne in axils of tubercles       **Mammillaria**
                                      **Sg. Cochemiea**
  68 Perianth straight-tubed; stamens at least included
    71 Receptacle tube naked or scaly but without hairs, bristles or spines
      72 Receptacle tube naked or with a few small scales above, but ovary and fruit smooth
        73 Plants with ribs, flowering from the spine-bearing areoles around the crown
          74 Ribs horizontally wrinkled and pleated as if the whole stem had been vertically compressed       **Aztekium**
          74 Ribs not so           **Copiapoa**
      73 Plants with tubercles, flowering from the axil or from a groove above the spine cluster, or from near the centre of the woolly crown
        75 Mature areoles spineless
          76 Plant body soft with low, rounded tubercles     **Lophophora**
          76 Plant body firm, with pointed, triangular tubercles in a flat rosette     **Ariocarpus**
        75 Mature areoles spiny
          77 Flowers arising from the spine-bearing areoles
            78 Spines minute, very numerous, totally covering the stems which appear white     **Epithelantha**
            78 Spines acicular and weak, curling or flat and papery, or pectinate     **Strombocactus**
          77 Flowers arising from the axils of tubercles     **Mammillaria**
          77 Flowers arising from the base of a groove running from the spine cluster at least halfway to the base of the top side of the tubercle
            79 Seed coat smooth or verrucose; outer tepals not fimbriate
              80 Seeds black, ± verrucose     **Neolloydia**
              80 Seeds brown, smooth
                81 Tubercles conical, neither axe-shaped nor scale-like, grooved above when adult     **Coryphantha**
                81 Tubercles vertically compressed and axe-like or horizontally compressed and overlapped like scales in a pine cone     **Pelecyphora**
            79 Seed coat pitted; seeds reddish brown to black; outer tepals fimbriate     **Escobaria**

72 Receptacle tube scaly, without hairs, bristles or spines
  82 Ribs narrow, wing-like and ± wavy edged, 20–100 or more (10–14 and straight in *E. coptonogonus*)   **Echinofossulocactus**
  82 Ribs not as above, or undeveloped
    83 Plant with finger-like tubercles 8–12 cm long crowned with flat, papery spines   **Leuchtenbergia**
    83 Plant not as above
      84 Fruit dehiscing by an apical pore and usually crowned by a few narrow persistent scales   **Copiapoa**
      84 Fruit not as above
        85 Scales on receptacle tube broader than long, rounded, with thin pallid margins; tubercles prominent, mostly arranged in ribs with a chin beneath each areole   **Gymnocalycium**
        85 Scales on receptacle tube longer than broad, not rounded or pallid edged
          86 Fruit dehiscing by vertical splits and a cap; spines never hooked   **Pediocactus**
          86 Fruit dehiscing by a basal pore; central spines sometimes hooked
            87 Ribs ± tuberculate; tubercles mostly grooved above; seeds ± verrucose to nearly smooth, often constricted midway   **Thelocactus**
            87 Ribs scarcely tuberculate, without grooves; seeds pitted or reticulate   **Ferocactus**
71 Receptacle tube scaly and hairy or bristly
  88 Receptacle tube hairy or felted but not bristly or spiny
    89 Stems ± covered in white flecks; seeds large, helmet-shaped   **Astrophytum**
    89 Stems not white-flecked (but may be white waxy); seeds not helmet-shaped
      90 Plants minute, with bodies up to 2 cm ∅ without ribs, tubercles or spines   **Blossfeldia**
      90 Plants larger, ribbed or tuberculate and spiny
        91 Fruit dehiscing at the apex   **Copiapoa**
        91 Fruit breaking apart at the base
          92 Fruit densely woolly towards the top, naked below   **Echinocactus**
          92 Fruit naked or scaly or at most thinly hairy
            93 Tubercles mostly shortly grooved above; central spines often hooked; fruit dry   **Thelocactus**
            93 Tubercles not grooved; spine not hooked; fruit fleshy, at least at first
              94 Stems solitary, depressed globose; flowers short and rather broadly campanulate; seeds wrinkled and irregularly pitted   **Oroya**
              94 Stems globose or somewhat elongated, mostly unbranched; flowers short funnelform; seeds rugose and minutely verrucose   **Neoporteria**

94 Stems short-cylindric, branching; flowers small, subcampanulate with a
  slender tube; seeds verrucose                                    **Mila**
88 Receptacle tube bristly or spiny
  95 Large unbranched cacti 20–50 cm ⌀ and 30–100 cm tall; flowers short,
    squat; spines extending to upper areoles of receptacle tube   **Eriosyce**
  95 Smaller plants without spines extending up receptacle tube
    96 Some spines hooked, or seeds as fine as dust
      97 Small shrubs with rather elongated, ribbed stems; seeds black, shield-
        shaped and flattened, rugose, to 2 mm ⌀                **Austrocactus**
      97 Plants ± globose, tuberculate or ribbed, with very small brown, hemi-
        spherical to subglobose, smooth seeds                      **Parodia**
    96 Spines not hooked; seeds not dust-like
      98 Tiny plants rarely above 6 cm high and 4 cm ⌀, unbranched; flowers
        commonly cleistogamous; seeds glossy brown or blackish, hemi-
        spherical, beaked, with a concave hilum                     **Frailea**
      98 Generally larger plants; flowers opening normally
        99 Seeds brown, strongly rugose, obliquely ovoid to pear- or helmet-
          shaped with a depressed hilum; perianth small, yellow
                                                              **Uebelmannia**
        99 Seeds dull brownish black to black, subglobose to hemispherical,
          verruculose, with a very broad truncate hilum; perianth rotate,
          commonly yellow                                       **Notocactus**
        99 Seeds black with a small basal hilum, verrucose and often rugose;
          perianth not opening out flat or rotate, commonly some shade of
          red                                                    **Neoporteria**

## ACANTHOCEREUS

(Bgr.) B. & R. in *Contr. U.S. Nat. Herb.* 12: 432, 1909.
Typ. *A. pentagonus* (L.) B. & R.

Small genus of rank-growing climbers from Central America with 3–5(–7)-
angled long-jointed stems and large, white, nocturnal flowers. The small scales
on the receptacle tube distinguish it from *Hylocereus*.

## × APORECHINOPSIS*

Rowl.
SYN. *Aporotrichocereus* Willis.
= *Aporocactus* × *Echinopsis*.
Few cultivars.

## × APOREPIPHYLLUM*

Rowl.
= *Aporocactus* × *Epiphyllum.*
Non × *Aporophyllum* Johnson.
Few cultivars.

## APOROCACTUS

Lemaire in *Ill. Hort.* 7 Misc. 67, 1860.
Typ. *A. flagelliformis* (L.) Lem.

The 'Rat's-tail Cactus': a very small Mexican genus of epiphytes with long, slender, finely spined, pendent stems and oblique-limbed, rather small, diurnal, red flowers.
Intergeneric hybrids: × *Aporechinopsis,* × *Aporepiphyllum,* × *Aporochia,* × *Aporodisocactus,* × *Heliaporus,* × *Seleniaporus.*

## × APOROCHIA

Rowl in Epiphytes 4 (13): 12, 1972.
= *Aporocactus* × *Nopalxochia.*
Few cultivars.

## × APORODISOCACTUS

Knebel in *Phyllocactus* 18, 1949.
= *Aporocactus* × *Disocactus.*
Few cultivars.

## ARIOCARPUS

Scheidweiler in *Bull. Acad. Sci. Brux.* 5: 491, 1838.
Typ. *A. retusus* Scheidw.
SYN. *Neogomesia, Roseocactus.*

Very small genus of singular appearance from N. Mexico and S. Texas. Plant body top-shaped, the flat surface level with the soil and covered in horny, spiralled tubercles with woolly axils but no spines. Flowers short-tubed, diurnal, purple, pink, white or yellowish.
ANDERSON, E. F. in *Amer. J. Bot.* 47: 582–589, 1960; 49: 615–622, 1962; 50: 724–732, 1963; 51: 144–151, 1964; and *Cact. Succ. J. Amer.* 37: 39–49, 1965. **Key** to species.

## ARTHROCEREUS

(Bgr.) Back. & Knuth *Kaktus ABC:* 211, 1935.
Typ. *A. microsphaericus* (K. Sch.) Back. & Knuth.
SYN. *Pygmaeocereus, Setiechinopsis.*

Very small genus from Argentina and Brazil, doubtfully distinct from *Echinopsis* by the constriction of the stem into short joints. The long-tubed, white, nocturnal flowers are, however, similar.

## ASTROPHYTUM

Lemaire *Cact. Gen. Nov. Sp. Nov. Hort. Monv.* 3, 1839.
Typ. *A. myriostigma* Lem.

Very small Mexican genus composed of two spiny and two spineless species, among the most popular of dwarf, solitary cacti and immediately recognizable from the few (4–8 usually), prominent ribs and surface covering of white flecks (which may, however, be ± absent in selected cultivars). The body is top-shaped, spherical or short columnar in age, and the showy blooms are some shade of yellow, sometimes with a red 'eye'.

GILKEY, J. E. in *Cact. Succ. J. Amer.* 16: 143–151, 1944. **Key** to species and varieties.

## AUSTROCACTUS

B. & R. *The Cactaceae* 3: 44, 1922.
Typ. *A. bertinii* (Cels) B. & R.

Very small (monotypic?) genus from Patagonia and Chile, forming branching shrublets, sometimes with aerial roots; with tuberculate ribs and hooked central spines. Flowers funnelform, yellowish pink, very spiny on the outside. Rare in cultivation.

## AZTEKIUM

Boedeker in *Monatsschr. D.K.G.* 1: 52, 1929.
Typ. *A ritteri* Boed.

Monotypic genus from Mexico at once recognizable from all other cacti by the horizontal pleats giving a wizened appearance as if the main axis had been compressed. Plant body small, top-shaped, sometimes offsetting, with 9–11 low ribs, spineless except for bristles in the woolly crown. Flowers minute, white or pink.

## BERGEROCACTUS

B. & R. in *Contr. U.S. Nat. Herb.* 12: 435, 1909.

Typ. *B. emoryi* B. & R.

Monotypic genus from Baja California forming thickets of slender, stiffly erect stems wholly covered in golden yellow spines. The flowers are diurnal and yellow, and the spiny globose fruit extrudes the pulp and seeds through an apical pore like purple toothpaste.

Intergeneric hybrids: × *Myrtgerocactus,* × *Pachgerocereus*

## BLOSSFELDIA

Werdermann in *Kakteenkunde* 11: 162, 1937.

Typ. *B. liliputana* Werd.

Monotypic genus from Argentina, the smallest of all cacti, with solitary or clustered unarmed bodies from a tuberous root, and small, diurnal, campanulate white flowers. The short receptacle tube without bristles distinguishes it from *Frailea.*

## BORZICACTUS

Riccobono in *Boll. R. Ort. Bot. Palermo* 8: 261, 1909.

Typ. *B. sepium* (H. B. & K.) B. & R.

SYN. *Akersia, Arequipa, Bolivicereus, Clistanthocereus, Hildewintera, Loxanthocereus, Maritimocereus, Matucana, Morawetzia, Oreocereus, Seticereus, Submatucana, Winteria, Winterocereus.*

Small but diverse genus of both cereiform and cactiform plants from S. America characterized by the red or orange, smallish, bird-pollinated flowers: diurnal, with an expanded, oblique limb, long narrow receptacle tube and abundant nectar, for which there is a well-developed nectar chamber roofed over by the bases of the lower filaments.

KIMNACH, M. in *Cact. Succ. J. Amer.* 32: 8–13, 57–60, 92–96, 109–112, 1960.

Intergeneric hybrid: × *Borzimoza.*

## × BORZIMOZA*

Rowl.

= *Borzicactus* × *Denmoza.*

1 cultivar.

## BROWNINGIA

B. & R. in *The Cactaceae* 2: 63, 1920.

Typ. *B. candelaris* (Mey.) B. & R.

SYN. *Azureocereus, Castellanosia, Gymnanthocereus, Gymnocereus, Rauhocereus.*

Small S. American genus of massive, tree-like, columnar cacti with a distinct trunk and crown of erect or curving thick, many-ribbed branches. The flowers, not often seen in cultivation, are nocturnal, funnelform and clothed with broad scales on the tube.

## CALYMMANTHIUM

Ritter in Back. *Die Cactaceae* 2:886, 1959 and *Kakt. u. and. Sukk.* 13: 25, 1962.

Typ. *C. substerile* Ritt.

Monotypic genus from N. Peru with 3–4-angled long-jointed climbing stems. It is unique among flowering plants for having the bud completely enclosed within what looks like a normal green branch, which has to split apart in order to expose the small pinkish-white flower.

## CARNEGIEA

B. & R. in *J. N.Y. Bot. Gard.* 9: 187, 1908.

Typ. *C. gigantea* (Eng.) B. & R.

Monotypic genus, the giant saguaro of Arizona, N. Mexico and S.E. California, with a massive trunk and few, thick, erect side branches. Flowers at the tips of the stems, ± campanulate, with very numerous stamens. The habit is matched by *Pachycereus*, but *Carnegiea* lacks the copious spines on the fruit.

## CEPHALOCEREUS

Pfeiffer in *Allg. Gartenz.* 6: 142, 1838.

Typ. *C. senilis* (Haw.) Pfeiff.

SYN. *Arrojadoa, Austrocephalocereus, Backebergia, Buiningia, Coleocephalocereus, Haseltonia, Micranthocereus, Mitrocereus, Neobuxbaumia, Neodawsonia, Pilocereus, Pilosocereus, Pseudopilocereus, Rooksbya, Stephanocereus, Subpilocereus.*

Medium to large Central American genus of mostly columnar cacti (*C. aureus* is globose) characterized by producing a conspicuous cephalium of copious wool and bristles from the flowering areoles all over the stem apex or in a vertical band down one side. *Melocactus* is distinguishable by the very small size of its mammillaria-like flowers.

Intergeneric hybrid; × *Cepheliocereus.*

## × CEPHELIOCEREUS*

Rowl.

SYN. *Heliosocereus* Gl. & F.
= *Cephalocereus* × *Heliocereus.*
1 cultivar.

## CEREUS

Mill. *Gard. Dict. Abr.* Edn. IV, 1754.

Typ. *C. hexagonus* (L.) Mill.

SYN. *Piptanthocereus.*

Medium-sized S. American and W. Indian genus of shrubby to tree-like cacti, with numerous erect branches with 4–8 prominent ribs (Fig. 7.9) and large, funnelform nocturnal flowers. The best spot character is the complete absence of wool, bristles or spines from the receptacle tube which is smooth and has small scales only towards the top. After anthesis the perianth drops off cleanly.

## CLEISTOCACTUS

Lemaire in *Ill. Hort.* 8 *Misc.* 35, 1861.

Typ. *C. baumannii* Lem.

SYN. *Cephalocleistocactus, Seticleistocactus.*

Medium-sized genus of S. American cacti with long, slender stems forming shrubs or thickets or in part climbing, with many ribs and closely spiny. It runs close to *Borzicactus* in many species, the distinction lying in the long, narrow, tubular flowers that do not open and have the style (and sometimes stamens also) exserted. *Denmoza* has shorter, stouter stems and a clearly defined nectar chamber.

Intergeneric hybrid: × *Cleistopsis.*

## × CLEISTOPSIS

Strigl in *Kakt. u.a. Sukk.* 30(9): 226–227, 1979.

= *Cleistocactus* × *Echinopsis.*

1 cultivar.

## COPIAPOA

B. & R. *The Cactaceae* 3: 85, 1922.
Typ. *C. marginata* (S. D.) B. & R.
SYN. *Pilocopiapoa.*

Small and ill-defined genus from Chile with many more names than species. The solitary or occasionally caespitose stems are globose to short cylindric with age and have many ribs ± divided into tubercles, commonly dark purplish brown or covered in white wax. The broad, bell- to funnel-shaped flowers are yellow, diurnal and borne in the woolly crown.

## CORRYOCACTUS

B. & R. *The Cactaceae* 2: 66, 1920.
Typ. *C. brevistylus* (K. Sch.) B. & R.
SYN. *Erdisia, Samaipaticereus.*

Small Andean genus of thicket-forming or shrubby columnar cacti branching mainly from the base or suckering. The small diurnal flowers come in shades from red to yellow.

## CORYPHANTHA

(Eng.) Lemaire *Les Cactées* 32, 1868.
Typ. *C. sulcolanata* Lem.
SYN. *Lepidocoryphantha.*

Medium-sized genus from Mexico and the S.W. U.S.A. with spiralled tubercles like a *Mammillaria* but set apart from other genera (*cf. Escobaria*) by the groove on the upper surface of an adult tubercle connecting the apical spine cluster with a point in the axil from which the flower arises. Flowers showy, campanulate, yellow or less frequently purplish.

## DENMOZA

B. & R. *The Cactaceae* 3: 78, 1922.
Typ. *D. rhodacantha* (S. D.) B. & R.

Very small Argentinian genus with a solitary globose to short columnar stem, distinguishable by the curious cylindrical flower with a slight S bend to the tube which is clothed in broad, acute, overlapping scales and hairs. The stamens and style are exserted in a long brush.
Intergeneric hybrid: × *Borzimoza.*

## DISCOCACTUS

Pfeiffer in *Allg. Gartenz.* 5: 241, 1837 and *Nov. Act. Cur.* 19: 117, 1839.
Typ. *D. placentiformis* (Lehm.) K. Sch.

Small genus from Brazil and Paraguay with solitary, depressed globose stems (rarely with offsets) with 10–20 low, ± tuberculate ribs. The moderately large, white, scented flowers arise from a central cephalium similar to, but usually smaller than, that in *Melocactus,* open at dusk and last only a few hours.

## DISOCACTUS

Lindley in *Bot. Reg.* 31 t. 9, 1845.
Typ. *D. biformis* Lindl.
SYN. *Bonifazia, Chiapasia, Pseudorhipsalis, Wittia.*

Small genus of terete to flat-stemmed unarmed epiphytes from tropical America with slim flowers having a long, quite smooth tube and rather few linear to oblanceolate tepals. *D. amazonicus* has the tepals tipped in blue.
KIMNACH, M. in *Cact. Succ. J. Amer.* 51: 166–171, 1979. Partial key to species.
Intergeneric hybrid: × *Aporodisocactus.*

## × ECHINOBIVIA

Rowl. in *Nat. Cact. Succ. J.* 21: 82, 1966.
SYN. *Lobiviopsis* Johnson non Fric.
= *Echinopsis* × *Lobivia.*
Many cultivars.

## ECHINOCACTUS

Link & Otto in *Verh. Ver. Beförd. Gart. Preuss. Staat.* 3: 420, 1827.
Typ. *E. platyacanthus* Link & Otto.
SYN. *Homalocephala.*

Small genus from Mexico and the S.W. U.S.A. familiar through *E. grusonii,* the 'Golden Barrel' or 'Mother-in-law's Armchair'. Some species are solitary and massive ('barrel cacti'), some low and clustering; all are fiercely spiny. Flowers are broad funnelform to campanulate, yellow to red, from the woolly crown.

## ECHINOCEREUS

Engelmann in Wislizenus *Mem. Tour Northern Mexico* 91, 1848.
Typ. *E. viridiflorus* Eng.

Large and diverse genus centred in the S.W. U.S.A. and Mexico but extending north to Wyoming and Utah (*E. viridiflorus*, hardiest of dwarf cacti). All are compact to moderate-sized solitary or clustering plants with globose to short cylindric soft-fleshed stems branching mainly near the base. The diurnal, coloured flowers are usually showy. Spot characters are the combination of green stigma lobes, very spiny receptacle and fruit, and a tendency for innovations to break out through the flesh of the stem.

## ECHINOFOSSULOCACTUS

Lawrence in *Loudon Gard. Mag.* 17: 317, 1841.
Typ. *E. coptonogonus* (Lem.) Lawr.
SYN. *Stenocactus.*

Very small genus, although 30 or more species have been separated on the flimsiest characters. They all come from Mexico and have small, ± globose and usually solitary stems immediately recognizable by the thin ribs with distant areoles, the ribs in all but one species being wavy and very numerous. The flower is distinctive, being small, mostly sombre shades of greenish, pinkish or yellowish, only half open and with broad, papery scales but no hairs or spines covering the receptacle.
TAYLOR, N. P. in *Cact. Succ. J. Gt. Brit.* 41(2): 35–42, 1979. Provisional key to species.
Intergeneric hybrid: × *Ferofossulocactus.*

## ECHINOPSIS

Zuccarini in *Abh. Bayer. Akad. Wiss. München* 2: 675, 1837.
Typ. *E. eyriesii* (Turp.) Zucc.
SYN. *Helianthocereus, Lasiocereus, Leucostele, Pseudolobivia* p.p.,
*Roseocereus, Trichocereus.*

Large S. American genus of both columnar and dwarf cacti ranging from a small solitary globose stem to tall 'organpipe' trees. The common feature is the large, long-tubed, funnelform, nocturnal flower which is white or rarely pink. The receptacle tube carries a series of scales with hairs but no spines in their axils (Figs. 14.1–3).
Intergeneric hybrids: × *Aporechinopsis,* × *Cleistopsis,* × *Echinobivia.*

## Epicacti

This hybrid complex covers a wide range of popular cacti bred and grown for their large and mostly spectacular flowers in white or shades of pink, red, purple, orange and rarely yellow. These remain open by day and last longer than those of the parent species. The plants are derived from multigeneric crosses between species of *Nopalxochia, Epiphyllum, Heliocereus* and other mostly epiphytic genera. The habit is close to that of the first two, with unarmed or weakly bristly flat or three-winged shoots.

HASELTON, S. E. *Epiphyllum Handbook.* Abbey Garden Press, Pasadena 1946.
ROWLEY, G. D. in *Epiphytes* 4: 3–21, 26–45, 47, 1972. **Key** to genera and bigeneric hybrids. See also BACKEBERG, C. *Die Cactaceae* Vol. 6.
*Directory of Epiphyllums and related Epiphytes.* Rainbow Gardens, La Habra 1980.

## EPIPHYLLUM

Haworth *Syn. Pl. Succ.* 197, 1812, non Pfeiffer 1837.
Typ. *E. phyllanthus* (L.) Haw.
SYN. *Marniera, Phyllocactus.*

Small genus of unarmed epiphytes with long-jointed, leaf-like, flat or sometimes 3-winged stems producing aerial roots, native to the hotter, moister parts of Central America. The mostly nocturnal flowers are very long (up to 30 cm, 12 in), white and often scented. The species are much less often seen in cultivation than the numerous intergeneric hybrids (epicacti) whose flowers are often coloured and stay open by day.
Intergeneric hybrids: × *Aporepiphyllum*, × *Epixochia*, × *Heliphyllum*, × *Seleniphyllum.*

## EPITHELANTHA

Weber ex B. & R. *The Cactaceae* 3: 92, 1922.
Typ. *E. micromeris* (Eng.) B. & R.

Monotypic genus of miniature cacti from N. Mexico and W. Texas forming a cluster of tiny globose heads appearing snow-white from the complete covering of fine spines on small spiralled tubercles. From similar looking species of *Mammillaria* it differs in that the flower arises from the tip of a tubercle, not from it axil.

GLASS, C. & FOSTER, R. in *Cact. Succ. J. Amer.* 50 (4): 184–186, 1978. **Key** to varieties.

## × EPIXOCHIA

Rowl. in Backeberg *Die Cactaceae* 6: 3556, 1962.
= *Epiphyllum* × *Nopalxochia.*
Many cultivars.

## ERIOSYCE

Philippi in *Anal. Univ. Chile* 41: 721, 1872.
Typ. *E. ceratistes* (Otto) B. & R.

Monotypic genus from the Andes in Chile resembling a giant *Neoporteria*, with globose to short columnar stems and a more spiny receptacle tube. It is uncommon in cultivation and shy flowering.

## ESCOBARIA

B. & R. *The Cactaceae* 4: 53, 1923.
Typ. *E. tuberculosa* (Eng.) B. & R.
SYN. *Cochiseia, Escobesseya, Neobesseya, Ortegocactus.*

One of several hotly disputed genera for which seed characters (notably the intracellular pits) and grooved tubercles alone afford reliable separation. From *Coryphantha* it differs in being smaller in all parts, with narrower stems, a taproot rather than fibrous roots, straighter spines, paler flowers and smaller seeds. The habitat is Mexico and the S.W. U.S.A., with one outlier (*E. vivipara*) reaching as far north as Canada.

CASTETTER, E. F., PIERCE, P. & SCHWERIN, K. H. in *Cact. Succ. J. Amer.* 47: 60–70, 1975.

TAYLOR, N. P. in *Cact. Succ. J. Gt. Brit.* 40 (2): 31–37, 1978; 41 (1): 17–20, 1979. Partial key to species.

## ESCONTRIA

Rose in *Contr. U.S. Nat. Herb.* 10: 125, 1906.
Typ. *E. chiotilla* (Web.) B. & R.

Monotypic genus of tall tree cacti from Mexico with small, yellow, diurnal flowers followed by globose, juicy fruits bearing on the outside broad, triangular, papery scales. The fruits are stated to taste like gooseberries and are marketed as 'chiotillas'.

## ESPOSTOA

B. & R. *The Cactaceae* 2: 60, 1920.
Typ. *E. lanata* (H. B. & K.) B. & R.
SYN. *Facheiroa, Pseudoespostoa, Thrixanthocereus, Vatricania.*

Small genus of S. American columnar cacti favoured by collectors for the beautiful mantle of snow-white hairs covering the stems. The flowering areoles become more densely woolly and form a cephalium down one side of the stem. *Cephalocereus* differs in having almost no hair on the receptacle tube.

## EULYCHNIA

Philippi in *Fl. Atac.* 23, 1860.
Typ. *E. spinibarbis* (Otto) B. & R.
SYN. *Philippicereus.*

Very small Chilean genus best known for those seedlings that combine white wool and very long central spines. The receptacle tube is short, scaly and spiny or bristly, but the fruit is fleshy and ± smooth.

## × FEROBERGIA

Glass in *Cact. Succ. J. Amer.* 38: 177, 1966.
= *Ferocactus* × *Leuchtenbergia.*
Few cultivars.

## FEROCACTUS

B. & R. *The Cactaceae* 3: 123, 1922.
Typ. *F. wislizeni* (Eng.) B. & R.

'Barrel cacti', small to very large, with strong spination. The genus is medium-sized and comes from Mexico and the S.W. U.S.A. It is similar to *Echinocactus* but differs by lacking wool in the axils of the scales covering the receptacle. The spines are distinctive, the centrals especially being usually broad and stout, often curved or hooked and clearly cross-furrowed like a file. Intergeneric hybrids: × *Ferobergia*, × *Ferofossulocactus.*

## × FEROFOSSULOCACTUS*

Rowl.
= *Echinofossulocactus* × *Ferocactus.*
At least one spontaneous hybrid.

## FRAILEA

B. & R. *The Cactaceae* 3: 208, 1922.

Typ. *F. cataphracta* (Dams) B. & R.

Small genus of miniature S. American cacti mostly at home in a 6 cm (2½ in.) pot. The plant body is solitary or clustered, with low tubercles arranged ± in ribs, and weak, tiny spines. Flowers, when produced, are funnelform and yellow. But most species are cleistogamous and set relatively large pods of seed without opening a bloom.

## GYMNOCALYCIUM

Pfeiffer *Abbild. Beschr. Cact.* 2: tt. 11, 12, 1845.

Typ. *G. denudatum* (Link & Otto) Pfeiff.

SYN. *Brachycalycium, Neowerdermannia, Spegazzinia, Weingartia.*

Medium to large genus of S. American globular cacti, mostly small and solitary with straight or spiralled ± tuberculate ribs, often with a characteristic 'chin' below each areole. The flowers are diurnal, off-white to pink or rarely red, orange or yellow. The best spot character is the smooth, cylindrical receptacle tube bearing appressed, rounded, thin scales without any hair or spines.

PUTNAM, E. W. *Gymnocalyciums.* Nat. Cact. & Succ. Soc., Leicester 1979.

GINNS, R, *Gymnocalyciums.* Succ. Pl. Trust 1967.

## HAAGEOCEREUS

Back. in *Blätter f. Kakteenf.* 1934–6.

Typ. *H.pseudomelanostele* Back.

SYN. *Floresia, Neobinghamia, Peruvocereus, Weberbauerocereus.*

Medium-sized genus of prostrate to erect cereiform cacti from Peru with funnelform, usually white, sometimes oblique-limbed flowers. The species most cherished by collectors are those with dense acicular spines in golden yellow, white or dark shades.

## HARRISIA

Britton in *Bull. Torrey Bot. Club* 35: 561, 1908.

Typ. *H. gracilis* (Mill.) B.

SYN. *Eriocereus.*

Small genus of Central American climbing cacti with long rather slender stems with 4–12 ribs or angles and large, showy, white flowers opening at dusk. A pest genus in Australia where it has run wild, it is valued elsewhere as a grafting stock.

## × HELIAPORUS

Rowl. in *Cact. Succ. J. Gt. Brit.* 13: 54, 1951.
SYN. *Aporoheliocereus* Knebel.
= *Aporocactus* × *Heliocereus.*
Several cultivars.

## HELIOCEREUS

(Bgr.) B. & R. in *Contr. U.S. Nat. Herb.* 12: 433, 1909.
Typ. *H. speciosus* (Cav.) B. & R.
Very small Mexican genus of shrubby to scrambling plants with long, few-angled, spiny stems bearing aerial roots, and showy, diurnal, usually coloured, funnelform flowers. *H. speciosus* with brilliant red flowers with a bluish sheen is parent of most epicacti.
Intergeneric hybrids: × *Cepheliocereus,* × *Heliaporus,* × *Heliochia,* × *Heliphyllum,* × *Seleliocereus.*

## × HELIOCHIA

Rowl. in Backeberg *Die Cactaceae* 6: 3551, 1962.
= *Heliocereus* × *Nopalxochia.*
Many cultivars.

## × HELIPHYLLUM

Rowl. in Backeberg *Die Cactaceae* 6: 3555, 1962.
= *Epiphyllum* × *Heliocereus.*
SYN. *Heliocactus* Janse, *Phylleliocereus* Guill., *Phyllocereus* Knebel.
Several cultivars.

## HYLOCEREUS

(Bgr.) B. & R. in *Contr. U.S. Nat. Herb.* 12: 428, 1909.
Typ. *H. triangularis* (L.) B. & R.
SYN. *Wilmattea.*
Small genus of strong-growing climbers from the hotter, more humid parts of Central America. The long-jointed stems reach several metres in length and are usually 3–4-winged and produce copious aerial roots which attach to rock faces and tree bark. The very large nocturnal flowers are white and readily distinguish the genus by the broad, overlapping scales covering the receptacle. The scaly fruit can be as large as an orange.

## LEUCHTENBERGIA ────────────────

Hooker in *Curtis Bot. Mag.* 1848 t. 4393.

Typ. *L. principis* Hook.

Monotypic genus from Mexico, one of the most easily recognizable of cacti from the spiralled, finger-like tubercles up to 12 cm (4¾ in.) long, each tipped by equally long, white, papery spines. The whole plant, which may have one or several heads, looks in habitat like an agave. The large, yellow flowers arise from the tips of young tubercles.

Intergeneric hybrids: × *Ferobergia*, × *Thelobergia*.

## LOBIVIA ────────────────

B. & R. *The Cactaceae* 3: 49, 1922.

Typ. *L. pentlandii* (Hook) B. & R.

SYN. *Acanthocalycium, Acantholobivia, Chamaecereus, Cylindrorebutia, Digitorebutia, Hymenorebutia, Mediolobivia* p.p., *Pseudolobivia* p.p., *Soehrensia.*

Medium-sized S. American genus of dwarf, compact, free-flowering cacti popular with collectors. The globose to short cylindric stems have ± tuberculate ribs and are usually clustering. The genus is separated from *Echinopsis* by the smaller size and generally shorter flowers which are diurnal and coloured, and from *Rebutia* by the stouter, more hairy receptacle tube and by flowering higher up the stems.

RAUSCH, W. *Lobivia*, Parts I–III. Vienna 1975–77.

Intergeneric hybrid: × *Echinobivia.*

## LOPHOCEREUS ────────────────

(Bgr.) B. & R. in *Contr. U.S. Nat. Herb.* 12: 426, 1909.

Typ. *L. schottii* (Eng.) B. & R.

Very small (monotypic?) genus from Mexico to Arizona, forming shrubs of stiffly erect cereiform stems branched mainly from the base. The flowering stem tips develop copious bristles at the large areoles, which sometimes bear more than one flower. Flowers small, funnelform, dull pinkish-white. A monstrous variant without ribs or spines is much in demand by collectors.

LINDSAY, G. in *Cact. Succ. J. Amer.* 35: 176–192, 1963. **Key** to species, etc.

## LOPHOPHORA

Coulter in *Contr. U.S. Nat. Herb.* 3: 131, 1894.

Typ. *L. williamsii* (Lem.) Coult.

Monotypic genus from Mexico to S. Texas, the peyote, peyotl, L.S.D. or dumpling cactus, long esteemed by the Mexican Indians for its hallucinogenic alkaloids. From all other cacti it differs in having a soft, grey stem the size of a small apple, sometimes offsetting, and covered in low tubercles in 8–10 indistinct ribs (Fig. 3.1). There are no spines; instead a brush of soft hair extrudes from each areole. The small flowers, usually white to pink, appear in the wool at the apex and are followed by smooth, red fruits.

## MAIHUENIA

Philippi in *Gartenflora* 32: 260, 1883.

Typ. *M. poeppigii* (Otto) Web.

Very small genus of miniature hardy cacti from the mountains of Chile and Argentina, of uncertain affinities. The habit is that of dwarf cylindric opuntias; but there are no glochids, and differences in seed and other microscopic features.

## MAMMILLARIA

Haworth *Syn. Pl. Succ.* 177, 1812, Nom. cons.

Typ. *M. mammillaris* (L.) Karst.

SYN. *Bartschella, Chilita, Cochemiea, Dolichothele, Ebnerella, Krainzia, Leptocladodia, Mamillopsis, Mammilloydia, Neomammillaria, Oehmea, Phellosperma, Porfiria, Pseudomammillaria, Solisia.*

Very large genus centred in Mexico, with outlying species in the S.W. U.S.A., W. Indies, and S. America. Plants dwarf and solitary or clustering, globose to short cylindric and covered in tubercles in spiralled rows, sometimes with hairs in the axils. Flowers small to medium-sized, in rings round the stem apex, followed by obovoid to elongated, red (rarely green), smooth, juicy fruits (Fig. 37.62). The feature that sets this very popular and familiar genus apart from all others is the siting of the flower in the axil of a tubercle rather than at its spiny tip.

CRAIG, R. T. *The Mammillaria Handbook.* Pasadena 1945. **Key** to species.

HUNT, D. R. *Review of Mammillaria names in current usage* in *J. Mamm. Soc.* June 1967–August 1975, seriatim.

## MELOCACTUS

Link & Otto in *Verh. Ver. Beförd. Gart. Preuss. Staat.* 3: 417, 1827, Nom. cons.

Typ. *M. communis* (Ait.) Link & Otto.

SYN. *Cactus.*

The 'Turk's-cap Cactus' from the hotter parts of Central America. The genus is probably small although hundreds of near-identical ''species'' have been described. All are solitary unless damaged, ± globose and form a stout, central, domed to cylindric cephalium of dense hairs and bristles in which the tiny, tubular, pink flowers and smooth, cylindrical, red fruits are ± imbedded. *Cephalocereus* and *Discocactus* are both distinguishable by having much larger nocturnal flowers.

## MILA

B. & R. *The Cactaceae* 3: 211, 1922.

Typ. *M. caespitosa* B. & R.

Monotypic genus of dwarf cacti from Peru with short cylindric stems bearing small yellow flowers from near the tips. The receptacle tube and ovary are almost naked, as is the fruit—a distinction from the closely related *Echinocereus*, and *Mila* never has a green stigma.

DONALD, J. D. in *Ashingtonia* 3 (2): 31, 1978 et seq.

## MONVILLEA

B. & R. *The Cactaceae* 2: 21, 1920.

Typ. *M. cavendishii* (Monv.) B. & R.

SYN. *Brasilicereus*

A slender counterpart of *Cereus*, *Monvillea* is a small genus native to the W. Indies and S. America distinguishable from *Cereus* by the persistence of the perianth on the fruit.

## MORANGAYA

Rowley in *Ashingtonia* 1: 44, 1974.

Typ. *M. pensilis* (Brand.) Rowl.

Monotypic genus endemic to rock faces in S. Baja California, having the long, trailing stems of an *Aporocactus* but a medium-sized, actinomorphic red flower.

## × MYRTGEROCACTUS ────────────

Moran in *Cact. Succ. J. Amer.* 34: 186, 1962.
= *Bergerocactus* × *Myrtillocactus*.
1 wild hybrid.


## MYRTILLOCACTUS ────────────

Console in *Boll. R. Ort. Bot. Palermo* 1: 8, 1897.
Typ. *M. geometrizans* (Mart.) Cons.

Very small (monotypic?) genus from Mexico and Guatemala forming stiffly erect, branching shrubs with 6–8-angled glaucous bluish stems and stout black spines. The tiny, whitish diurnal flowers have a very short tube and spreading perianth, and two or more commonly arise from one areole. Intergeneric hybrids: × *Myrtgerocactus,* × *Stenomyrtillus.*


## NEOLLOYDIA ────────────

B. & R. in *Bull. Torrey Bot. Club* 49: 251, 1922.
Typ. *N. conoidea* (DC.) B. & R.
SYN. *Cumarinia, Gymnocactus, Rapicactus.*

Small genus from Mexico and S. Texas, very close to *Mammillaria* and *Coryphantha.* From the former it differs in bearing the flower from the base of a groove on the upperside of a young tubercle; from the latter by its dissimilar form of seed.


## NEOPORTERIA ────────────

B. & R. *The Cactaceae* 3: 94, 1922.
Typ. *N. subgibbosa* (Haw.) B. & R.
SYN. *Chileorebutia, Delaetia, Horridocactus, Islaya, Neochilenia, Nichelia, Pyrrhocactus, Reicheocactus, Thelocephala.*

Medium-sized genus not sharply differentiated from others in S. Peru and Chile, composed of dwarf, usually unbranched, globular to short-columnar cacti with ± tuberculate ribs and small to medium short funnelform flowers from near the stem tips, occasionally more than one per areole.

## NEORAIMONDIA

B. & R. *The Cactaceae* 2: 181, 1920.
Typ. *N. macrostibas* (K. Sch.) B. & R.
SYN. *Neocardenasia.*

Very small genus of shrubby to tree-like cereiform plants from Peru, Chile and Bolivia. Stems with 4–8 deep ribs, distinct from other cacti by the large furry areoles which proliferate when bearing flowers, often more than one per areole. It is rare in cultivation.

## NOPALXOCHIA

B. & R. *The Cactaceae* 4: 204, 1923.
Typ. *N. phyllanthoides* (DC.) B. & R.
SYN. *Lobeira, Pseudonopalxochia.*

Very small but esteemed genus of unarmed epiphytes from Mexico with long, leaf-like stems similar to *Epiphyllum*, but broadly funnelform, many-tepalled, showy pink or red, diurnal flowers. *N. phyllanthoides* is a key figure in the ancestry of the modern epicacti.

ROWLEY, G. D. in *Ashingtonia* I: 11, 1973. **Key** to 4 species.
Intergeneric hybrids: × *Aporochia,* × *Epixochia,* × *Heliochia.*

## NOTOCACTUS

(K. Sch.) Back. & Knuth *Kaktus ABC* 253, 1935.
Typ. *N. ottonis* (Lehm.) Back. & Knuth.
SYN: *Brasilicactus, Eriocactus, Malacocarpus, Wigginsia.*

Medium-sized genus of compact, solitary or clumping, globose to short cylindric cacti from S. America, justly popular in collections. The short funnelform to campanulate flowers are diurnal and typically sparkling yellow, less commonly red; the stigmas are red or purple.

MACE, A. W. *Notocactus.* Nat. Cact. & Succ. Soc., Sussex 1975.

## NYCTOCEREUS

(Bgr.) B. & R. in *Contr. U.S. Nat. Herb.* 12: 423, 1909.
Typ. *N. serpentinus* (Lag. & Rodr.) B. & R.

Very small genus of rather thin-stemmed clambering cacti with 7–13 ribs covered in acicular white spines and native to Central America. The medium to large white to pinkish blooms are nocturnal, and the fruit is scaly and spiny.

## OPUNTIA

Miller *Gard. Dict. Abr.* Edn. IV, *1754.*

Typ. *O. humifusa* Raf.

SYN. *Austrocylindropuntia, Brasiliopuntia, Consolea, Corynopuntia, Cylindropuntia, Grusonia, Maihueniopsis, Micropuntia, Nopalea, Tephrocactus.*

Very large genus—the largest in Cactaceae—covering the full geographical spread from Canada and the N. U.S.A. down to S. Chile, and naturalized in many parts of the Old World. Opuntias are dwarf and tufted or creeping, shrubby or tree-like, with jointed stems which may be cylindrical (cholla, tuna) or flattened and plate-like (prickly pear) or ± globose. They bear leaves which are deciduous and scale-like (or terete and up to 10 cm (4 in.) long and subevergreen in *O. subulata*) and almost always glochids as well as, or in place of, spines. The ± rotate perianth falls off cleanly from a rim on the top of the fruit (prickly pear, Fig. 14.4) which is covered in spiny areoles at first. Seedlings have two large flat cotyledons. Some are cultivated for the fruits and as emergency cattle fodder; several are frost hardy.

## OROYA

B. & R. *The Cactaceae* 3: 102, 1922.

Typ. *O. peruviana* (K. Sch.) B. & R.

Very small Peruvian genus; stems mostly solitary, small and globose with (12–)20–35 low ribs and small, squat, coloured flowers. From *Copiapoa* it is distinguished by the bright green stem and the slightly fleshy fruit which detaches from the base.

## × PACHGEROCEREUS

Moran in *Cact. Succ. J. Amer.* 34: 93, 1962.

= *Bergerocactus* × *Pachycereus.*

1 wild hybrid.

## PACHYCEREUS

(Bgr.) B. & R. in *Contr. U.S. Nat. Herb.* 12: 420, 1909.

Typ. *P. pringlei* (Wats.) B. & R.

SYN. *Marginatocereus, Pseudomitrocereus*

Very small genus of massive tree cacti, the Mexican counterpart of Arizona's saguaro (*Carnegiea*). The flowers are smaller and the best single diagnostic feature is the large, dry fruit covered in wool and spines like a chestnut burr.

Intergeneric hybrid: × *Pachgerocereus.*

## PARODIA

Spegazzini in *Ann. Soc. Cient. Argent.* 96: 70, 1923.

Typ. *P. microsperma* (Web.) Speg.

Small S. American genus of widely grown dwarf cacti for which large numbers of superfluous names have been coined on the basis of individual specimens. The usually solitary, globose to short cylindric stems have numerous ribs divided up into tubercles. The areoles are spiny and often woolly too. About the only diagnostic characters separating *Parodia* from the rest of the complex of dwarf S. American cacti are the minute, dust-like seeds and the tendency for the central spines to be hooked.

BUINING, A. F. H. in *Succulenta* 33: 65–71, 1954. **Key** to species in Dutch.

## PEDIOCACTUS

B. & R. in Britton & Brown *Ill. Fl.* Edn. II, 2: 569, 1913.

Typ. *P. simpsonii* (Eng.) B. & R.

SYN. *Navajoa, Pilocanthus, Toumeya, Utahia*

Small or very small genus of dwarf cacti from the W. U.S.A., uncommon in collections because of cultural difficulties. The solitary or sometimes clustered stems are globose or short cylindric, diverse in form and spination. The flowers arise from the upper edge of young areoles, and the fruit has a few scales towards its top and splits vertically, to open by a cap.

BENSON, L. in *Cact. Succ. J. Amer.* 33: 49–54, 1961; 34: 163–168, 1962. **Key** to species.

## PELECYPHORA

Ehrenberg in *Bot. Zeit.* 1: 737, 1843.

Typ. *P. aselliformis* Ehr.

SYN. *Encephalocarpus.*

Very small genus of dwarf, slow-growing, solitary or clustering Mexican cacti popular with collectors. In *P. aselliformis* the tubercles are hatchet-shaped and the tiny spines arranged like two combs; in *P. strobiliformis* the tubercles are scale-like, acute and overlap as in a pine cone, with minute deciduous bristles at each tip. The small flowers are purple; their colour and point of origin distinguishes this genus from some similar strombocacti.

## PENIOCEREUS

(Bgr.) B. & R. in *Contr. U.S. Nat. Herb.* 12: 428, 1909.
Typ. *P. greggii* (Eng.) B. & R.
SYN. *Cullmannia, Neoevansia.*

Small genus of climbing cacti from Mexico and the S.W. U.S.A. notable for the massive underground rootstock. The long, slender, woody and sparingly succulent stems have 4–5 angles and very closely set areoles with minute spines; the large white flowers are nocturnal. *Pterocactus* differs in having scale leaves and glochids, no ribs and no flower tube.

H. SANCHEZ-MEJORADA *Revision del Genero Peniocereus* (*Las Cactaceas*). Mexico 1974. **Key** to 12 species in Spanish.

## PERESKIA

Miller *Gard. Dict.* Abr. Edn. IV, 1754.
Typ. *P. aculeata* Mill.
SYN. *Rhodocactus.*

Small genus of only slightly succulent shrubs, climbers or large trees with conspicuous, broad, flat, deciduous leaves and little resemblance to other cacti apart from the obvious spiny areoles. The flowers are superficially reminiscent of single roses, having few, free, spreading tepals. The species are native to tropical America, and in gardens require much warmth, water and space.

## PERESKIOPSIS

B. & R. in *Smiths. Misc. Coll.* 50: 331, 1907.
Typ. *P. porteri* (Brand.) B. & R.

Small genus from Mexico and Guatamala, in habit like *Pereskia* but closer to *Opuntia* in seed structure and in possessing glochids. The leaves are fleshier than those of *Pereskia.* It is valued as a vigorous, though tender, rootstock for accelerating seedling growth.

## PTEROCACTUS ———————————————

K. Sch. in *Monatsschr. Kakteenk.* 7: 6, 1897.

Typ. *P. tuberosus* (Pfeiff.) B. & R.

SYN. *Marenopuntia.*

Very small genus of small, slow-growing Mexican and Argentinian cacti composed of thin, weak, cylindrical branches from a massive tuberous root. New growths have scale leaves and glochids are present as well as spines. The solitary, sessile flowers are mostly terminal, confluent with the stem tip, and yellow or yellow and red. The seed is large and kidney-shaped or winged. KIESLING, R. in *Bol. Soc. Argentina Bot.* 14 (1–2): 111–116, 1971. **Key** to 8 spp. in Spanish.

## QUIABENTIA ———————————————

B. & R. *The Cactaceae* 4: 252, 1923.

Typ. *Q. zehntneri* B. & R.

Very small genus of S. American straggly shrubs or small trees with the habit of cylindrical-stemmed opuntias but with flat and ± persistent fleshy leaves. The flower is similar to that of *Pereskia.*

## RATHBUNIA ———————————————

B. & R. in *Contr. U.S. Nat. Herb.* 12: 414, 1909.

Typ. *R. alamosensis* (Coult.) B. & R.

Very small (monotypic?) Mexican genus of thicket-forming straggly shrubs with 4–8-ribbed stems and a flower that makes it easily recognizable: scarlet, diurnal, with a narrow scaly tube and ± oblique, spreading or reflexing limb.

## REBUTIA ———————————————

K. Sch. in *Monatsschr. Kakteenk.* 5: 102, 1895.

Typ. *R. minuscula* K. Sch.

SYN. *Aylostera, Mediolobivia* p.p., *Sulcorebutia.*

Medium-sized genus of solitary or tufted cacti justly popular for combining small, compact habit with a profusion of small but superb blooms in red, purple, pink, orange, yellow or almost white. Diagnostic features are the lack of ribs, tubercles in spirals, flowers in rings round the base of the stems, and the narrow, smooth receptacle tube. It is native to Bolivia and Argentina. Species with the areoles extended upwards in a woolly groove towards the axil of the tubercle are classed by some as *Sulcorebutia.*

## RHIPSALIS

Gaertner *Fruct. Sem.* 1: 137, 1788, Nom. cons.

Typ. *R. baccifera* (Mill.) Stearn.

SYN. *Acanthorhipsalis, Epiphyllopsis, Erythrorhipsalis, Hariota, Hatiora, Lepismium, Pfeiffera, Pseudozygocactus, Rhipsalidopsis.*

Large genus of ± unarmed, sparingly succulent epiphytes of the tropical and subtropical forests of America but with outliers, perhaps introduced, in parts of Africa, Madagascar, India and Sri Lanka. The stems are extremely diverse: terete, flat and leaf-like, winged or angled, sometimes long- and short-jointed on the one plant, with minute areoles which may have hair or fine weak bristles; very exceptionally spines. The flowers are mostly tiny, with rather few, spreading, free tepals, few stigmas, and are followed by smooth round fruits with a sticky juice ('Mistletoe Cactus' alludes to these fruits and the general habit).

## SCHLUMBERGERA

Lemaire in *Rev. Hort.* Ser. IV, 7: 253, 1858.

Typ. *S. russelliana* (Hook.) B. & R.

SYN. *Epiphyllanthus, Zygocactus.*

Very small but horticulturally important genus of unarmed epiphytes from Brazil, parents of the 'Christmas Cactus' and 'Easter Cactus', popular as house plants. The shoots are composed of a series of leaf-like joints from a small basal trunk, and have areoles in the marginal notches or scattered over the surface like a miniature opuntia pad (but without glochids). The flowers are relatively large and zygomorphic, with a well-defined nectar chamber, red, purplish or almost white.

## × SELELIOCEREUS

Guill. in *Plantes Utiles, ornementales ou interessantes des Pays Chauds.* II *Plantes Grasses.* 51, 1937.

SYN. *Helioselenius* Rowl.

= *Heliocereus* × *Selenicereus.*

Few cultivars.

## × SELENIAPORUS

Rowl. in Epiphytes 4 (13): 13, 1972.

= *Aporocactus* × *Selenicereus.*

Few cultivars.

## SELENICEREUS

(Bgr.) B. & R. in *Contr. U.S. Nat. Herb.* 12: 429, 1909.

Typ. *S. grandiflorus* (L.) B. & R.

SYN. *Cryptocereus, Deamia, Mediocactus, Strophocactus.*

Small genus of long-stemmed climbers and epiphytes with copious aerial roots, native to the hotter forest regions of Central America. The stems are variously armed and ribbed or angled; the flowers large to very large, white, scented and nocturnal, among the most splendid of all flowering plants, justly earning the name 'Queen of the Night' for *S. grandiflorus.*
Intergeneric hybrids: × *Seleliocereus*, × *Seleniaporus*, × *Seleniphyllum.*

## × SELENIPHYLLUM

Rowl. in Backeberg *Die Cactaceae* 6: 3557, 1962.

SYN. *Phyllenicereus* Guill., *Phylloselenicereus* Knebel.

= *Epiphyllum* × *Selenicereus.*

Few cultivars.

## STENOCEREUS

(Bgr.) Ricc. in *Bol. R. Orto Bot. Palermo* 8: 253, 1909.

Typ. *S. stellatus* (Pfeiff.) Ricc.

SYN. *Anisocereus, Heliabravoa, Hertrichocereus, Isolatocereus, Lemaireocereus, Machaerocereus, Marshallocereus, Polaskia, Pterocereus, Ritterocereus.*

Rather loosely-defined medium-sized 'dump' genus of cereiform plants from which some have segregated many smaller genera. The majority are erect, shrubby or tree-like; *S. eruca* creeps along the ground. The usually short funnelform or campanulate flowers have a stout, scaly receptacle tube with hairs and sometimes bristles. The fleshy fruit bears spines at first which fall as it ripens.
Intergeneric hybrid: × *Stenomyrtillus.*

## × STENOMYRTILLUS*

Rowl.

= *Stenocereus* × *Mytillocactus.*

1 cultivar.

## STETSONIA ————————————————————

B. & R. *The Cactaceae* 2: 64, 1920.
Typ. *S. coryne* (S. D.) B. & R.

Monotypic genus from Argentina; a slow-growing tree cactus with trunk and crown of erect, 8–9-ribbed branches and recognizable from other tree cacti by the base of the receptacle being covered in thin overlapping scales like a pine cone.

## STROMBOCACTUS ————————————————

B. & R. *The Cactaceae* 3: 106, 1922.
Typ. *S. disciformis* (DC.) B. & R.
SYN. *Normanbokea, Obregonia, Turbinicarpus.*

Small genus of miniature, mostly solitary, spirally tubercled, top-shaped or subglobose cacti from Mexico. The stem surface is greyish and the spines weak and often papery or pectinate. The short funnelform, freely borne flowers arise near the woolly apex and are mainly whitish. The presence of spines distinguishes this genus from *Ariocarpus*; the less scaly receptacle from *Pediocactus*. (See also note under *Pelecyphora*.) Some authorities retain *Strombocactus* in a narrower sense for species with a dry, thin-walled fruit and minute (0.3 mm ⊘) subrotund, red-brown seeds, classing all others as *Turbinicarpus*.

## TACINGA ————————————————————

B. & R. *The Cactaceae* 1: 39, 1919.
Typ. *T. funalis* B. & R.

Very small (monotypic?) genus of scrambling shrubs from Brazil, uncommon in cultivation, with the habit of slender, cylindrical-stemmed opuntias but segregated on account of the peculiar flower, which has the tepals rolled back and a ring of hairs separating them from the tall brush of exserted stamens.

## × THELOBERGIA ———————————————————

Hirao in *Colour Encyclopaedia of Cacti:* 30, 1979.
= *Thelocactus* × *Leuchtenbergia.*
One cultivar.

## THELOCACTUS————————————————————

(K. Sch.) B. & R. in *Bull. Torrey Bot. Club* 49: 251, 1922.

Typ. *T. hexaedrophorus* (Lem.) B. & R.

SYN. *Ancistrocactus, Brittonia, Coloradoa, Echinomastus, Glandulicactus, Hamatocactus, Sclerocactus.*

Small or medium-sized, ill-defined 'dump' genus which, despite classification problems, contains many fine collectors' cacti. The solitary or rarely clumping stems are globose to short cylindric with ± tuberculate ribs. One spot character is the upward extension of the areole as a short felted groove on the top side of the tubercle, but to a much lesser extent than in *Coryphantha*. The fruit dehiscence and seed form are also diagnostic.

GLASS, C. & FOSTER, R. in *Cact. Succ. J. Amer.* 49: 213 *et seq.*, 1977. Key to 7 species from Chihuahua.

Intergeneric hybrid: × *Thelobergia*.

## UEBELMANNIA ————————————————————

Buining in *Succulenta* 46: 159, 1967.

Typ. *U. gummifera* (Back. & Voll) Buin.

Very small genus from Brazil of globose to short columnar cacti with many acute, ± tuberculate ribs and closely set, sometimes confluent areoles forming crests, with fine bristly spines. The plant surface is ± deep purplish, pustulate and sometimes silver scaly, recalling *Astrophytum* (q.v.). The tiny flowers are yellowish.

## WEBEROCEREUS ————————————————————

B. & R. in *Contr. U.S. Nat. Herb.* 12: 431, 1909.

Typ. *W. tunilla* (Web.) B. & R.

SYN. *Eccremocactus, Werckleocereus.*

Small genus of ± unarmed epiphytes from Central America with the flat, leaf-like stems of an *Epiphyllum* but much smaller, less showy, white or pink nocturnal flowers.

## WILCOXIA ————————————————————

B. & R. in *Contr. U.S. Nat. Herb.* 12: 434, 1909.

Typ. *W. poselgeri* B. & R.

Very small genus of thin-stemmed climbing cacti from Mexico and S. California similar in habit to *Peniocereus* but, instead of a single large tuber, having many smaller, elongated tubers, and smaller, red or purple, diurnal flowers.

**Figs. 15.1-15.4   Commelinaceae:** *Tradescantia navicularis*

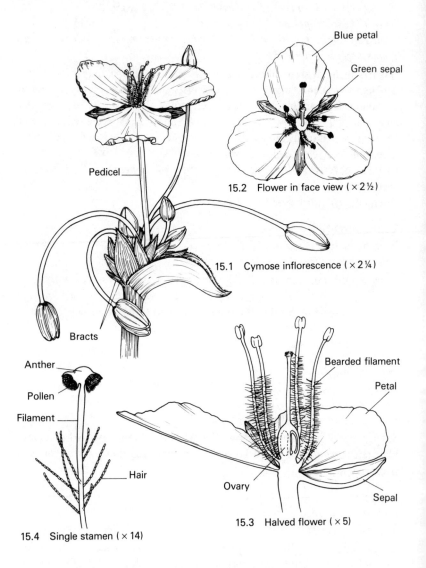

Blue petal

Green sepal

Pedicel

15.2   Flower in face view ( × 2 ½ )

15.1   Cymose inflorescence ( × 2 ¼ )

Bracts

Anther

Pollen

Filament

Bearded filament

Petal

Hair

Ovary

Sepal

15.3   Halved flower ( × 5)

15.4   Single stamen ( × 14)

# CHAPTER 15

# Commelinaceae

This medium-sized Family is distinguished from its allies among Monocotyledons by having three green sepals and three coloured petals; Agavaceae, Dioscoreaceae and Liliaceae have a perianth of six more or less similar tepals. The plants are tropical or subtropical herbs with jointed stems and alternate, sheathing leaves, sometimes in rosettes. The inflorescence is typically a cincinnus. The flowers are commonly blue, a colour very rarely found elsewhere in succulents.

Several genera, such as *Zebrina* and *Rhoeo*, are valued as house plants, and a few *Tradescantia* species will stand frost. All plants are soft and juicy, and in addition to the species mentioned below others of *Tradescantia* and *Cyanotis* verge on true succulence.

Genus including Succulents: *TRADESCANTIA* Only.

## TRADESCANTIA

L. *Sp. Pl.* Edn. I: 288, 1753; *Gen. Pl.* Edn. V: 139, 1754.
Typ. *T. virginiana* L.

Large genus of herbaceous American perennials of which the one with greatest claim to succulence is *T. navicularis* (Figs. 15.1–4). This has small, thick, keel-like leaves overlapped and sheathing the short shoots, and elongated prostrate stems that root from the nodes. The flowers with 3 mauvish-pink petals, 3 small green sepals and 6 hairy stamens at once set it apart from any other succulent.

**Figs. 16.1-16.6   Compositae: 16.1-16.3 *Senecio stapeliiformis*; 16.4-16.6 *Senecio crassissimus***

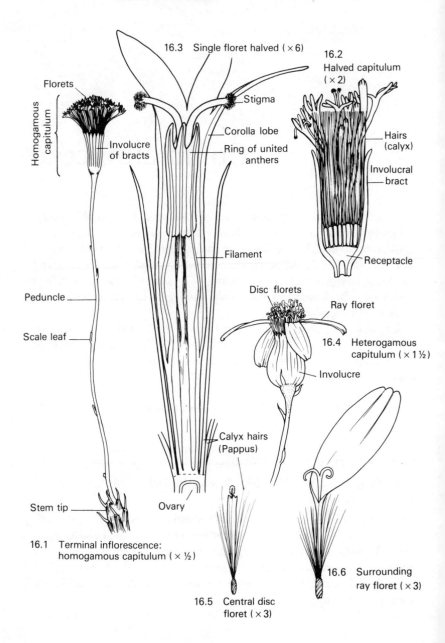

16.3   Single floret halved ( × 6)

Stigma

Corolla lobe

Ring of united anthers

Filament

16.2
Halved capitulum
( × 2)

Hairs
(calyx)

Involucral
bract

Receptacle

Florets

Homogamous capitulum

Involucre
of bracts

Peduncle

Scale leaf

Disc florets

Ray floret

16.4   Heterogamous
capitulum ( × 1 ½)

Involucre

Calyx hairs
(Pappus)

Stem tip

Ovary

16.1   Terminal inflorescence:
homogamous capitulum ( × ½)

16.5   Central disc
floret ( × 3)

16.6   Surrounding
ray floret ( × 3)

# CHAPTER 16

# Compositae

Arguably the largest of all Families of flowering plants, this has an estimated 1100 genera, of which *Senecio* with 2000 to 3000 species is a strong competitor as the largest of all genera. The worldwide success of the Family is no doubt due to the evolution of a highly specialized and very uniform compound flower head, ideally suited both for efficient cross-pollination and, later, for seed dispersal. Individual flowers are minute (**florets**) and tubular, packed tightly together on a disc-like inflorescence called a **capitulum** ('little head'), and surrounded by a cylindrical protective **involucre** made up of bracts. The whole simulates a single large flower, and is called such by the layman, but to be botanically correct we should speak of the flower-head (or **pseudanthium**) of a dahlia or chrysanthemum, made up of individual florets.

Taking *Senecio* as an example (Figs. 16.1–3), we find that in *S. stapeliiformis* the florets are all tubular and actinomorphic, with five short equal corolla lobes: we refer to them as **disc florets**. In other species, as *S. crassissimus* (Figs. 16.4–6), there are two sorts of flowers: disc florets at the centre and **ray florets** round the outside. The latter have a zygomorphic corolla, extended on one side into a long strap-like ray. The rays all extend outwards, adding to the illusion of a single flower with many-petalled corolla.

Each floret (Fig. 16.3) is made up of five petals united into a long narrow tube, enclosing five stamens whose anthers are also united into a long narrow cylinder around the style. The calyx is represented only by a ring of hairs round the base of the corolla. Pollen is released inside the anther tube and slowly pushed out by the style, which acts as a piston—you can see the tiny blobs of golden pollen atop a newly expanded capitulum. Later, when most of the pollen has been taken, the two stigma lobes curl apart and become receptive.

A capitulum scores over a single large flower in a number of ways. Structurally it is more robust and better protected: raindrops bounce off and do not wash away the pollen and nectar (which is at the bottom of the tube); and boring and biting insects have to attack each seed in turn rather than finding 'all the eggs in one basket' as in a single large ovary. Also the functional life of such a flower-head is longer than that of the equivalent solitary flower.

The fruit that ripens from each floret is distributed (in the succulent species, at least) by a parachute developed from the enlarged calyx hairs—a mechanism all too familiar in the floating seeds of the common dandelion, one plant of which can disperse 23 000 seeds in a year. Unfortunately for the grower of succulents, these do not seem to set viable seed away from their native habitat, even after hand-pollination.

In general habit the Compositae are enormously diverse, from tiny annuals to shrubs and small trees. Although succulence has developed to a marked degree only in two genera in South Africa, all three basic life-forms are found: leaf-, stem- and caudiciform succulents. The Mexican *Senecio praecox* is also a good candidate for consideration as a stem-succulent.

## KEY TO GENERA INCLUDING SUCCULENTS

| | |
|---|---:|
| 1  Bracts of involucre in 1 or 2 series, free | **Senecio** |
| 1  Bracts of involucre in 1 series only, connate at least at the base into cup | **Othonna** |

### OTHONNA

L. *Sp. Pl.* Edn. I: 924, 1753; *Gen. Pl.* Edn. V: 396, 1754.

Typ. *O. coronopifolia* L.

Large genus of African xerophytes including leaf- and caudiciform succulents. *O. capensis (crassifolia)* is a common and easily grown carpeter with soft, watery, cylindrical green leaves. The caudiciform species are more for the specialist grower. *O. euphorbioides* has cactus-like clusters of spines, some of which are forked (Fig. 37.76).

JACOBSEN: **Key** to cultivated species.

### SENECIO

L. *Sp. Pl.* Edn. I: 866, 1753; *Gen. Pl.* Edn. V: 373, 1754.

Typ. *S. vulgaris* L.

SYN. *Kleinia, Notonia.*

Very large cosmopolitan genus (2000–3000 species) that in temperate countries is most conspicuous for the weedy ragworts and groundsels. All three types of leaf-, stem- (Fig. 7.7) and caudiciform succulent have been evolved in Africa. The plants are of extremely diverse habit, but all have the standardized capitulate inflorescences that make the Family at once recognizable (Figs. 16.1–6). The distinction from *Othonna* rests only on the structure of the involucre.

JACOBSEN: Synopsis of cultivated species.

# CHAPTER 17

# Convolvulaceae

The bindweed Family is of medium size and comprises plants of diverse habit, some shrubby and self-supporting, but many climbing, such as the persistent invaders of our gardens, the species of *Convolvulus*. The large bell-shaped white or pink flowers make them easily recognizable, and it is a short step to the non-invasive annual morning glories (*Ipomoea*) with their large and showy coloured blooms. Some African species of *Ipomoea* are perennial and form massive underground caudices that have caught the eye of collectors and are now exposed to view in many glasshouses. At least the pinkish-purple flowers are more showy than in many caudiciforms. But the interest does not, apparently, also extend to the closely related *I. batatas*, the sweet potato, a widely grown agricultural crop of hot countries.

Genus including Succulents: *IPOMOEA* only.

IPOMOEA ————————————————————————————————

L. *Sp. Pl.* Edn. I: 159, 1753; *Gen. Pl.* Edn. V: 76, 1754.
Typ. *I. pestigridis* L.

Very large, cosmopolitan genus of warm temperate and tropical countries that includes annuals and perennials, twiners and even trees. Only a handful of species with an underground caudex and slender annual shoots need concern us here, however.

**Figs. 18.1-18.5    Crassulaceae: 18.1-18.3 *Sedum anglicum;* 18.4-18.5
*Sempervivum* hybrid**

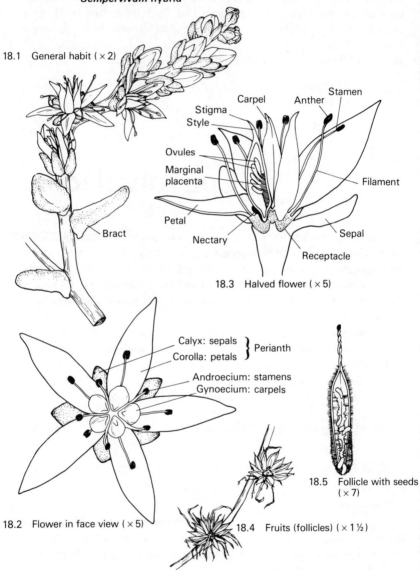

18.1   General habit ( × 2)

Carpel   Anther   Stamen

Stigma
Style

Ovules
Marginal
placenta

Petal

Nectary

Filament

Sepal

Receptacle

Bract

18.3   Halved flower ( × 5)

Calyx: sepals
Corolla: petals   } Perianth

Androecium: stamens
Gynoecium: carpels

18.5   Follicle with seeds
( × 7)

18.2   Flower in face view ( × 5)

18.4   Fruits (follicles) ( × 1 ½ )

# CHAPTER 18

# Crassulaceae

A medium-sized cosmopolitan Family, the Crassulaceae is the third largest of Families containing exclusively succulent plants, following Cactaceae and Mesembryanthemaceae. In addition to herbaceous, soft, fleshy perennials there are a few annuals and biennials rarely grown by collectors, whereas a few species grow into small trees with fat fleshy trunks up to 2 m (6½ ft.) tall. Leaf succulence, however, is the rule. The habit ranges from sparingly fleshy shrublets of fairly conventional look (*Kalanchoe*) down to extreme xerophytes showing surface reduction, close packing of foliage in square or round columns, hairy or waxy covering and all the recognized apparatus for water conservation. Overall they have the widest adaptability of all succulents: *Sedum rosea* occurs in the arctic north, and the one genus *Crassula* runs the gamut from some of the most drought resistant of all plants in the deserts of S.W. Africa to submerged aquatics which only break the water surface in order to flower. The many hardy species of *Sedum* and *Sempervivum* are a subject to themselves: the province of rock and alpine garden enthusiasts.

Crassulaceae have small, star-like or tubular, isomerous flowers with stamens as many as the sepals, petals and carpels (*Crassula*) or twice as many. Structurally the flowers are the simplest of all in succulents, with carpels almost always free and superior, and the flowers actinomorphic and usually bisexual. Each carpel ripens to a small follicle shedding abundant dust-like seed. The flowers are usually massed in corymbs and sometimes scented, although not always pleasantly. White, yellow and red are the commonest colours; blue occurs only in *Sedum coeruleum*. Closely parallel is the saxifrage Family, Saxifragaceae, but these are never truly succulent.

## General References

BERGER, A. 1930 Crassulaceae in ENGLER & PRANTL: *Die Natürlichen Pflanzenfamilien* Edn. II 18a. **Keys** to all genera and species, in German.

PRAEGER, R. L. 1932 An account of the Sempervivum Group. (London).

## KEY TO GENERA

1 Stamens as many as petals
  2 Leaves opposite                                                      Crassula
  2 Leaves alternate, in rosettes                                Sinocrassula
1 Stamens twice as many as petals
  3 Flower parts in fours; leaves opposite                        Kalanchoe
NOTE: *Diamorpha* (unc.) is an annual with alternate, not opposite, leaves.
  3 Flowers parts in fives or higher numbers
    4 Flower parts in fives
      5 Inflorescence terminal; leaves not or only rarely rosulate
        6 Petals free or nearly so
          7 Inflorescence equilateral, with branches in all planes
            8 Petals erect, spreading only at the tips; leaves opposite
                                                                     Lenophyllum
            8 Petals spreading from low down; leaves not opposite    Orostachys
          7 Inflorescence secund-cymose, all in one plane               Sedum
        6 Petals ± united
          9 Sepals small, shorter than the corolla tube
NOTE: *Mucizonia* and *Pistorinia* (unc.) are sedum-like annuals with alternate,
    subterete leaves.
            10 Leaves alternate
              11 Leaves deciduous, passing over gradually into bracts
                12 Plant dying back to a subterranean tuber        Umbilicus
                12 Plant with persistent, thick aerial stems        Tylecodon
              11 Leaves persistent, abruptly passing over into bracts
                                                                    Adromischus
            10 Leaves opposite
              13 Flowers erect, yellow                          Chiastophyllum
              13 Flowers nodding, not yellow                         Cotyledon
          9 Sepals conspicuous, as long as or longer than the corolla tube
                                                                        Villadia
      5 Inflorescence lateral; leaves commonly rosulate
        14 Petals united into a ± long campanulate tube
          15 Flowers up to 2 cm ∅, yellowish or reddish           Rosularia
          15 Flowers 2–3 cm ∅, bright purplish magenta              Tacitus
        14 Petals free or only shortly united
          16 Petals spreading radially from midway
            17 Inflorescence a narrow, equilateral panicle or thyrse with many
                short few-flowered branches                       Thompsonella

17 Inflorescence not as above
    18 Petals red spotted; stamens reflexed                **Graptopetalum**
    18 Petals not spotted; stamens erect                     **Dudleya**
16 Petals erect or only slightly spreading above
    19 Petals appendiculate within                      **Pachyphytum**
    19 Petals not appendiculate within
        20 Corolla not convolute in the bud, red or yellow, rarely green
              or white, showy, usually strongly pentagonal; petals thick
              and fleshy, sharply keeled; sepals ± spreading; leaves
              narrow-based, readily detached          **Echeveria**
        20 Corolla convolute in the bud, pallid, slightly angled only;
              petals thin, scarcely keeled; sepals erect or appressed;
              leaves broad-based, not readily detached    **Dudleya**
4 Flower parts in sixes (rarely fives) or higher numbers
  21 Flower parts (5–)6–16
    22 Scales at base of carpels large and petaloid       **Monanthes**
    22 Scales at base of carpels small, not petaloid
        23 Rosettes stemless, tufted; plants hardy
           24 Petals united into a short, wide, 6–8-angled tube    **Rosularia**
           24 Petals free or only shortly united
              25 Flower parts 6–7; flower bell-shaped       **Jovibarba**
              25 Flower parts 8–16; flower star-shaped   **Sempervivum**
        23 Plants developing a stem; tender
           26 Perennials with terminal leaf rosettes; nectar glands ± 4-sided
                                         **Aeonium**
           26 Annuals or biennials (rarely perennial) with ± scattered leaves;
              nectar glands 1–2-horned            **Aichryson**
  21 Flower parts 17–32                             **Greenovia**

## ADROMISCHUS

Lemaire in *Jard. Fleur.* 2 *Misc.* 59, 1852.
*Typ. A. hemisphaericus* (L.) Lem.

Small genus of dwarf shrublets from S. and S.W. Africa, originally classified in *Cotyledon* and with intermediate species to that and to *Tylecodon*. The leaves are highly succulent, very diverse in form, often waxy or spotted with purple and are more showy to look at than the slim, erect, tubular flowers.
TOELKEN, H. in *Bothalia* 12, 377–393, 1978. **Key** to species.
JACOBSEN: Synopsis.

## AEONIUM

Webb & Berthelot *Hist. Nat. Iles Can.* 3: 184, 1840.

Typ. apparently not yet designated.

Medium-sized genus endemic to the Canary Islands except for outliers in N. Africa to Arabia and other Atlantic islands. From *Sempervivum* they differ by the often large rosettes which are borne on simple or branching stems. Flowers are yellow to whitish or rarely red, carried terminally from a rosette that dies after flowering.

BRAMWELL, D. *Wild flowers of the Canary Islands*, 139–145, 1974. **Key** to species.

JACOBSEN: Synopsis.

Intergeneric hybrid: × *Greenonium*.

## AICHRYSON

Webb & Berthelot *Hist. Nat. Iles Can.* 3: 180, 1840.

Typ. *A. laxum* (Haw.) Bramw.

SYN. *Macrobia.*

Small genus from Atlantic islands (one species in Portugal) composed of mostly monocarpic herbs with flat, mostly downy leaves in lax rosettes and scattered along the branches. Flowers yellow.

BRAMWELL, D. in *Bol. 59 Inst. Nac. Inv. Agron,* 203–213, 1968; in *Wild flowers of the Canary Islands*, 137–139, 1974. Both with **key** to species.

## CHIASTOPHYLLUM

(Led.) Stapf in Engler and Prantl *Die Natürl. Pflanzenf.* Edn. II, 18a: 418, 1930.

Typ. *C. oppositifolium* (Led.) Bgr.

Monotypic genus from the Caucasus segregated from *Umbilicus* and *Sedum. C. oppositifolium* is hardy and grown on rock gardens for its elegant nodding sprays of pale yellow flowers.

## COTYLEDON

L. *Sp. Pl.* Edn. I: 429, 1753; *Gen. Pl.* Edn. V: 196, 1754.

Typ. *C. orbiculata* L.

Medium-sized genus ranging from S. Africa to S. Arabia and forming small to medium shrubs with opposite leaves. From *Adromischus* it differs in the opposite leaves and more showy, usually hanging flowers; from *Kalanchoe* by the number of floral parts.

TOELKEN, H. in *Bothalia* 12: 377–393, 1978.

JACOBSEN: Synopsis.

### CRASSULA

L. *Sp. Pl.* Edn. I: 282, 1753; *Gen. Pl.* Edn. V: 136, 1754.

Typ. *C. perfoliata* L.

SYN. *Dinacria, Kalosanthes, Pagella, Rhopalota, Rochea, Tillaea, Vauanthes.*

Very large cosmopolitan genus found in all types of habitat from bog and marsh to desert, and accordingly diverse in life form although all are succulent (Figs. 7.1, 7.3). The small, weedy annuals are rarely cultivated. The spot characters are the combination of opposite leaves and a single whorl of (3–)5(–9) stamens (Figs. 1.8–16).

TOELKEN, H. in *J. S. Afr. Bot.* 41: 93–124, 1975; *Contr. Bolus Herb.* 8, 1977. **Key** to S. African species.

JACOBSEN: Synopsis.

Intergeneric hybrid: × *Echesula.*

### × DUDLEVERIA

Rowl. in *Nat. Cact. Succ. J.* 13: 75, 1958.

= *Dudleya* × *Echeveria.*

The one cultivar reported here seems more likely to be *Echeveria* × *Villadia.*

### DUDLEYA

B. & R. in *Bull. N.Y. Bot. Gard.* 3: 12, 1903.

Typ. *D. lanceolata* (Nutt.) B. & R.

SYN. *Hasseanthus, Stylophyllum.*

Medium-sized genus of rosette leaf succulents from the S.W. U.S.A. and N.W. Mexico, close to *Echeveria* but distinct by the combination of usually glaucous sheathing leaves, usually spreading petal tips and other minor features of the flowers.

JACOBSEN: Synopsis.

Intergeneric hybrid: × *Dudleveria.*

## × ECHESULA

Gossot in Marnier-Lapostolle *Liste des Plantes Grasses sauf Cactées du Jardin Botanique des Cèdres* 24, 1949.

= *Crassula* × *Echeveria.*

No certain example; the one reported hybrid is not of this parentage.

## ECHEVERIA

DC. *Prodr.* 3: 401, 1828.

Typ. *E. coccinea* (Cav.) DC.

SYN. *Cremneria, Cremnophila, Oliveranthus, Urbinia.*

Large genus of compact, rosette-forming leaf succulents from Mexico, with outliers in the S. U.S.A. and S. America. The colourful rosettes have a flower-like appearance, and the hardier species are valued for summer bedding displays. The leaves have a range of forms and shapes, colours and surface adornments (wax, hairs, etc.).

WALTHER, E. *Echeveria.* San Francisco 1972. **Key** to species.

JACOBSEN: Synopsis.

Intergeneric hybrids: × *Dudleveria,* × *Echesula,* × *Graptoveria,* × *Pachyveria,* × *Sedeveria.*

## × GRAPSONELLA*

Rowl.

= *Graptopetalum* × *Thompsonella.*

Few cultivars.

## GRAPTOPETALUM

Rose in *Contr. U.S. Nat. Herb.* 13: 296, 1911.

Typ. *G. pusillum* Rose.

Small genus from the S.W. U.S.A. to Mexico distinguished from *Echeveria* by the more open flowers with spotted petals on lax cymosely branched inflorescences instead of erect spikes or racemes as in *Echeveria.*

Intergeneric hybrids. × *Grapsonella,* × *Graptophytum,* × *Graptosedum,* × *Graptoveria,* × *Lengraptophyllum.*

WALTHER, E. in *Cact. Succ. J. Amer.* 1: 183–186, 1930. **Key** to 6 species.

× GRAPTOPHYTUM ——————————————————————————

Gossot in Marnier-Lapostolle *Liste des Plantes Grasses sauf Cactées du Jardin Botanique des Cèdres* 27, 1949.
= *Graptopetalum* × *Pachyphytum.*
Several cultivars.

× GRAPTOSEDUM* ———————————————————————

Rowl.
= *Graptopetalum* × *Sedum.*
Several cultivars.

× GRAPTOVERIA ——————————————————————————

Gossot in Marnier-Lapostolle *Liste des Plantes Grasses sauf Cactées du Jardin Botanique des Cèdres* 27, 1949.
SYN. *Echepetalum* Gossot.
= *Echeveria* × *Graptopetalum.*
Few cultivars.

× GREENONIUM ——————————————————————————

Rowl. in *Nat. Cact. Succ. J.* 13: 75, 1958.
SYN. *Aeoniogreenovia* Vogg.
= *Aeonium* × *Greenovia.*
Few wild hybrids.

GREENOVIA ——————————————————————————————

Webb & Berthelot *Hist. Nat. Iles Can.* 3: 198, 1841.
Typ. *G. aurea* (Sm.) Webb & Berth.

Very small genus of Canarian endemics with sessile, blunt leaves in sempervivum-like rosettes which are monocarpic and close up like bulbs during the dry season. The flowers are golden yellow and have the highest number of flower parts in the Family.
BRAMWELL, D. *Wild flowers of the Canary Islands*, 145, 1974. **Key** to species.
Intergeneric hybrid: × *Greenonium.*

## JOVIBARBA

Opiz *Seznam Rostlin Květeny České* 54, 1852.

Typ. *J. hirta* (Jusl.) Opiz.

SYN. *Diopogon.*

Very small European genus of two polymorphic species included by many in *Sempervivum*, to which they are similar in habit and hardiness.

SMITH, A. C. *The Genus Sempervivum and Jovibarba*. Kent 1975. **Key** to species.

Intergeneric hybrid: × *Jovivum.*

## × JOVIVUM*

Rowl.

= *Jovibarba* × *Sempervivum.*

Few cultivars.

## KALANCHOE

Adanson *Fam. Pl.* 2: 248, 1763.

Typ. *K. laciniata* (L.) DC.

SYN. *Bryophyllum, Kitchingia.*

Large genus, widespread throughout the tropics, of xerophytic but not very succulent shrubs or climbers, rarely annual or biennial. Many grow plantlets from their leaves that afford a ready means of propagation. The usually showy, hanging or erect, colourful flowers have a long corolla tube and parts in fours, which distinguishes the genus from *Cotyledon* (parts in fives).

HAMET, R. & MARNIER-LAPOSTOLLE, J. in *Arch. Mus. Nat. d'Hist. Nat.* Ser. 7 VIII: 1–110, Paris 1964.

JACOBSEN: Synopsis.

BALDWIN, J. T. in *Amer. J. Bot.* 25: 572–9, 1938. **Key** to 26 commonly cultivated species.

## × LENGRAPTOPHYLLUM*

Rowl.

= *Lenophyllum* × *Graptopetalum.*

1 cultivar.

## LENOPHYLLUM

Rose in *Smiths. Misc. Coll.* 47: 159, 1904.
Typ. *L. guttatum* Rose.

Very small genus from Mexico and the S.W. U.S.A. with affinities with both *Sedum* and the *Echeveria* complex. The terminal inflorescences, which are racemose or spicate, are the most distinctive feature. The opposite leaves are mostly purplish brown or dark-spotted.
Intergeneric hybrid: × *Lengraptophyllum.*

## MONANTHES

Haworth in *Rev. Pl. Succ.* 68, 1821.
Typ. *M. polyphylla* Haw.

Small genus of diminutive shrublets from Atlantic islands and N. Africa. The leaves are mostly in rosettes and sometimes rough-papillate, and the main spot character is the presence of large, flat, nectar scales in the flower, almost like a second whorl of petals. One species is annual.
BRAMWELL, D. *Wild flowers of the Canary Islands*, 135–137, 1974. **Key** to species.
JACOBSEN: Synopsis.

## OROSTACHYS

Fischer *Cat. Jard. Pl. Comte A. de Razoumoffsky Gor. Moscow* 99, 1808.
Typ. *O. malacophylla* (Pall.) Fisch.

Small S. Asiatic genus segregated from *Sedum* by the monocarpic rosettes which produce a tall, spicate raceme or panicle of many small white (or less frequently yellowish or reddish) flowers. Some species have a sharp white bristle tip to each leaf.

## PACHYPHYTUM

Lk. Kl. & O. in *Allg. Gartenz.* 9: 9, 1841.
Typ. *P. bracteosum* Klotzsch.

Small Mexican genus related to *Echeveria*, from which it can be differentiated by the presence of a pair of scales inside each petal and about half its length. The very fleshy leaves are commonly glaucous and ± in rosettes (Fig. 7.4), and the cup- to bell-shaped flowers are borne on an erect cincinnus.

JACOBSEN: Synopsis.

POELLNITZ, K. v. in *Cact. J. Gt. Brit.* 5: 72, 1937. **Key** to species.

Intergeneric hybrids: × *Graptophytum*, × *Pachysedum*, × *Pachyveria.*

## × PACHYSEDUM

Jacobsen in *Sukk. Lexicon* 274, 1970.

= *Pachyphytum* × *Sedum.*

1 cultivar.

## × PACHYVERIA

Haage & Schmidt in *Haupt-Verzeichnis über Samen und Pflanzen mit Verkaufsbedingungen* 193, 1926.

SYN. *Echephytum* Gossot, *Pachyrantia* Walth., *Urbiphytum* Gossot.

= *Echeveria* × *Pachyphytum.*

Several cultivars.

WALTHER, E. in *Cact. Succ. J. Amer.* 6: 53–66, 1934. **Key** to 14 hybrids.

## ROSULARIA

(DC.) Stapf in *Curtis Bot. Mag.* 1923 t. 8985.

Typ. *R. pallida* (Sch. & Kot.) Stapf.

SYN. *Afrovivella, Sempervivella.*

Medium-sized S. Asiatic genus intermediate between *Sedum* and *Sempervivum*, having a rosette like the latter but lateral, cymose inflorescences, flower parts 5–8 and petals ± united into a tube. All the species are hardy.

## × SEDADIA

Moran in *Baileya* 19: 147, 1975.

= *Sedum* × *Villadia.*

1 wild hybrid.

## × SEDEVERIA

Walth. in *Cact. Succ. J. Amer.* 25: 20, 1953.

= *Echeveria* × *Sedum.*

Few cultivars.

**SEDUM** ────────────────────────────────

L. *Sp. Pl.* Edn. I: 430, 1753; *Gen. Pl.* Edn. V: 197, 1754, non Adanson.
Typ. *S. acre* L.
SYN. *Meterostachys, Pseudosedum, Rhodiola.*

Very large 'dump' genus, the stonecrops, including a heterogeneous
assortment of species after removal of *Orostachys* and other segregates. It
covers the N. Hemisphere and extends southwards with a single species in
Peru. Many are hardy—more so than in any other genus of succulents—and
in favour with rock and alpine gardeners for hot, dry, sunbaked spots and
chinks in walls. Some species are dioecious and caudiciform (*S. rosea*, the
roseroot, Fig. 7.11); some annual (*S. coeruleum*, unique in having pale blue
flowers) or biennial (*S. pilosum, sempervivoides*), and while most are dwarf, a
few reach 1½ m (5 ft.) high in Mexico with thick fleshy trunks (Figs.
18.1–3).

FROEDERSTROEM, H. in *Acta Hort. Goth.* 5: 3–75, 1930; 6: 5–111, 1931;
7: 3–126, 1932; 10: 2–262, 1935. **Key** to species.
PRAEGER, R. L. in *J. Roy. Hort. Soc.* 46: 1–314, 1921.
JACOBSEN: Synopsis.
CHITTENDEN, F. J. *Dictionary of Gardening* 4: 1919–1927, 1951. **Key** to
cultivated species.
CLAUSEN, R. T. *Sedum of the Trans-Mexican Volcanic Belt,* 380 pp. New
York 1959. Various **keys**.
CLAUSEN, R. T. *Sedum of North America North of the Mexican Plateau,*
743 pp. New York and London 1975. Various **keys**.
Intergeneric hybrids: × *Graptosedum,* × *Pachysedum,* × *Sedadia,* ×
*Sedeveria.*

**SEMPERVIVUM** ──────────────────────────

L. *Sp. Pl.* Edn. I: 464, 1753; *Gen. Pl.* Edn. V: 209, 1754.
Typ. *S. tectorum* L.
SYN. *Hypagophytum.*

Medium-sized genus of hardy, stemless rosette plants from the mountains of
Europe, W. Asia and N. Africa. The rosettes are monocarpic and mostly
offset freely forming a tuft or carpet. Flowers are red or yellow and rotate.
The houseleeks are very tenacious of life, and valued by rock and alpine
gardeners for planting on top of walls and in bare, sunny patches where little
else would survive (Figs. 18.4–5).

SMITH, A. C. *The Genus Sempervivum and Jovibarba.* Kent 1975. **Key** to species.
JACOBSEN: Synopsis.
Intergeneric hybrid: × *Jovivum.*

## SINOCRASSULA

Berger in Engler & Prantl *Die Natürl. Pflanzenf.* Edn. II 18a; 462, 1930.
Typ. *S. indica* (Decne.) Bgr.

Very small, dwarf genus from the Himalayas to W. China distinctive for having only a single whorl of stamens. Otherwise, the species, which include annuals as well as perennials, belong with *Sedum.*

## TACITUS

Moran in *Cact. y Suc. Mex.* 19: 76, 1974.
Typ. *T. bellus* Mor. & Meyr.

Monotypic genus from W. Mexico with a flat, echeveria-like rosette of bristle-tipped leaves, immediately distinct from all other Crassulaceae by the few, very large (2–3 cm; ¾–1¼ in.) brilliant red flowers with the petals united into a tube almost closed at the mouth by incurved lips. Offsets form sparingly with age.

## THOMPSONELLA

B. & R. in *Contr. U.S. Nat. Herb.* 12: 391, 1909.
Typ. *T. minutiflora* B. & R.

Very small Mexican genus scarcely separable from *Echeveria* by the thin petals which curl outwards at the tips. Adventitious buds may be produced from the inflorescences which afford a ready means of propagation.
Intergeneric hybrid: × *Grapsonella.*

## TYLECODON

Toelken in *Bothalia* 12: 377–382, 1978.
Typ. *T. papillaris* (L.) Rowl.

Medium-sized S. African genus of very dwarf to large shrubby succulents with pachycaul stems and spirally arranged deciduous leaves; flowers as for *Cotyledon* (Fig. 3.2).
TOELKEN, H. in *Bothalia* 12: 377–382, 1978.

## UMBILICUS

DC. in *Bull. Sci. Soc. Phil.* 3: 1, 1801.

Typ. *U. rupestris* (Sal.) Dandy.

Small genus of very similar species from Europe, the Canary Islands and W. Asia, of which *U. rupestris* is the common wall pennywort or navelwort. From a perennial fleshy tuber arise soft, pale green peltate leaves and an annual terminal racemose inflorescence with a diminishing series of leaves and small, greenish-white, cupshaped flowers.

## VILLADIA

Rose in *Bull. N.Y. Bot. Gard.* 3: 3, 1903.

Typ. *V. parviflora* (Hemsl.) Rose.

SYN: *Altamiranoa.*

Medium-sized genus of compact shrublets to creepers (rarely annuals) from Mexico and the Andes, infrequent in cultivation. From *Sedum* they differ in having the petals united into a distinct tube, and in the rather large sepals. Intergeneric hybrid: × *Sedadia.*

CHAPTER 19

# Cucurbitaceae

This large Family can be exemplified by the marrows and melons, pumpkins and cucumbers of our gardens: robust, quick-growing annual climbers with alternate leaves and tendrils. The plants are monoecious or dioecious, the female flowers being recognizable even in the bud by the fat ovary developing beneath the perianth. The Family is mainly tropical and has adapted in various ways in the advance into drier country. Thus, in Madagascar the result has been shrubby climbers with simple, fleshy, circular or elliptical, glossy green leaves (*Xerosicyos*). In Socotra we find the extraordinary endemic *Dendrosicyos*, giant of them all up to 6 m (20 ft.) tall, and in southern Malaysia the no less bizarre *Neoalsomitra podagrica* with a small, jointed, spiny green caudex. *Ibervillea* from the S.W. U.S.A. and the remaining African genera have a massive lumpish, perennial caudex abruptly tapered into long, thin, annual climbing shoots bearing usually palmately lobed leaves and tendrils. The flowers are small and inconspicuous, but those genera with berries are more ornamental and it is worth the effort of hand-pollination to try to induce them to set. Jacobsen lists several other genera, but of all these only *Kedrostis* and perhaps an occasional *Ibervillea* can be said to be at all common or easy in cultivation.

## General References

GENTRY, H. S. 1964 Cucurbitaceae in SHREVE, F. & WIGGINS, I. L. *Vegetation and Flora of the Sonoran Desert* II, pp. 1417–1434.

HUTCHINSON, J. 1967 Cucurbitaceae in *The Genera of Flowering Plants* II, pp. 376–419. **Key** to genera.

JEFFREY, C. 1967 Cucurbitaceae in *Fl. Trop. E. Afr.* 157 pp. (London). **Keys** to genera and species.

# KEY TO GENERA INCLUDING SUCCULENTS

1 Leaf succulents of shrubby habit with simple, entire leaves                    **Xerosicyos**
1 Caudiciform plants with thin, palmately veined, lobed or incised leaves
  2 Çaudex spiny, often jointed                                        **Neoalsomitra**
  2 Caudex neither spiny nor jointed
    3 Caudex erect, tapering, without thin, vining, annual branches; tendrils
      absent
      4 Leaves prickly                                               **Dendrosicyos**
      4 Leaves hairy                                                 **Corallocarpus**
                                           *(C. glomeruliflorus)*
NOTE: Both the above are rare.
    3 Caudex squat, abruptly passing over into long, thin, vining, annual
      branches; tendrils usually present
      5 Caudex with vertical pleats and furrows                      **Momordica**
      5 Caudex not pleated, ± terete
        6 Tendrils branched, spiralling below the branch as well as above; fruit a
          dry capsule splitting at the apex              **Gerrardanthus**
        6 Tendrils simple or absent, rarely bifid and then never spiralling below
          the branch; fruit a red or yellow fleshy berry
          7 Stamens inserted at the mouth of the receptacle; ovules numerous
                                                 **Ibervillea**
          7 Stamens inserted on the tube of the receptacle; ovules usually few
                                                 **Kedrostis**

## CORALLOCARPUS

Welwitsch in Benth. & Hook. *Gen. Pl.* 1: 831, 1867.

Typ. *C. welwitschii* (Naud.) Hook. ex Welw.

Small genus from Africa, Madagascar, Arabia and India composed mostly of
tendril climbers but with a single aberrant species, *C. glomeruliflorus* from S.
Arabia and Yemen which has a grotesque, fat caudex and thick branches
without tendrils. It is of interest to collectors, but rare in cultivation.

## DENDROSICYOS

Balfour in *Proc. Roy. Phys. Soc. Edinb.* 11: 513, 1882.

Typ. *D. socotrana* Balf.

Giant of the Family, a striking monotypic genus endemic to Socotra. The
massive tapering trunk is said to reach 6 m (20 ft.) tall and 1 m (40 ins.) in
diameter, and bears rough, bristly leaves. It is a rarity in collections.

## GERRARDANTHUS

Harvey in Benth. & Hook. *Gen. Pl.* 1: 820, 840, 1867.

Typ. *G. macrorrhiza* Harv.

Very small African genus similar to *Kedrostis* but distinguished by having a dry, dehiscent fruit and tendrils forked at the apex.

## IBERVILLEA

Greene in *Erythea* 3: 75, 1895.

Typ. *I. lindheimeri* (Gray) Greene.

SYN. *Maximowiczia.*

New World counterpart of *Kedrostis,* this is a very small (monotypic?) genus from S.W. U.S.A. and N.W. Mexico differentiated on minor details of the flower only.

## KEDROSTIS

Medikus *Phil. Bot.* 2: 69, 1791.

Typ. *K. africana* (L.) Cogn.

Medium-sized genus of the Old World tropics and sub-tropics with long, slender, climbing stems from a massive, smooth, lumpish caudex that grows typically partly above ground. The stalked leaves are ± palmately lobed and the tendrils are unbranched. The fleshy fruits are usually red.

## MOMORDICA

L. *Sp. Pl.* Edn. I: 1009, 1753; *Gen. Pl.* Edn. V: 440, 1754.

Typ. *M. balsamina L.*

Medium-sized tropical genus similar to *Kedrostis* in habit but most readily distinguishable by the different form of the caudex, which is ± bottle-shaped with vertical fissures so that it appears lobed in cross-section. *M. rostrata* from Kenya is occasionally cultivated.

## NEOALSOMITRA

Hutchinson in *Ann. Bot.* Ser. II. 6: 97, 1942.

Typ. *N. sarcophylla* (Wall.) Hutch.

Small genus spreading from India to Polynesia and Australia, of which the rare and delicate species *N. podagrica* is outstanding for the fusiform thickening of the stem bases which are constricted into green joints covered in large green prickles.

**XEROSICYOS** ─────────────────────────────

Humbert in *C.R. Acad. Sci. Paris* 208: 220, 1939.

Typ. *X. danguyi* Humb.

Very small genus endemic to Madagascar and forming climbing shrubs with tendrils and alternate, entire, fleshy, green circular to elliptic leaves. The flowers are minute and the plants dioecious.

ROWLEY, G. D. in *Ashingtonia* 2: 177, 1977. **Key** to species.

# CHAPTER 20

# Didiereaceae

This is a small but extremely curious Family endemic to S.W. Madagascar—'the cacti of the Old World'. The cylindrical or conical pachycaul stems recall those of some cacti, euphorbias and *Fouquieria*; spines are much in evidence in a surprisingly varied assortment of patterns, and there are also simple, deciduous leaves which may be linear, elliptical or orbicular. Most cactus-like of all is *Didierea*, with tubercles tipped with clusters of usually four diverging spines. The presence of thin, grass-like leaves during the growing season, and the fact that the areole is horny and shield-like, not felted, distinguish this genus from cacti. The siting of leaves in relation to spines separates euphorbia and fouquieria—the latter, in particular, has petiolar spines.

The flowers of Didiereaceae are also quite unlike those of cacti, being small and unisexual, but unfortunately they are rarely seen in cultivation. All species are in demand by collectors; they require warmth and care, and propagation is almost entirely limited to seed, which is in short supply.

## General References

MONTAGNAC, R. 1958 *Cactus* (France) 61: 73–80. **Keys** to species.

RAUH, W. 1963. Didieréacées in HUMBERT, H. *Flore de Madagascar*, 121e *Famille*. (Paris). **Key** to genera and species in French.

## KEY TO GENERA

1 Spines in clusters of 4 (–5) at the tips of the tubercles      **Didierea**
1 Spines solitary or in pairs (minute in *Alluaudia dumosa*)
     2 Branches strongly zigzagged      **Decaryia**
     2 Branches not strongly zigzagged
         3 Much branched shrubs with slender, woody, sparingly succulent shoots;
            leaves linear      **Alluaudiopsis**
         3 Shrubs or trees with stout branches; leaves orbicular or broadly obovate
            (scale-like and dropping very soon in *A. dumosa*)      **Alluaudia**

## ALLUAUDIA ─────────────────────────────

Drake in *Bull. Mus. Hist. Nat. Paris* 9: 37, 1903.

Typ. apparently not yet designated.

Very small genus of shrubs or trees with a ± succulent trunk, in nature up to 12 m (40 ft.) tall, with long wandlike branches covered in solitary spines in the axils of horizontal flat leaves; later short spur shoots develop below the spines, each with a pair of vertical leaves. *A. dumosa* is exceptional in having the leaves reduced to scales on the young shoots only.

JACOBSEN: **Key** to species.

## ALLUAUDIOPSIS ─────────────────────────

Humbert & Choux in *C.R. Acad. Sci. Paris* 199: 1651, 1934.

Typ. *A. fiherensis* Humb. & Ch.

Very small genus of scarcely succulent prickly shrubs 2–4 m (6½–13 ft.) in height with either solitary or paired spines, distinct from *Alluaudia* by the later paired leaves being sited above rather than below the spines.

JACOBSEN: **Key** to species.

## DECARYIA

Choux in *C.R. Acad. Sci. Paris* 188: 1620, 1929.

Typ. *D. madagascariensis* Choux.

Ultimately a small tree to 6 m (20 ft.) tall but seen in cultivation more as a dense, twiggy, sparingly succulent shrub with curiously zigzagged branches, each angle carrying two outwardly directed prickles with a small, flat, oval leaf between. The genus is monotypic.

## DIDIEREA

Baillon in *Bull. Soc. Linn. Paris* 1880: 258.

Typ. *D. madagascariensis* Baill.

Very small genus of singular, cereiform appearance, with one or more fleshy, tapered trunks and ± tuberculate thick branches carrying clusters of narrow leaves and radiating spines, the latter simulating the areole of a cactus but without the felt. *D. madagascariensis* is erect, with a central trunk and long tubercles; *D. trollii* is prostrate at first and later throws up erect stems with low tubercles.

**Figs. 21.1-21.10    Dioscoreaceae: *Dioscorea* spp.**

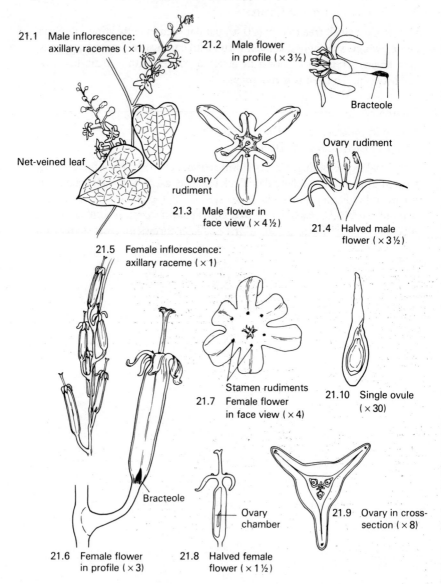

21.1    Male inflorescence:
axillary racemes ( × 1)

21.2    Male flower
in profile ( × 3 ½ )

Bracteole

Net-veined leaf

Ovary rudiment

Ovary
rudiment

21.3    Male flower in
face view ( × 4 ½ )

21.4    Halved male
flower ( × 3 ½ )

21.5    Female inflorescence:
axillary raceme ( × 1)

Stamen rudiments

21.7    Female flower
in face view ( × 4 )

21.10    Single ovule
( × 30)

Bracteole

Ovary
chamber

21.9    Ovary in cross-
section ( × 8)

21.6    Female flower
in profile ( × 3)

21.8    Halved female
flower ( × 1 ½ )

# CHAPTER 21

# Dioscoreaceae

A small Family of Monocotyledons, this is represented in the British flora by *Tamus communis*, the black bryony, which gives a good image of the Family as a whole: long, slender, twining, annual branches with heart-shaped leaves, arising from a perennial underground tuber that may reach great size and many pounds in weight. The flowers, borne in racemes, are small, inconspicuous, and have parts in threes; male and female are borne on separate plants.

The principal genus, *Dioscorea*, is pantropical and very large, including among its species the edible yams—a parallel to *Ipomoea* (p. 145). In two parts of its range where *Dioscorea* encounters very hot, dry conditions—Mexico and Southern Africa—there has been parallel development of a more or less overground caudex covered in large, polygonal, corky tubercles. These four species form the Section Testudinaria, regarded by some as a separate genus *Testudinaria* although linked to the other yams by intermediates.

From the other Monocotyledon Families including succulents, *Dioscorea* stands apart by the unique habit and the net-veined leaves (similar to Dicotyledons). *D. elephantipes*, with the caudex tessellated with conical warts, is the justly popular 'Elephant's Foot'; where the tubercles are less prominent the trimerous flowers serve as the surest distinction from other caudiciforms.

Genus including Succulents: *DIOSCOREA* only.

167

## DIOSCOREA

L. *Sp. Pl.* Edn. I: 1032, 1753; *Gen. Pl.* Edn. V: 456, 1754.

Typ. *D. sativa* L.

SYN. *Testudinaria.*

Very large genus of which 3 species from S. Africa and 1 from Mexico are highly rated in succulent collections. They are recognizable by the spherical or lumpish caudex, up to 1 m (40 in.) or more in diameter in nature, covered in bark ± cracking into polygonal warts, most pronounced in *D. elephantipes* (Figs. 7.12, 21.1–10). The leaves are glossy green and heart-shaped.

JACOBSEN: **Key** to species (as *Testudinaria*).

## A CLOSER LOOK

For examining tiny flowers, a ×8 or ×10 pocket lens is very helpful.

Ideally, a low-power binocular microscope with overhead illumination is worth every penny of the cost of buying it, for the new world of beauty and intricacy that it reveals.

To cut a delicate flower in half vertically, trim off the pedicel to just below the base of the bloom, hold this part between thumb and forefinger, and gently slide a sharp razor through it upwards towards the petals, which can finally be gently torn apart. This is much easier than trying to cut from the top downwards.

**Figs. 22.1-22.4  Euphorbiaceae: *Euphorbia milii***

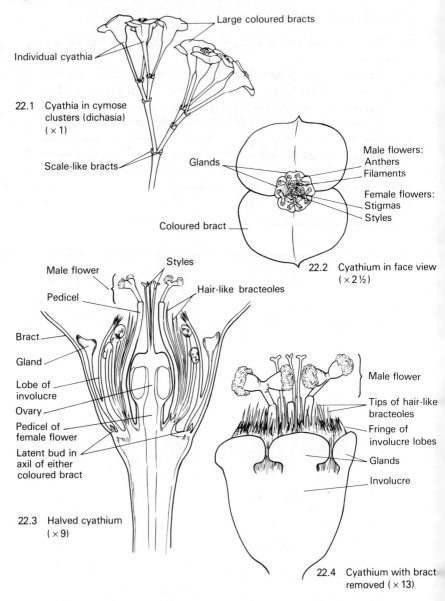

Large coloured bracts

Individual cyathia

22.1  Cyathia in cymose
      clusters (dichasia)
      (×1)

Scale-like bracts

Glands

Male flowers:
Anthers
Filaments

Female flowers:
Stigmas
Styles

Coloured bract

22.2  Cyathium in face view
      (×2½)

Styles

Male flower

Hair-like bracteoles

Pedicel

Bract

Gland

Lobe of
involucre

Ovary

Pedicel of
female flower

Latent bud in
axil of either
coloured bract

22.3  Halved cyathium
      (×9)

Male flower

Tips of hair-like
bracteoles

Fringe of
involucre lobes

Glands

Involucre

22.4  Cyathium with bract
      removed (×13)

# CHAPTER 22

# Euphorbiaceae

A very large, cosmopolitan and heterogeneous Family, the Euphorbiaceae are represented in the European flora only by a handful of annual or perennial weeds: *Mercurialis*, the dog's mercury, and *Euphorbia*, the spurges, for example. In the tropics, however, there are many shrubs and trees, among them economically important genera like *Hevea* and *Manihot*, sources of rubber, and the castor oil plant, *Ricinus*. The unifying characters of the Family lie in the flowers, which are always small, much reduced in structure and unisexual. *Jatropha* provides a good starting point: the cymose inflorescences bear a single terminal female flower and from 7 to 20 lateral males. The male flowers have 5 sepals and 5 petals; the female lacks a corolla. The remaining genera including succulents—*Euphorbia* and its allies—show a much more specialized type of inflorescence (Figs. 22.1–4) in which the flowers are reduced to the barest essentials: a single stamen standing on a jointed pedicel in the male, and an ovary with three styles in the female. A lone female flower stands in the centre, surrounded by many males, and the whole enveloped by an **involucre** of often coloured or ornate bracts. The overall arrangement is called a **cyathium** and runs parallel in effect to the capitulum of Compositae, resembling a single flower (pseudanthium) to the eye of a visiting insect. Sometimes the cyathia contain flowers of one sex only, and some *Euphorbia* species are dioecious.

*Euphorbia* cyathia secrete copious nectar that is freely available to a wide range of insect and other visitors, but *Pedilanthus* and *Monadenium* are much more selective, the cyathium being zygomorphic and hooded or slipper-shaped and excluding all but the one, long-tongued insect appropriate to pollination. After fertilization, the three-lobed ovary swells up and finally flies apart into three part-fruits (**mericarps**), each containing a single large seed.

Once having studied the make-up of the euphorbiaceous inflorescence, the reader is unlikely to confuse it with any other Family, despite the superficial resemblance of many of the species to cacti, Stapelieae, Didiereaceae or Fouquieriaceae. A further useful spot character is the white milky latex which flows freely from a wound. It is usually irritant or poisonous, so one must respect these plants, wash off any latex at once and avoid getting it in cuts or the eyes.

## General References

BROWN, N. E., HUTCHINSON, J. and PRAIN, D. 1915–20, Euphorbiaceae in *Fl. capensis* 5: 216–515; and 1913 *Fl. Trop. Afr.* 6: 441–1020. Synopsis of genera and key to species.

WHITE, A., DYER, R. A. and SLOANE, B. L. 1941 *The Succulent Euphorbieae (Southern Africa)* 2 Vols. (Pasadena) *Euphorbia*: key to species of S. Africa only.

## KEY TO GENERA INCLUDING SUCCULENTS

1 Thick-stemmed to caudiciform shrubs with palmately veined, usually long-petiolate leaves and branching, glandular stipules; flowers staminate or pistillate, some with petals, not aggregated within a common involucre    **Jatropha**
1 Leaves sessile or very shortly petiolate; stipules absent or developed as simple spines or scales; flowers minute, apetalous, one female surrounded by several males within a common involucre (cyathium)
  2 Cyathium symmetrical about two axes, one vertical and one horizontal
    3 Glands of cyathium united in a ring; large, sparingly succulent smooth shrubs with flat, entire, ovate to obovate leaves 5–18 cm long
                                                              **Synadenium**
    3 Glands of cyathium free                                 **Euphorbia**
NOTE: *Elaeophorbia* (unc.) differs only in having a fleshy fruit (drupe).
  2 Cyathium symmetrical about one vertical axis only
    4 Smooth-stemmed erect shrubs with terete, green or grey-green, sparingly succulent shoots which are often waxy or downy at first and few, distant leaves; cyathium lopsided, with a conspicuous spur-like appendage ('slipper flowers')                        **Pedilanthus**
    4 Plants of various habit but, if smooth stemmed, then with many, close, spiralled leaves or leaf scars; cyathium without a conspicuous one-sided spur                                                    **Monadenium**
NOTE: *Endadenium* (unc.) differs only in minor features of the nectary.

## EUPHORBIA

L. *Sp. Pl.* Edn. I: 450, 1753; *Gen. Pl.* Edn. V: 208, 1754.

Typ. *E. antiquorum* L.

Very large and cosmopolitan genus of extremely diverse habit: annuals and perennials, herbs, shrubs and trees. Stem succulence has evolved in many different ways in Africa and also in parts of India, Ceylon, the Canary Islands and America (Fig. 7.10). Prickles and thorns are common, but there is no felted areole as in cacti, and the flowers are utterly different. The milky latex also serves to distinguish the spurges from almost all other cactiform and cereiform succulents. The more symmetrical cyathium with separate glands serves to differentiate it from other succulent Euphorbiaceae (Figs. 22.1–4).

JACOBSEN: Synopsis.

## JATROPHA

L. *Sp. Pl.* Edn. I: 1006, 1753; *Gen. Pl.* Edn. V: 437, 1754 ('Jatropa').

Typ. *J. urens* L.

Large genus widespread throughout the tropics and subtropics and showing a degree of stem succulence in some species of desert regions of N. America and S. Africa. Notable features are the alternate, petiolate, often large and thin leaves, the usually conspicuous and branched stipules, and the separate, unisexual flowers—one apetalous female surrounded by several males.

ROWLEY, G. D. in *Ashingtonia* 2: 124–128, 1976.

PAX, F. in ENGLER, A. *Das Pflanzenreich* IV. 147 Vol. 42: 1–148, 1910 and 68: 39, 1919. **Key** to species in Latin.

## MONADENIUM

Pax in *Engl. Bot. Jahrb.* 19: 126, 1894.

Typ. *M. coccineum* Pax.

Medium-sized genus from mainly the tropics of Africa, running parallel to *Euphorbia* in diversity of life forms from dwarf caudiciforms to shrubs and trees, but generally unarmed. The curious, lop-sided cyathium, without a nectar spur, sets it apart from allied genera.

BALLY, P. R. O. *The Genus Monadenium.* Bern 1961. **Key** to species.

JACOBSEN: Synopsis.

## PEDILANTHUS

Poiteau in *Ann. Mus. Hist. Nat. Paris* 19: 388, 1812, Nom. cons.
Typ. *P. tithymaloides* (L.) Poit.
SYN. *Tithymalus.*

Small genus of Central American much-branched shrubs with moderately succulent, cylindrical, usually grey glaucous or pubescent stick-like shoots with long internodes and small to scale-like leaves. The popular name 'slipper flower' refers to the lop-sided cyathium with a long nectar spur.
DRESSLER, R. L. *The Genus Pedilanthus.* Contr. Gray Herb. Harvard Univ. 182, Mass. 1957. **Key** to species.

## SYNADENIUM

Boissier in DC. *Prodr.* 15: 187, 1862.
Typ. *S. cupulare* (Boiss.) Wheel.

Small genus of very poisonous tropical African shrubs with thick, fleshy, smooth green branches and large, flat, pale green leaves. The cyathia differ from those of *Euphorbia* mainly in having the glands united into a 2–5-lobed rim-like nectary.

# CHAPTER 23

# Fouquieriaceae

This monotypic Family is native to Mexico and the S.W. U.S.A. The eight species of *Fouquieria* are extremely xerophytic, hard-wooded, prickly shrubs with a tendency to pachycauly, notably in *F. columnaris* of Baja California and *F. fasciculata* and *F. purpusii* of southern Mexico. These develop succulence of a sort and certainly have a cactus-like appearance. The thin, wiry branches from the main trunk bear spines derived from persistent, woody petioles after the small, entire, elliptical leaves have fallen. This distinguishes *Fouquieria* from all other succulents except some Geraniaceae, which are quite dissimilar in general habit. The flowers, rarely seen in cultivation, have 5 united petals, 10–15 stamens and 3 united carpels which ripen as a trilocular capsule.

## General References

HENRICKSON, J. 1972 *Aliso* 7: 439–537. **Key** to species.

NASH, G. V. 1956 *Cact. Succ. J. Amer.* 38: 86–91. **Key** to species.

Genus including Succulents: *FOUQUIERIA* only.

## FOUQUIERIA

Kunth in H. B. & K. *Nov. Gen. Sp.* 6: 81, 1823.
Typ. *F. formosa* H. B. & K.
SYN. *Idria*.

Small genus of fiercely armed xerophytes with the characters of the Family as set out above. Only the 3 species named are strictly eligible for inclusion in a succulent collection.

# CHAPTER 24

# Geraniaceae

The gardener's geraniums—descendants of tough, xerophytic species of *Pelargonium* from South Africa—give an introduction to one life form within this small Family. Another is to be seen in the wild cranesbills of our native flora—the true *Geranium*. The flowers are pentamerous and, in the succulents at least, there is a highly efficient dispersal mechanism in which the carpels split away from the central columnar style and the seed is either catapulted out or floats away with a hygroscopic awn whose contortions in response to changes in air humidity effectively screw the seed into the soil. Habit and leaf form are extremely diverse, although many are hairy, some aromatic, and stipules are commonly present. There are many variations on the caudiciform and stem succulent theme; a few species almost qualify as leaf succulent.

## KEY TO GENERA INCLUDING SUCCULENTS

1  Plants mostly unarmed (exc. *P. spinosum, echinatum*); flowers ± zygomorphic, with 2–7 functional stamens and a long, narrow nectar spur adnate to the pedicel (Fig. 37.77)                                **Pelargonium**
1  Plants mostly spiny (exc. *S. multifidum*); flowers actinomorphic, with 15 functional stamens and without a nectar spur adnate to the pedicel      **Sarcocaulon**

## PELARGONIUM———————————————————————

L'Heritier ex Aiton *Hort. Kew* Edn. I, 2: 417, 1789.

Typ. *P. cucullatum* (L.) L'Her. ex Ait.

Very large genus of xerophytic perennials centred in S. Africa but with outliers in many far-flung places. Jacobsen lists 26 as of interest to collectors of succulents: some caudiciform, some stem-succulent, and a few almost leaf-succulent also. Lobed or compound leaves with stipules (Figs. 37.72–73) are the rule, and many are aromatic when crushed. The spot character is the nectar spur adnate to the pedicel, which in consequence feels oval when rolled between the fingers, and the long tubular cavity can be seen with a pocket lens if the flower is sectioned vertically in the correct plane, and horizontally.

CLIFFORD, D. *Pelargoniums,* Edn. II. London 1970.

WALT, J. J. A. v.d. *Pelargoniums of Southern Africa,* 1977.

## SARCOCAULON ———————————————————————

(DC.) Sweet *Hort. Brit.* Edn. I: 73, 1827.

Typ. *S. l'heritieri* Sweet

SYN. *Monsonia.*

Small genus of extremely xerophytic dwarf stem succulents from S. and S.W. Africa. Most are armed with spines formed from the persistent hardened petioles. The stems are resinous and the regular flowers come in a range of colours.

MOFFETT, R. O. *The Genus Sarcocaulon.* Bothalia 12(4): 581–613, 1979.

**Key** to 14 species.

# CHAPTER 25

# Gesneriaceae

I may be taken to task for including this Family on the strength of a single caudiciform species now in succulent collections, while omitting tuberous begonias, cyclamens and other ornamentals of similar habit. Where does one draw the line? Apparently the only arbiter here is relative obscurity: everyone knows begonias and cyclamens, but who ever heard of *Rechsteineria* until a few years ago?

The Gesneriaceae form a large Family of warmth- and moisture-loving plants that are mostly herbaceous and often have tubers, as in the gloxinias (*Sinningia*) of our conservatories. Some develop fleshy leaves, as for instance *Streptocarpus saxorum*, but these are not xerophytes so are omitted here. The flowers are mostly showy, zygomorphic and quite specialised in structure.

Genus including Succulents: *RECHSTEINERIA* only

### RECHSTEINERIA

Regel in *Flora* 31: 247, 1848, Nom. cons.

Typ. *R. allagophylla* (Mart.) Reg.

A single species of this large genus from Mexico to N. Argentina, *R. leucotricha* from W. Parana, Brazil is not rare in succulent collections and accommodates well to a dry winter rest. The globose caudex can be up to 30 cm (12 in.) across and is usually planted above soil level. It produces annual shoots with a whorl of 4 large, soft, white-felted, obovate leaves. Flowers are tubular and orange-pink.

# BOTANICAL NEXT-OF-KIN

Plants relations are determined almost entirely by study of similarities in flower and fruit structure. Do not be deceived into thinking that plants are close relatives because of vegetative likenesses—the rosettes of *Anacampseros* and *Sempervivum*, for instance, or the stems of cacti and euphorbias. We refer to such superficial similarities as results of convergent evolution.

# CHAPTER 26

# Labiatae

This is another large, predominantly non-succulent Family that infiltrates succulent collections via a handful of African xerophytes with somewhat fleshy leaves. The fact that the foliage is often agreeably scented, and the flowers are blue—a rare colour in succulents—adds to their charms.

Labiatae are herbs or small shrubs with opposite, decussate leaves borne on square stems. Many are aromatic and find a place in the herb garden: mint (*Mentha*), thyme (*Thymus*), sage (*Salvia*) and several others. The small, strongly zygomorphic blooms come in clusters in the upper leaf axils (**verticillasters**) and have a two-lipped corolla tailor-made for bee or butterfly visitors. A further spot character is the form of the ovary, which is divided into four lobes like a hot cross bun. This can best be observed by peering down the calyx tube after the corolla has fallen away.

## KEY TO GENERA INCLUDING SUCCULENTS

1 Flowers in lax clusters, the filaments free           **Plectranthus**
1 Flowers in dense clusters, the filaments united        **Coleus**

## COLEUS

Loureiro *Fl. Cochinch.* 358, 372, 1790.
Typ. *C. amboinicus* Lour.

Large, widespread genus of tropical herbs and small shrubs of which one—*C. scutellarioides* (SYN. *C. blumei*)—from Java is the source of the popular house plant with vividly coloured foliage. A few African species are xerophytic and have developed somewhat succulent foliage.

180

## PLECTRANTHUS

L'Heritier *Stirp. Nov.* 84, 1788, Nom. cons.

Typ. *P. fruticosus* L'Her.

Large to very large genus parallel to *Coleus* and distinguished only by minute floral characters. It has also evolved a degree of leaf succulence in certain species from the drier parts of Africa.

## POLLINATION MECHANISMS

The often complex architecture of flowers is related to the need to attract pollinators and the advantages of cross- rather than self-pollination. For an illustrated account of floral biology see Rowley: *Illustrated Encyclopedia of Succulents,* Chapter 4.

**Figs. 27.1-27.4   Liliaceae: *Aloe aristata***

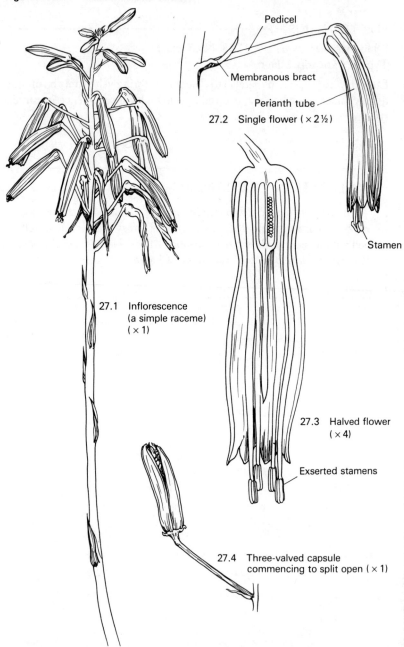

Pedicel

Membranous bract

Perianth tube

27.2   Single flower ( × 2 ½ )

Stamen

27.1   Inflorescence
(a simple raceme)
( × 1 )

27.3   Halved flower
( × 4 )

Exserted stamens

27.4   Three-valved capsule
commencing to split open ( × 1 )

# CHAPTER 27

# Liliaceae

The very large lily Family is considered a cornerstone of Monocotyledon evolution, with its simple, unspecialized, trimerous flowers the prototype of the more advanced types met with in arums, orchids and palms. Typically the plants have bulbs or rhizomes with long, narrow, parallel-veined, sessile leaves with sheathing bases. The usually showy, actinomorphic, bisexual flowers have a perianth of 3 + 3 tepals, not distinguishable into sepals and petals, 3 + 3 stamens and a 3-lobed ovary. They are borne in racemes or are sometimes solitary. The Family contributes generously to our gardens: tulips, hyacinths and many spring bulbs; later the lilies and autumn crocuses. In some ways a bulb is succulent, and many growers are prepared to admit a few of the more exotic bulbs into their succulent collections: species of South African *Ornithogalum, Albuca, Scilla* and so on, as well as Amaryllidaceae like *Haemanthus* and *Ammocharis.* Again we are up against the problem of defining a succulent. Africa has an enormous wealth of bulbs and if one is admitted, all should logically be included. Few would agree to this. So here, as a token, a single genus of bizarre appearance is keyed out, being hallowed by long tradition as a 'succulent'.

Leaf succulence has evolved to a high degree in one of the 28 Tribes into which the Family is divided, the Aloineae, and to a lesser extent in one (or two?) genera of the Asphodeleae. In the Aloineae the perianth is tubular and a rosette habit predominates, either single rosettes or clumps and lying flat on the ground or elevated on simple or sparingly branched stems. In *Aloe* some species attain tree-like stature, with massively enlarged fibrous to fleshy trunks of curious anatomy. The leaves are more or less fleshy, long and tapered, sometimes with marginal teeth, tubercles or other adornments, and the inflorescences are lateral racemes or panicles.

For distinctions from other Monocotyledons, see under Agavaceae (p. 78). Crassulaceae differ in the number of flower parts (never in threes) and in lacking a leaf sheath.

## General References

BERGER, A. 1908 Aloineae in ENGLER, A. *Das Pflanzenreich* 33. Keys to genera and species in Latin.

HUTCHINSON, J. 1959 Liliaceae in *The Families of Flowering Plants* 2nd Edn: 591–612 (London). Keys to genera.

## KEY TO GENERA INCLUDING SUCCULENTS

1  Plant bulbous, the large greenish bulb producing long, twining annual stems with
    thread-like foliage          **Bowiea**
NOTE: *Ornithogalum, Scilla, Albuca* and many other genera of Liliaceae, as well as
    Amaryllidaceae like *Haemanthus* and *Ammocharis*, sometimes find their
    way into succulent collections. But there is a general feeling that bulbs
    deserve a class by themselves.
1  Plants not bulbous or, if so (*Haworthia* and *Aloe* p.p.) then without long twining
    annual stems
  2  Perianth rotate; filaments bearded          **Bulbine**
  2  Perianth tubular; filaments not bearded
    3  Inflorescences thin and wiry, bearing rather inconspicuous greenish-white
       flowers held erect or ascending
      4  Perianth radially symmetrical          **Astroloba**
      4  Perianth two-lipped          **Haworthia**
    3  Inflorescences stiff and rather stout, bearing showy red, yellow or rarely
      white flowers which hang down or project at an angle
      5  Perianth curved to S-shaped with a swollen belly; leaves commonly in two
        series, entire; stamens included          **Gasteria**
      5  Perianth rarely more than slightly curved and slightly bellied; leaves
        spiralled (except *Aloe plicatilis, haemanthifolia*), commonly spiny
        edged; stamens ± exserted          **Aloe**

## ALOE

L. *Sp. Pl.* Edn. I: 319, 1753; *Gen. Pl.* Edn. V: 150, 1754.

Typ. *A. perfoliata* L.

SYN. *Aloinella, Chamaealoe, Guillauminia, Leptaloe, Lomatophyllum, Poellnitzia.*

Very large genus of rosette succulents centred in S. Africa but extending to Madagascar, N. Africa and Arabia. The fleshy, lanceolate to linear, sheathing leaves are often large and prickly at the edges. From *Agave, Aloe* is distinguishable by the generally less stiff, less fibrous and less sharply armed leaves; the presence of a stem in many species, and the lateral inflorescence which does not end the life of the main rosette. The small, tubular, usually red to yellow flowers are borne in racemes, panicles or spikes (Figs. 27.1–4), and the fruit is a 3-lobed dry capsule, rarely a fleshy berry. *A. vera* and other species provide the bitter aloes of medicine.

REYNOLDS, G. W. *The Aloes of South Africa.* 520 pp. Cape Town 1950. Edn. II Cape Town 1970. Synopsis of sections; **keys** to species.

REYNOLDS, G. W. *The Aloes of Tropical Africa and Madagascar.* 537 pp. Swaziland 1966. Synopsis of sections; **keys** to species.

JACOBSEN: Synopsis.

Intergeneric hybrids: × *Aloloba* × *Alworthia*, × *Gastrolea.*


## × ALOLOBA

Rowl. in *Nat. Cact. Succ. J.* 22: 74, 1967.
SYN. *Chamaeloba* Cumm.
= *Aloe* × *Astroloba.*
Few cultivars.


## × ALWORTHIA

Rowl. in *Nat. Cact. Succ. J.* 28: 7, 1973.
SYN. *Alolirion* Rowl.
= *Aloe* × *Haworthia.*
2 cultivars.


## ASTROLOBA

Uitewaal in *Succulenta* 1947: 53.
Typ. *A. pentagona* (Haw.) Uit.
SYN. *Apicra.*

Small genus from the Eastern Cape doubtfully distinct from *Haworthia* by the actinomorphic perianth. The overlapping, stiff, acute leaves are arranged in 5 straight or spiralling rows up short stems.

Intergeneric hybrids: × *Aloloba,* × *Astroworthia,* × *Gastroloba.*

## × ASTROWORTHIA

Rowl. in *Nat. Cact. Succ. J.* 22: 74, 1967.
SYN. *Apworthia* v.P.
= *Astroloba* × *Haworthia.*
2 wild hybrids and 1 cultivar.

## BOWIEA

Harvey in Curtis *Bot. Mag.* 1867 t. 5619, Nom. cons.
Typ. *B. volubilis* Harv. ex Hook.
SYN. *Schizobasopsis.*

Very small genus of peculiar bulbous plants from S. and E. Africa easily recognizable by the bulb which is usually planted above soil and green, and by the long, asparagus-like, annual, twining shoots with small, greenish-white flowers. Leaves are reduced to minute, ephemeral scales.

## BULBINE

Wolf *Gen. Sp. Pl.* 84, 1776 non Gaertner 1788, Nom. cons.
Typ. *B. frutescens* (L.) Willd.
SYN. *Bulbinopsis.*

Medium-sized genus of leaf succulents recognizable by the trimerous, rotate, usually yellow perianth and conspicuously bearded filaments. Some species are shrublets with evident stems; *B. alooides* resembles an aloe, and the majority are stemless with rosettes of soft, pale green, terete leaves, often from an underground fleshy rootstock. Although centred in Africa, the genus has a few species also in Australia.
JACOBSEN: **Key** to cultivated species.
BAIJNATH, H. Monograph in preparation, with **keys**.

## × GASTERHAWORTHIA

Guill. in *Bull. Mus. Hist. Nat. Paris* 3: 339, 1931.
SYN. *Gastrolirion* Walth.
= *Gasteria* × *Haworthia.*
Few cultivars.

## GASTERIA

Duval *Pl. Succ. Alenc.* 6, 1809.

Typ. *G. verrucosa* (Haw.) Duv.

Medium-sized genus of ± stemless rosette plants from S. and S.W. Africa. The species are poorly defined and a modern revision is badly needed. Leaves start in 2 series, alternating, but often go over to a spiral arrangement when adult; the juvenile and adult foliage can look strikingly different. The leaves are typically tongue-shaped, dark green, entire and with paler spots or stripes or sometimes pustulate or verrucose. The usually pendulous flowers have an inflated base to the perianth.

WALTHER, E. in *Cact. Succ. J. Amer.* 1: 234–238, 1930. **Key** to cultivated spp.

Intergeneric hybrids: × *Gasterhaworthia*, × *Gastrolea*, × *Gastroloba*.

## × GASTROLEA

Walth. in *Cact. Succ. J. Amer.* 2: 306, 1930.

SYN. *Chamaeteria* Cumm., *Gasteraloe* Guill., *Lomateria* Guill., *Poellneria* Rowl.

= *Aloe* × *Gasteria.*

Many cultivars.

WALTHER, E. in *Cact. Succ. J. Amer.* 2: 303–307, 1930. **Key** to 5 hybrids.

## × GASTROLOBA

Cumm. in *Bull. Afr. Succ. Pl. Soc.* 9: 36, 1974.

= *Astroloba* × *Gasteria.*

Few cultivars.

## HAWORTHIA

Duval *Pl. Succ. Alenc.* 7, 1809, Nom. cons.

Typ. *H. arachnoidea* (L.) Duv.

SYN. *Chortolirion.*

Large genus of dwarf, ± stemless, solitary or clustering leaf succulents from S. and S.W. Africa. The leaves are extremely diverse in form; the flowers constantly racemose, whitish and with an oblique, two-lipped perianth—the surest distinction from other genera.

BAYER, M. B. *Haworthia Handbook.* 184 pp. 1976. **Key** to species.

JACOBSEN: Synopsis.

Intergeneric hybrids: × *Alworthia*, × *Astroworthia*, × *Gasterhaworthia*.

**Figs. 28.1-28.5    Mesembryanthemaceae: 28.1-28.2** *Pleiospilos* **sp.; 28.3 and 28.5**
***Bergeranthus multiceps;* 28.4 *Glottiphyllum linguiforme***

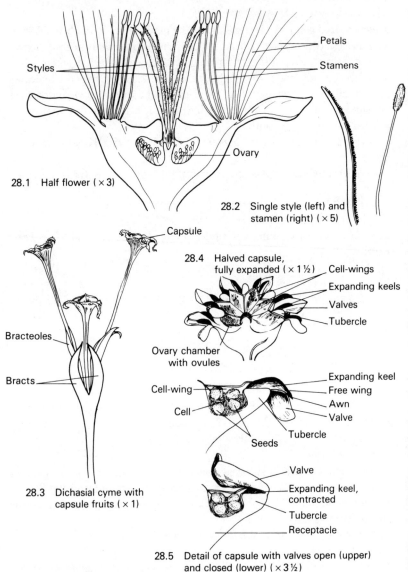

Petals

Styles

Stamens

Ovary

28.1    Half flower ( × 3)

28.2    Single style (left) and
         stamen (right) ( × 5)

Capsule

28.4    Halved capsule,
         fully expanded ( × 1 ½ )

Cell-wings

Expanding keels

Valves

Tubercle

Bracteoles

Bracts

Ovary chamber
with ovules

Cell-wing

Cell

Expanding keel

Free wing

Awn

Valve

Seeds

Tubercle

28.3    Dichasial cyme with
         capsule fruits ( × 1)

Valve

Expanding keel,
contracted

Tubercle

Receptacle

28.5    Detail of capsule with valves open (upper)
         and closed (lower) ( × 3 ½)

# CHAPTER 28

# Mesembryanthemaceae

Rivalling Cactaceae as the largest wholly succulent Family, the Mesembry-anthemaceae are centred in South Africa where they form one of the most characteristic and singular features of the flora of the hotter, drier regions, despite the modest size of most of the plants. Basically these are annual or perennial herbs or small shrubs with simple, exstipulate leaves that are generally opposite and decussate and always more or less soft and fleshy. There is amazing diversity in the plant body, running through a whole series from the least modified (as *Aptenia*, with long stems and flat, stalked, sparingly fleshy foliage) to extreme xerophytes with contracted internodes, chunky near-spherical leaves, minimal surface exposure and all manner of adornments such as wax, hair and papillae associated with reducing transpiration. Some genera are heterophyllous, with a different type of foliage for the growing and resting seasons; some retreat underground and present to the light only the windowed tips of their leaves; some match their backgrounds so closely in colour and markings that they are extremely difficult to find at all in habitat when not in flower.

The flowers are mostly showy and come in all colours except blue. The large number of linear petals and stamens sets them apart from the flowers of other succulents; cacti differ in having a distinct tube to the bloom. But one must be careful not to confuse these with the many-rayed capitula of Compositae (p. 142), made up of separate tiny blooms within an involucre of bracts.

The fruit is also unlike that of any other plant. The commonest type is a **hygroscopic capsule** that opens star-like when wetted and closes again on drying out. Growers will already be familiar with the sudden change when plants are watered overhead, the open capsules almost resembling flowers. Structurally, the fruits are complex, and since they provide the main characters for distinguishing genera, it is necessary to look at them closely. This can best be done by slicing a ripe, dry capsule in half up the middle, and wetting one half, so that one can examine the fruit both closed and open. The opening is achieved by means of **expanding keels** (Fig. 28.5), one on either side of the valve which roofs the cell or locule. These swell up when wetted and hinge the valve open. Further elaborations are the presence of a **tubercle** and of **wings** arching the cell. These are concerned with the dispersal of seeds from the often deep cells by the impact of raindrops: a 'splash-cup mechanism'. Droplets hitting the conical centre are deflected down into the cells in such a way that seeds are ejected a distance of many centimetres. The whole system is doubtless related to the need for germination to take place during the comparatively brief and long-separated periods of rain. Variations on the above pattern are capsules that expand once but do not close again when dry; **schizocarps** which fall apart in pieces, each containing one seed, and a single instance (*Carpobrotus*) where the fruit remains intact and fleshy, somewhat like a fig.

---

## QUICK SPOTS

Certain genera or groups of genera here are immediately recognizable by spot characters, saving the time of working through the full key. A selection of these follows:

'Living stones' or 'Pebble plants': *Lithops*

Plantlike lumps of granite: *Didymaotus, Pleiospilos*

Plantlike downy greengages: *Muiria*

Plant with windowed leaf tips: *Conophytum* p.p., *Fenestraria, Frithia* and to some extent *Lithops* p.p.

Stems bead-like: *Monilaria, Psilocaulon*

Plant thorny: *Eberlanzia* p.p.

Plant with a caudex and annual shoots: *Sphalmanthus* p.p.

Leaves pearly white encrusted all over tips: *Titanopsis* (and to a lesser extent other genera)

Leaf tipped with bristles: *Trichodiadema*

Petals spatulate: *Kensitia*

Fruit fleshy and berry-like: *Carpobrotus.*

# General References

HERRE, H. 1971 *The Genera of Mesembryanthemaceae* (Cape Town). Two **keys** to genera.

JACOBSEN, H. 1960 *Handbook of Succulent Plants*, Vol. 3. (London). 1977 *Lexicon of Succulent Plants*. 2nd Edn. (Poole). **Keys** to genera, and to species of several genera also.

## KEY TO GENERA

1 Annuals or biennials with flat, crystalline papillate leaves
  2 Flowers showy, 3.5 cm or more ∅, white or coloured     **Cleretum**
  2 Flowers not showy, 2–3 cm ∅, creamy white     **Mesembryanthemum**
NOTE: The following genera are unc. annuals, some with terete leaves, a few without papillae: *Aethephyllum, Amoebophyllum, Apatesia, Carpanthea, Eurystigma, Hymenogyne, Micropterum, Pherolobus, Skiatophytum, Synaptophyllum.*
1 Perennials; leaves if papillate then not flat
  3 Leaves petiolate, thin and flat
NOTE: *Caryotophora* (unc.) has alternate or sub-opposite lanceolate leaves.
    4 Leaves cordate; flower pink or purple     **Aptenia**
    4 Leaves ovate-lanceolate; flowers yellow     **Platythyra**
  3 Leaves sessile, rarely more than 4 times as wide as thick
    5 Some leaves at least appearing spirally arranged
NOTE: Some unc. species of *Aridaria, Prenia* and *Sphalmanthus* have the bracts alternate; see 64. *Aspazoma* (unc.) has semiterete sheathing leaves; *Saphesia* (unc.) has long, flat, narrow leaves and a tuberous rootstock.
      6 Leaves ± trigonous, linear, acute     **Conicosia**
NOTE: *Herrea* (unc.) differs only in fruit structure.
      6 Leaves terete, not over 6 times as long as wide, blunt
        7 Leaves finger-like, 2–3 alternating on one shoot     **Dactylopsis**
        7 Leaves club-shaped, window-tipped, several in a flat rosette     **Frithia**
NOTE: Compare *Fenestraria*, with opposite, decussate leaves.
    5 All leaves opposite and decussate
      8 Shoots reduced to a single pair of leaves united into a subglobose or short-cylindric body, flat or domed on top, or with two lobes not above half as long as the body
        9 Stigmas and fruit cells 4–7; cell roofs undeveloped
          10 Plant body like a velvety, grey-green plum, with the fissure below the apex     **Muiria**
          10 Fissure central
            11 Plant bodies flat-topped, grey or brown or variously mottled, commonly resembling stones; sepals free, style absent     **Lithops**
            11 Plant bodies ± globose or two-lobed, not usually resembling stones; sepals ± united below into a tube; style usually present     **Conophytum**
        9 Stigmas and fruit cells 6–19; cell roofs present
          12 Bracts present; sepals 4–5; placental tubercle large     **Cheiridopsis**
          12 Bracts absent; sepals 5–10; placental tubercle absent

13  Flowers yellow                                                 **Dinteranthus**
13  Flowers white, pink or purple                                  **Gibbaeum**
8 Shoots with more than one leaf pair or, if reduced to 2 leaves, then these free
 for the upper half and not united into a ± spherical body
 14  Heterophyllous, with leaf pairs of at least two types, a widely expanded
  pair alternating with one united into a conical body
 15  Plant prostrate or stemless
  16  Plant papillate, with 5–7 stigmas and fruit cells      **Meyerophytum**
  16  Plant glabrous, with 8–19 stigmas and fruit cells     **Cheiridopsis**
 15  Plant erect, suffruticose
  17  Stems thin, not above 3 mm ∅
   18  Stigmas and fruit cells 10                        **Vanzijlia**
   18  Stigmas and fruit cells 4–5                       **Ruschia**
NOTE: *Dicrocaulon* (unc.) is a miniature shrublet differing from *Meyerophytum* in
 fruit structure.
  17  Stems thick, 5 mm or more ∅
   19  Stem often jointed like a necklace; resting leaf pair globose   **Monilaria**
   19  Stem with sheathing leaf bases but not jointed like a necklace;
    resting leaf pair conical                          **Mitrophyllum**
 14  Homophyllous, with successive leaf pairs not strongly dissimilar
  20  Leaves and sepals tipped by a cluster of bristles    **Trichodiadema**
  20  Leaves and sepals without an apical cluster of bristles
   21  Leaves sticky, readily picking up grains of sand     **Psammophora**
   21  Leaves not sticky
    22  Leaf pairs, if more than 1, juxtaposed, without evident internodes
     23  One leaf pair only per shoot (except during growth); leaves obtuse,
      not much longer than thick
      24  Flowers lateral, one on either side of the plant body   **Didymaotus**
      24  Flowers appearing terminal
       25  Stigmas connate into a sessile disc           **Argyroderma**
       25  Stigmas free
        26  Stigmas and fruit cells 4–5               **Ruschia** p.p.
         *(R. dualis, elevata, pygmaea* etc.)
       26  Stigmas and fruit cells 6 or more
        27  Bracts absent
         28  Deciduous geophytes with leaves of a pair almost
          or quite equal (although they may be more
          united along one margin than the other), with
          translucent papillae or dots            **Diplosoma**
         28  Dwarf evergreen chamaephytes with leaves of a
          pair usually very unequal, rarely equal, without
          translucent papillae or dots            **Gibbaeum**
        27  Bracts present
         29  Plant heavily covered in dark spots giving a
          brownish, granite-like appearance; sepals almost
          free                                    **Pleiospilos**

29 Plant immaculate or with only scattered spots, appearing green or whitish green
  30 Flowers usually pedicellate; sepals free; cells blocked by a tubercle       **Cheiridopsis**
  30 Flowers sessile; sepals united below; tubercle absent   **Vanheerdea**
23 More than 1 leaf pair per shoot, or with 2 nearly free leaves much longer than thick
31 Leaves club-shaped, with an apical window       **Fenestraria**
NOTE: Compare *Frithia* with spiral rosettes
31 Leaves not windowed
  32 Leaves ± in two series in a horizontal plane, each oblique and the decumbent branches lying on the soil       **Glottiphyllum**
  32 Leaves decussate, not turned in one plane
    33 Leaf surfaces quite smooth, without dots
      34 Leaves entire
        35 Flowers yellow or white
          36 Highly succulent plants with leaves not above 3 times as long as wide
            37 Bracts and placental tubercles present; stigmas and fruit cells 5       **Bijlia**
            37 Bracts and placental tubercles absent; stigmas and fruit cells 6–7       **Lapidaria**
          36 Less highly succulent, with leaves more than 3 times as long as wide
NOTE: *Ruschianthus* (unc.) keys out here.
            38 Petals stiff, with staminodes between them and the stamens; stigmas and fruit cells 5       **Nelia**
            38 Petals limp; staminodes absent; stigmas and fruit cells 5–15       **Machairophyllum**
        35 Flowers pink to purple
          39 Staminodes present; filaments not bearded       **Cerochlamys**
          39 Staminodes absent; filaments bearded       **Jensenobotrya**
NOTE: *Namaquanthus* and *Zeuktophyllum* (unc.) have short-stalked flowers with bracts
      34 Leaves toothed
        40 Flowers yellow
          41 Bracts similar to foliage leaves; disc annular       **Schwantesia**
          41 Bracts distinct from foliage leaves; disc of separate glands       **Carruanthus**
        40 Flowers white to purple
          42 Bracts and placental tubercles present; stigmas and fruit cells 5       **Acrodon**
          42 Bracts and placental tubercles absent; stigmas and fruit cells 5–11       **Juttadinteria**

33 Leaf surface, at least on young leaves, covered with dots or papillae
   which may be rough to the touch
   43 Leaves united for ¼ to ⅓ their length
      44 Leaves glabrous; placental tubercle absent
         45 Sepals 6; staminodes present                              **Herreanthus**
         45 Sepals 4–5; staminodes absent                             **Juttadinteria**
      44 Leaves pubescent; placental tubercle present                 **Odontophorus**
   43 Leaves not united above ¼ of their length
      46 Nectar glands 5–10, separate
         47 Leaves mostly entire, smooth; placental tubercle present
            48 Pedicel and bracts present
               49 Leaves ± trigonous; placental tubercle a large ± 3-sided knob
                                                                      **Bergeranthus**
               49 Leaves not trigonous; placental tubercle otherwise
                  50 Rootstock fleshy; placental tubercle 2-humped  **Rhombophyllum**
                  50 Rootstock woody; placental tubercle small and not 2-humped
                                                                      **Hereroa**
            48 Pedicel and bracts absent                              **Orthopterum**
         47 Leaves mostly toothed or with raised dots; placental tubercle absent
            51 Stigmas squat, not filiform
               52 Leaves usually toothed; stigmas and fruit cells 5–6   **Stomatium**
               52 Leaves usually entire; stigmas and fruit cells 7–14   **Nananthus**
            51 Stigmas long, filiform
               53 Rootstock rhizomatous, little thickened; stigmas plumose
                                                                      **Chasmatophyllum**
               53 Rootstock thick and tuberous; stigmas not or scarcely plumose
                  54 Leaves with random, scattered teeth; stamens incurved in a cone
                                                                      **Rhinephyllum**
                  54 Leaves usually strongly and regularly toothed (entire in
                     *F. ryneveldiae*); stamens diffuse               **Faucaria**
      46 Nectar glands united into a crenate ring
         55 Rootstock thick and tuberous
            56 Stigmas and fruit cells 5 or, if more (*Titanopsis* p.p.) then
               leaf tips pustulate and bracts absent
               57 Bracts absent; cell roofs well developed
                  58 Leaves encrusted with prominent, white papillae; placental
                     tubercle absent                                  **Titanopsis**
                  58 Leaves smooth or at most dotted; placental tubercle
                     present, small                                   **Ebracteola**
               57 Bracts present; cell roofs undeveloped              **Rhinephyllum**
            56 Stigmas and fruit cells 6–14
               59 Cell roofs well-developed                           **Khadia**
               59 Cell roofs absent or very narrow                    **Nananthus**
         55 Rootstock not tuberous

60 Minute carpeter with short rhizomes not more than 2 mm thick; leaves
    irregularly encrusted at the tip with pustules; flower nocturnal  **Neohenricia**
60 Tufted plants with stems 5 mm or more in thickness; leaves not encrusted
    with papillae; flowers diurnal
   61 Bracts present; sepals 4; staminodes absent  **Calamophyllum**
   61 Bracts absent; sepals 5; staminodes present  **Cylindrophyllum**
22 Leaf pairs separate, with visible internodes (although these may be covered
    by the leaf sheaths)
   62 Stigmas 4–7 (8–12 in a few unc. species of *Ruschia*)
      63 Placentation axile
         64 Leaves flat
            65 Dead leaves persisting as skeletons; staminodes present  **Sceletium**
            65 Dead leaves not persisting as skeletons; staminodes absent  **Prenia**
         64 Leaves terete, sub- or semiterete
            66 Stems ± jointed, with sheathing, persistent leaf bases;
    staminodes absent  **Psilocaulon**
            66 Stems not or indistinctly jointed; leaves not conspicuously
    persistent; staminodes present
               67 Plants scarcely papillate, with wiry or woody branches;
    flowers nocturnal, in dichasial cymes  **Aridaria**
               67 Plants papillate, with herbaceous branches; flowers mostly
    diurnal, 1–3 together  **Sphalmanthus**
      63 Placentation parietal or basal
         68 Green parts of the plant conspicuously papillate
            69 Bracts present; some at least of the old inflorescences
    persisting and spinescent
               70 Leaves dotted; inner filaments bearded; staminodes present
    **Eberlanzia**
               70 Leaves plain; filaments not bearded; staminodes absent  **Mestoklema**
            69 Bracts not distinct from the foliage leaves; inflorescences not
    spinescent  **Drosanthemum**
         68 Green parts of the plant not conspicuously papillate (except in a
    few unc. species of *Ruschia*)
NOTE: *Ruschianthemum* (unc.) resembles *Ruschia* in habit but has a distinctly
different capsule.
            71 Placental tubercle present (sometimes undeveloped in
    *Disphyma australe*)
               72 Prostrate plant rooting at the nodes  **Disphyma**
               72 Erect or decumbent woody shrublets
                  73 Leaves free, plain; sepals and stigmas 6  **Astridia**
                  73 Leaves connate at the base, dotted; sepals and stigmas 4–5

74 Flowers yellow; staminodes absent; nectar glands absent or separate **Hereroa**

74 Flowers not yellow; staminodes usually present, nectar disc annular **Ruschia**

71 Placental tubercle absent

  75 Leaves 4 or more times as long as their maximum width

    76 Leaves acutely trigonous, with a cartilaginous, often serrate keel; filaments bearded **Erepsia**

    76 Leaves ± terete or, if trigonous, then without a cartilaginous keel; filaments not bearded

      77 Valve wings present **Lampranthus**

      77 Valve wings absent **Ruschia**

  75 Leaves less than 4 times as long as wide

    78 Leaves connate for ¼ to ½ their length **Braunsia**

    78 Leaves free or united up to ¼ their length

      79 Leaves commonly toothed; cell roofs present **Oscularia**

      79 Leaves entire; cell roofs absent or very narrow

        80 Flowers diurnal; keels of capsule with membranous marginal wings **Delosperma**

        80 Flowers nocturnal; keels of capsule not winged **Mossia**

62 Stigmas 8 or more (4–5 in a few unc. species of *Carpobrotus*)

  81 Plants prostrate or creeping or, if erect, then pruinose

    82 Leaves dotted; bracts present; placentation basal **Cephalophyllum**

    82 Leaves plain; bracts absent; placentation parietal

      83 Staminodes present; filaments bearded; fruit a hygroscopic capsule **Malephora**

NOTE: *Wooleya* (unc.) is an erect, pruinose shrublet

      83 Staminodes absent; filaments not bearded; fruit a fleshy berry **Carpobrotus**

  81 Plants erect or decumbent, not pruinose

NOTE: Some unc. species of *Ruschia* key out here.

    84 Filaments bearded; placental tubercle present

      85 Leaves pubescent, toothed, flowers solitary, yellow **Odontophorus**

      85 Leaves glabrous, entire; flowers 1–3 together, white, purple or red

        86 Leaves free, plain; inflorescences not spinescent; flowers without bracts; sepals 4 **Ruschia**

        86 Leaves connate at the base, dotted; inflorescences persistent and spinescent; bracts present; sepals 5–6 **Leipoldtia**

NOTE: *Schlechteranthus* (unc.) has connate leaves, 6 sepals and 11–12 stigmas and fruit cells.

    84 Filaments not bearded; placental tubercle absent

      87 Leaves with denticulate, cartilaginous margins; branches 2-angled; petals linear; capsules opening once and not closing again **Semnanthe**

      87 Leaves almost or quite entire; branches terete; petals spatulate; capsules opening when wet and closing again when dry **Kensitia**

## ACRODON

N. E. Brown in *Gard. Chron.* 81: 12, 1927.
Typ. *A. bellidiflorus* (L.) N. E. Br.

Very small genus from the S.W. Cape, composed of dwarf, stemless succulents with long narrow leaves distinguished by having small cartilaginous teeth towards the tip. The showy, stalked flowers are white, with or without a red border, and have 5 stigmas and cells.

## APTENIA

N. E. Brown in *Gard. Chron.* 78: 412, 1925.
Typ. *A. cordifolia* (L.) N. E. Br.

Very small genus of short-lived perennial weedy creepers with flat, stalked, heart-shaped leaves and small, pink to purple flowers. There are 4 stigmas and cells. *A. cordifolia* 'Variegata' is worth growing for its white leaf margins.

## ARGYRODERMA

N. E. Brown in *Gard. Chron.* 71: 92, 105, 1922.
Typ. *A. testiculare* N. E. Br.
SYN. *Roodia.*

Small genus of highly succulent stemless plants from the W. Cape. Shoots solitary or clustered, each producing 1 pair of smooth, isodiametric, silvery white to grey-green leaves—'silverskins' alludes to this distinctive appearance. The flowers are solitary, purple, yellow or white. The curious cushion-like stigma sitting on top of the 10–24-celled ovary distinguishes this genus from *Lithops, Gibbaeum* and other similar genera.
HARTMANN, H. in *Nat. Cact. Succ. J.* 28: 48–50, 1973.
JACOBSEN. **Key** to species.
Intergeneric hybrid: × *Argyrops.*

## × ARGYROPS

Kimnach in *Cact. Succ. J. Amer.* (in press).
= *Argyroderma* × *Lithops.*
1 cultivar.

## ARIDARIA

N. E. Brown in *Gard. Chron.* 78: 453, 1925.
Typ. *A. noctiflora* (L.) Schwant.
SYN. *Nycteranthus*.

Large Cape genus of perennial shrublets similar to *Lampranthus* and *Ruschia*, but distinguishable from both by the axile placentation (see also *Sphalmanthus*). There are 4–5 stigmas and cells.

## ASTRIDIA

Dinter in *Gard. Chron.* 80: 430, 447, 1926.
Typ. *A. dinteri* L. Bol.

Small genus of robust shrublets up to 75 cm (2½ ft.) tall with large, opposite, free, parallel-sided, semiterete leaves which are sometimes almost sickle-shaped. The flowers are white to red or almost yellow, and have 6 stigmas and cells. It is native to the W. Cape. *Ruschia* has leaves connate at the base; *Lampranthus* has a placental tubercle usually.
JACOBSEN: **Key** to species.

## BERGERANTHUS

Schwantes in *Zeitschr. f. Sukk.* 3: 180, 1926.
Typ. *B. scapiger* (Haw.) Schwant.

Small genus from the E. Cape and Orange Free State comprising dwarf, stemless, clumping growths with nearly trigonous, long-tapered, entire leaves which are ± dark spotted. The flowers are yellow or tinged red, have 5 stigmas and cells and are borne in dichasia. The conspicuous ± 3-sided placental tubercle and broad keels are diagnostic features (Figs. 28.3, 28.5).

## BIJLIA

N. E. Brown in *J. Bot. London* 66: 267, 1928.
Typ. *B. cana* (Haw.) N. E. Br.

Monotypic genus from the Prince Albert Division. *B. cana* has highly succulent, soft, chunky leaves like *Pleiospilos* but smooth and unspotted, glaucous and grey-green. The habit is stemless and tufted; the flowers are yellow and have 5 stigmas and cells.

## BRAUNSIA

Schwantes in *Gartenwelt* 32: 644, 1928.

Typ. *B. geminata* (Haw.) L. Bol. (Herre) or *B. nelii* Schwant. (Index Nom. Gen.)

SYN. *Echinus.*

Very small genus from the S. Cape, forming small erect or sprawling shrublets with leaves up to 25 mm (1 in.) long and 15 mm (⅗ in.) broad, united in pairs quarter to halfway and with a white cartilaginous margin. Flowers white or pink, with (4–)5(–7) stigmas and cells. A diagnostic feature is the echinate seed.

## CALAMOPHYLLUM

Schwantes in *Zeitschr. f. Sukk.* 3: 15, 28, 29, 106, 1927.

Typ. *C. teretifolium* (Haw.) Schwant.

Very small genus known only from long-cultivated material and apparently close to *Cylindrophyllum*, q.v. The flowers are solitary, stalked and red, and have 10–12 stigmas and cells.

## CARPOBROTUS

N. E. Brown in *Gard. Chron.* 78: 433, 1925.

Typ. *C. edulis* (L.) N. E. Br.

SYN. *Sarcozona.*

Medium-sized genus of vigorous trailing and rooting species that are cultivated as sand-binders for consolidating dunes in many countries; *C. edulis* is hardy on coasts of S. England. The genus is native to the S. Cape, with outliers in Chile, California, Australia and New Zealand. It is easily recognized from the robust habit, the large, trigonous, pointed leaves, the yellow or purple flowers up to 13 cm (5 in.) in diameter—and hence the largest in the Family—and the unique fruit, the edible 'hottentot's fig', which is fleshy and indehiscent. Stigmas and cells number (4–) 10–16. Intergeneric hybrid: × *Carpophyma.*

## × CARPOPHYMA*

Rowl.

= *Carpobrotus* × *Disphyma.*

Few wild hybrids in Australasia.

## × CARRUANTHOPHYLLUM*

Rowl.

= *Carruanthus* × *Machairophyllum.*

1 cultivar, presumed extinct.

## CARRUANTHUS

Schwantes ex N. E. Brown in *J. Bot.* 66: 325, 1928.

Typ. *C. ringens* (L.) Boom.

SYN. *Tischleria.*

Very small genus from the S. Cape with the habit of *Faucaria* but distinct by the smooth leaves without dots. The solitary, stalked flowers are yellow and have 5 stigmas and cells.

Intergeneric hybrid: × *Carruanthophyllum.*

## CEPHALOPHYLLUM

N. E. Brown in *Gard. Chron.* 78: 433, 1925.

Typ. *C. tricolorum* (Haw.) N. E. Br.

Medium or perhaps large genus from the W. Cape, valued for the large and showy flowers in most colours except blue. The habit is typically a central rosette throwing long, radiating, prostrate and rooting branches bearing tufts of long, parallel-sided, opposite, ± terete leaves. Diagnostic features are the shallow 8–20-celled fruits with basal placentation.

JACOBSEN: Synopsis.

## CEROCHLAMYS

N. E. Brown in *J. Bot.* 66: 171, 1928.

Typ. *C. pachyphylla* L. Bol.

Monotypic genus from the Little Karoo. *C. pachyphylla* is stemless, solitary or with a few branches of 1–3 pairs of very fleshy leaves shortly united at the base, blunt, keeled, smooth, glaucous and dotless. The flowers are purple and have 5 stigmas and cells.

## CHASMATOPHYLLUM

Dinter & Schwantes in *Zeitschr. f. Sukk.* 3: 15, 17, 30, 1927.
Typ. *C. musculinum* (Haw.) Dint. & Schw.

Very small genus scattered across S. and S.W. Africa. The plants are low, much-branched, twiggy shrublets with opposite, sheathing, semiterete leaves keeled and with usually 1–2 teeth at the tip. Flowers solitary, stalked, yellow, about 25 mm (1 in.) across, with 5 stigmas and cells.

## CHEIRIDOPSIS

N. E. Brown in *Gard. Chron.* 78: 433, 1925.
Typ. *C. tuberculata* (Mill.) N. E. Br.

Large genus from the W. Cape and S.W. Africa much valued by collectors for the diversity of peculiar leaf shapes and markings. All are compact growing and without visible internodes, and one sheathing leaf pair protects the next season's pair developing within. Many are ± heterophyllous, and the surface is typically greyish-green and spotted. The solitary flowers are yellow, orange, white or rarely purple, and have 8–19 stigmas and cells.
JACOBSEN: Synopsis.

## CLERETUM

N. E. Brown in *Gard. Chron.* 78: 412, 1925.
Typ. *C. bellidiforme* (Burm. f.) Rowl.
SYN. *Dorotheanthus.*

Small but horticulturally important genus of Cape annuals with radical or alternate, flat, elongated, soft leaves covered in glittering papillae. The popular garden 'Livingstone Daisies', *Mesembryanthemum criniflorum* of florists, with their brilliant blooms of all colours except blue, derive from hybrids of *C. bellidiforme* and *C. oculatum* mainly. There are 5 stigmas and cells.
JACOBSEN: **Key** to species (as *Dorotheanthus*).

## CONICOSIA

N. E. Brown in *Gard. Chron.* 78: 433, 1925.
Typ. *C. pugioniformis* (L.) N. E. Br.

Small but distinctive Cape genus of similar and ill-defined species having stout fleshy roots and rosettes of linear, trigonous, smooth, grass-green leaves. The flowers are large and yellow, borne on long leafy lateral inflorescences. Diagnostic features are the spiralled rather than opposite leaves and the extraordinary fruit, a large capsule opening once only by 10–20 valves and finally breaking up into wing-like segments, each carrying 1–2 seeds.

BROWN, N. E. in *Gard. Chron.* 90: 13 *et seq.,* 1931–32. **Key** to 12 species.

## CONOPHYTUM

N. E. Brown in *Gard. Chron.* 71: 198, 1922.

Typ. *C. minutum* (Haw.) N. E. Br.

SYN. *Berrisfordia, Derenbergia, Oophytum, Ophthalmophyllum.*

Very large genus from the W. Cape showing extreme surface reduction and xeromorphy. The minute, tufted, ± stemless plants are often lithophytes, growing sometimes with hardly any visible soil. Each shoot is composed of two leaves united to form a fleshy body which may be two-lobed, top-shaped or spherical, sometimes dotted or windowed, and with a short central fissure through which the solitary yellow, purple or white flower emerges (Fig. 7.6). Each leaf pair dies back after flowering to form a protective skin over the next during the long dry season. The small flowers have 4–7 stigmas and cells.

BOOM, B. K. *Het Geslacht Conophytum.* Wageningen 1973 (also in *Succulenta* 1973, seriatim). **Key** to species in Dutch.

JACOBSEN: Synopsis of sections.

RAWE, R. in *Cact. Succ. J. Amer.* 41: 147–150, 229–233, 1969; 47: 132, 186, 212, 1975. Synopsis and partial **keys.**

## CYLINDROPHYLLUM

Schwantes in *Zeitschr. f. Sukk.* 3: 15, 28, 1927.

Typ. *C. calamiforme* (L.) Schwant.

Very small genus scattered across the Cape region. Dwarf, clumping, short-stemmed succulents with ± terete, finger-like, opposite leaves up to 9 cm (3½ in.) long. Flowers whitish to pink, with 5–8 stigmas and cells.

## DACTYLOPSIS

N. E. Brown in *Gard. Chron.* 78: 413, 1925.

Typ. *D. digitata* (Ait.) N.E. Br.

Very small and easily recognized genus, but rare in collections because of cultural difficulties. From a cluster of stout, thong-like roots arise shoots composed of a few, alternating, sheathing, highly succulent, soft green finger-like leaves that die away in the dormant season. The small, white, brush-like flowers have 5 stigmas and cells and stay open for at least a fortnight.

## DELOSPERMA

N. E. Brown in *Gard. Chron.* 78: 412, 1925.

Typ. *D. pruinosum* (Thunb.) Ingr.

SYN. *Schoenlandia.*

Large and ill-defined genus from S. to E. Africa, Abyssinia and Arabia, comprising annual or perennial plants of diverse habit, sometimes with a caudex. The internodes are visible between the opposite, decussate pairs of ± free leaves, and the medium-sized flowers come in most colours except blue. The main characteristic is the 5-celled capsule which lacks placental tubercles and (usually) cell roofs, but generally has membranous marginal wings to the keel.

Intergeneric hybrid: × *Delosphyllum.*

## × DELOSPHYLLUM*

Rowl.

= *Delosperma* × *Glottiphyllum.*

1 cultivar.

## DIDYMAOTUS

N. E. Brown in *Gard. Chron.* 78: 433, 1925.

Typ. *D. lapidiformis* (Marl.) N. E. Br.

Monotypic genus from the Ceres Karoo in habit like *Pleiospilos bolusii* or *nelii* but with flowers borne laterally, one on either side of the main pair of leaves, each with a pair of bracts.

## DINTERANTHUS

Schwantes in *Zeitschr. f. Sukk.* 2: 184, 264–267, 1926.

Typ. *D. pole-evansii* (N. E. Br.) Schwant.

Very small genus of highly succulent miniatures from S.W. Africa and the N. Cape resembling *Argyroderma* and *Lithops.* The flowers are yellow and the stigmas and cells number 6–7(–15). A distinctive feature is the minute, dust-like seed.

JACOBSEN: **Key** to species.

## DIPLOSOMA

Schwantes in *Zeitschr. f. Sukk.* 2: 179, 1926.

Typ. *D. retroversum* (Kens.) Schwant.

SYN: *Maughania, Maughaniella.*

Very small genus from the W. Cape comprising tiny plants with one or a few growths of paired, soft, papulose, pulpy leaves that are united at the base symmetrically or asymmetrically so that they lie flat on the soil (cf. *Glottiphyllum*). The leaves are deciduous, and the flowers white to pink, with 5–7 stigmas and cells.

## DISPHYMA

N. E. Brown in *Gard. Chron.* 78: 433, 1925.

Typ. *D. crassifolium* (L.) L. Bol.

Very small but far-flung genus found in the Cape, Australia and New Zealand and in habit like a smaller version of *Carpobrotus*, with which it intercrosses. However, the fruit is a 5-celled, dry, hygroscopic capsule. The flowers are white to deep pink.

Intergeneric hybrid: × *Carpophyma.*

## DROSANTHEMUM

Schwantes in *Zeitschr. f. Sukk.* 3: 14, 29, 106, 1927.

Typ. *D. hispidum* (L.) Schwant.

SYN. *Anisocalyx, Jacobsenia.*

Large genus of shrubby plants from S. Africa with the habit of *Lampranthus* but simply distinguished by the glittering papillae on the narrow, trigonous to terete leaves. The flowers come in all colours except blue, and are often multicoloured and very showy. There are 4–6 stigmas and cells.

JACOBSEN: Synopsis.

## EBERLANZIA

Schwantes in *Zeitschr. f. Sukk.* 2: 189, 1926.

Typ. *E. clausa* (Dint.) Schwant.

Papillate shrublets like the foregoing, but distinct by the persistence of the old inflorescences in most species as branched, twiggy thorns. The flowers are smaller, white to purple, and have 5 stigmas and cells. This medium-sized S. African genus is infrequent in cultivation.

## EBRACTEOLA

Dinter & Schwantes in *Zeitschr. f. Sukk.* 3: 15, 24, 1927.
Typ. *E. montis-moltkei* (Dint.) Dint. & Schw.

Very small genus of dwarf, tufted succulents with a much thickened rootstock. The narrow, pointed, keeled leaves are 3–4½ cm (1¼–2¾ in.) long, glaucous and dotted; the flowers are white to purple and have 5 stigmas and styles. The genus is native to S.W. Africa.

FRIEDRICH, H. C. in *Prodr. Fl. Südwestafrika* 27: 44–46, 1970. Key to species in German.

## EREPSIA

N.E. Brown in *Gard. Chron.* 78: 433, 1925.
Typ. *E. inclaudens* (Haw.) N. E. Br.

Medium-sized genus of glabrous shrublets from the S. Cape. It runs close to *Lampranthus*, but the more sharply edged, trigonous leaves, with the keel cartilaginous or rough-edged, afford a distinction. The purple, white or rarely yellow flowers have numerous inarching staminodes, bearded filaments and (4–)5–6(–7) stigmas and cells.

## FAUCARIA

Schwantes in *Zeitschr. f. Sukk.* 2: 176, 1926.
Typ. *F. tigrina* (Haw.) Schwant.

Medium-sized, long-cultivated genus from the Karoo and E. Cape, popularly called 'Dog's Chaps', 'Tiger's Chaps' and similar names from the resemblance of a leaf pair to the gaping jaws of an animal. Each plant is composed of 1 or more stemless, compact rosettes of 4–6 pairs of decussate, very fleshy, lanceolate to acute-spatulate, spotted leaves with ± long marginal bristly teeth. The yellow to orange flowers have 5–6 stigmas and cells. The best spot character is the unique deep obconical capsule.

## FENESTRARIA

N.E. Brown in *Gard. Chron.* 78: 433, 1925.
Typ. *F. aurantiaca* N. E. Br.

Monotypic genus from S.W. Africa, 'Baby's Toes' in popular parlance. The opposite, club-shaped, inch-long (25 mm) leaves are packed in rosettes and grow in nature with only the truncate windowed tips showing above soil.

There are short underground rhizomes, and the long-stalked flowers are yellow or white, with 10–16 stigmas and cells.

## FRITHIA

N. E. Brown in *Gard. Chron.* 78: 433, 1925.
Typ. *F. pulchra* N.E. Br.

Monotypic genus from Pretoria, superficially very like the preceding but without rhizomes, the leaves all being in one spiral rosette. The purple to white flowers have 5 stigmas and cells, and are structurally unlike those of *Fenestraria.* With age the plants branch sparingly.

## × GIBBAEOPHYLLUM*

Rowl.
SYN. *Mentophyllum* Marn.
= *Gibbaeum* × *Glottiphyllum.*
1 cultivar.

## GIBBAEUM

N. E. Brown in *Gard. Chron.* 71: 129, 151, 1922.
Typ. *G. pubescens* (Haw.) N.E. Br.
SYN. *Antegibbaeum, Argeta, Imitaria, Mentocalyx, Rimaria* p.p.

Medium-sized genus of dwarf, stemless, clumping succulents from the Cape. The habit and growing season are diverse, but characteristically one leaf of a pair is ± different from the other, these being ± united below and soft, highly succulent, pale green and commonly pubescent. The white or purple flowers have 6–7(–9) stigmas and cells.

NEL, G. C. *The Gibbaeum Handbook.* London 1953. **Key** to species.
JACOBSEN: Synopsis.
Intergeneric hybrids: × *Gibbaeophyllum,* × *Muirio-gibbaeum.*

## GLOTTIPHYLLUM

N. E. Brown in *Gard. Chron.* 70: 311, 1921.
Typ. *G. linguiforme* (L.) N.E. Br.

This medium-sized genus of very soft, fleshy Cape succulents is easy to recognize from the way in which the pairs of opposite, often tongue-shaped leaves are ± turned to lie in two series, with the shoot prone on the soil. The

leaves, various in form, are always oblique and two of a pair are rarely identical; the surface is quite smooth and grass green, often overlaid with white or russet, and only rarely with dots. The large flowers are yellow (white in 1 cultivar) and have 8–20 stigmas and cells (Fig. 28.4).
BROWN, N. E. in *Gard. Chron.* 82: 290 *et seq.*, 1927–1928. Key to 27 species.
Intergeneric hybrids: × *Delosphyllum,* × *Gibbaeophyllum.*

HEREROA————————————————————————————————
(Schwantes) Dinter & Schwantes in *Zeitschr. f. Sukk.* 3: 23, 1927.
Typ. *H. puttkamerana* (Dint. & Bgr.) Dint. & Schw.

Medium-sized, ill-defined genus of tufted herbs or twiggy shrublets, the latter with visible internodes, from S. and S.W. Africa. The leaves are scarcely connate, semiterete or keeled, often notched or hatchet-shaped at the tip, and dark spotted. The yellow, pinkish or rarely white flowers have 5 stigmas and 5 or 10 cells.

HERREANTHUS ————————————————————————————————
Schwantes in *Gartenwelt* 32: 514, 1928.
Typ. *H. meyeri* Schwant.

Monotypic genus from Namaqualand: a dwarf, stemless, clumping plant with few pairs of thick, connate, whitish green leaves with acute tips and indistinct spots. The white flowers have 6 stigmas and cells.

JENSENOBOTRYA————————————————————————————————
Herre in *Sukkulentenkunde* 4: 79, 1951.
Typ. *J. lossowiana* Herre.

Monotypic genus from S.W. Africa comprising the distinct-looking highly succulent species *J. lossowiana.* It forms a thick-stemmed shrublet, long-lived in habitat and short-lived in cultivation, with pairs of opposite, connate, silver-grey leaves expanded into a knob-like tip. The flowers are deep pink with a paler centre, and have 5 stigmas and cells.

## JUTTADINTERIA

Schwantes in *Zeitschr. f. Sukk.* 2: 182, 1926.

Typ. *J. kovisimontana* (Dint.) Schwant.

SYN. *Dracophilus, Namibia.*

Small S.W. African genus of clumping plants or small shrublets with closely packed, chunky, whitish green, smooth or rough leaves often toothed at the edges like a *Faucaria*, from which it differs by the fruit structure. The white to purple flowers have 8–25 stigmas and cells.

JACOBSEN: **Keys** to species of *Dracophilus, Juttadinteria,* and *Namibia.*

## KENSITIA

Fedde in *Fedde Repert.* 48: 11, 1940.

Typ. *K. pillansii* (Kens.) Fedde.

SYN. *Piquetia.*

Monotypic genus from the W. Cape forming a shrub like *Erepsia* but distinct from all other Mesembryanthemaceae by the peculiar spatulate petals, with a very narrow claw and expanded red limb. There are 8–10 stigmas and cells.

## KHADIA

N. E. Brown in *Gard. Chron.* 88: 279, 1930.

Typ. *K. acutipetala* N.E. Br.

Very small genus from the Transvaal, segregated from *Nananthus* only on minor floral characters. The white to pink flowers have (6–)7–9(–10) stigmas and cells.

JACOBSEN: **Key** to species.

## LAMPRANTHUS

N. E. Brown in *Gard. Chron.* 87: 72, 211, 1930.

Typ. *L. tenuifolius* (L.) Schwant.

SYN. *Esterhuysenia.*

Large genus of free-flowering shrublets from S. Africa with flowers of every colour except blue, valued for use in vivid bedding displays in hot, sunny and dry sites in parks and gardens where frost allows. The opposite, decussate, almost free leaves are trigonous, semiterete or subterete, parallel-sided and smooth, rarely dotted, and up to 5 cm (2 in.) long (Fig. 7.2). The flowers have 4–7 stigmas and cells. *Ruschia* is a close parallel, but differs from

*Lampranthus* in usually having a placental tubercle and lacking cell wings, which are nearly always present in the latter.
JACOBSEN: Synopsis.

## LAPIDARIA

Dinter & Schwantes ex N. E. Brown in *Gard. Chron.* 84: 492, 1928.
Typ. *L. margaretae* Dint. & Schw. ex N.E. Br.

Monotypic genus from S.W. Africa resembling in habit *Argyroderma* and *Dinteranthus*. It has 3–4 pairs of smooth, chunky, reddish- or whitish-green leaves, the generic name referring to the stone-like appearance, and yellow flowers. From *Argyroderma* it differs in having 6–7 free, filamentous stigmas; from *Dinteranthus* in the presence of cell roofs, the less united leaves and the absence of dots.

## LEIPOLDTIA

L. Bolus in *Fl. Pl. S. Afr.* 7 t. 256, 1927.
Typ. *L. constricta* L. Bol.

Small genus of lampranthus-like shrublets from the W. Cape and S.W. Africa, infrequent in cultivation, and distinguished only by the higher number (10–12) of stigmas and cells and by the presence of a placental tubercle. The flowers are pale to dark purple.

## LITHOPS

N. E. Brown in *Gard. Chron.* 71: 44, 1922.
Typ. *L. lesliei* N.E. Br.

One of the wonders of the Plant Kingdom, the 'Pebble Plants' or 'Living Stones' form a medium-sized genus spread from S.W. Africa across the Cape to Transvaal. The solitary or clustered top-shaped bodies consist of a single pair of united leaves, renewed each year, having a central fissure through which the solitary white or yellow flower emerges. There are 4–7 stigmas and cells. The ± flat top of the body grows flush with the soil, and each species has its characteristic colourings which harmonize with the particular mineral background where it grows. *Conophytum* approaches *Lithops* in markings in some of its smaller species, the distinction lying in the union of sepals and the presence of a style.

JACOBSEN: Two **keys** to species.

NEL, G. C. *Lithops.* Stellenbosch 1946.

COLE, D. T. *Lithops: A checklist and index.* In *Excelsa* 3: 37–71, 1973.

Intergeneric hybrid: × *Argyrops.*

## MACHAIROPHYLLUM

Schwantes in *Möllers Deutsche Gärtnerz.* 42: 187, 1927.

Typ. *M. albidum* (L.) Schwant.

Small genus from the Cape composed of dwarf, stemless, tufted plants with very smooth, glaucous, elongated, pointed leaves and without visible internodes. The flowers are yellow, often suffused with red towards the outside, and have 5–15 stigmas and cells.

JACOBSEN: **Key** to the species.

Intergeneric hybrid: × *Carruanthophyllum.*

## MALEPHORA

N. E. Brown in *Gard. Chron.* 81: 12, 1927.

Typ. *M. mollis* (Ait.) N.E. Br.

SYN. *Crocanthus, Hymenocyclus.*

Small genus from S. and S.W. Africa composed of soft, often pruinose, prostrate or fruticose plants doubtfully distinct from *Lampranthus* by the 8–11 stigmas and cells and the presence of staminodes. The species are equally ornamental.

## MESEMBRYANTHEMUM

L. *Sp. Pl.* Edn. I: 688, 1753; *Gen. Pl.* Edn. V: 215, 1754, emend.

L. Bolus, Nom. cons.

Typ. *M. nodiflorum* L.

SYN. *Callistigma, Cryophytum, Derenbergiella, Halenbergia, Hydrodea, Opophytum.*

Originally including all species of Mesembryanthemaceae, this still large genus is reduced to those species of annual or perennial, fleshy herbs including the original 'Ice Plants', so-called from the covering of glittering papillae. The ± flat, often stalked and large leaves are at first opposite, later alternate. The flowers, which have (4–)5 stigmas and cells, are less showy than those of *Cleretum.* The range is wide: S. and N. Africa, Mediterranean regions, California and elsewhere, to some extent introduced.

## MESTOKLEMA

N. E. Brown in *Gard. Chron.* 100: 164, 1936.
Typ. *M. tuberosum* (L.) N.E. Br.

Very small genus from S. and S.W. Africa. Eberlanzia-like plants, with the green parts minutely papulose and glossy, but mostly with thickened or tuberous roots. The usually small flowers have 5 stigmas and cells and are borne in dichasia.
BROWN, N. E. in *Gard. Chron.* 100: 164–166, 1936. **Key** to 5 species.

## MEYEROPHYTUM

Schwantes in *Möllers Deutsche Gärtnerz.* 36: 436, 1927.
Typ. *M. meyeri* Schwant.

Very small heterophyllous genus from the W. Cape, like a prostrate-growing *Vanzijlia,* but papillate and with 5–7 rather than 10 stigmas and cells, and no staminodes.
JACOBSEN: **Key** to species.

## MITROPHYLLUM

Schwantes in *Zeitschr. f. Sukk.* 2: 181, 1926.
Typ. *M. mitratum* Schwant.
SYN. *Conophyllum, Mimetophytum.*

Medium-sized genus from the W. Cape of thick-stemmed, heterophyllous shrublets. First appear two long, pointed, spreading, semiterete leaves united only by the bases; then between them 2 leaves united almost to the tips into a conical body which envelops the growing apex during the resting season, the two types alternating up the axis as it grows. Flowers, rare in cultivation, are white, yellow or pink, with 5–7 stigmas and cells.

## MONILARIA

Schwantes in *Gartenwelt* 33: 69, 1929.
Typ. *M. moniliformis* (Thunb.) Schwant. (Herre) or *M. chrysoleuca* (Schlecht.) Schwant. (Index Nom. Gen.).

Small genus from the W. Cape, related to *Mitrophyllum* but readily told apart since the stem is constricted into short joints like a string of beads.

Flower and fruit characters are the same. *Psilocaulon* has thinner, more elongated stems, smaller ephemeral leaves, 4–5 stigmas and cells, and axile placentation.

## MOSSIA

N. E. Brown in *Gard. Chron.* 87: 71, 151, 1930.

Typ. *M. intervallaris* (L. Bol.) N.E. Br.

Monotypic genus from Transvaal and the E. Cape. *M. intervallaris* is a dwarf creeper similar to *Delosperma*, with small white flowers opening at night, and has (4–)5(–7) stigmas and cells.

## MUIRIA

N. E. Brown in *Gard. Chron.* 81: 116, 1927.

Typ. *M. hortenseae* N.E. Br.

Extraordinary monotypic genus from the Riversdale District of the Cape, related to *Gibbaeum*, with which it forms natural hybrids. Each plant of *M. hortenseae* consists of a circle of ovoid, velvety bodies, like greengages, each composed of a pair of leaves completely united, with a minute fissure obliquely sited below the top. As in *Conophytum* the dried skin of one growth protects the apex in the dormant season. The tiny pale pink flower bursts through the tip of the body and has 6–7 stigmas and cells.

Intergeneric hybrid: × *Muirio-gibbaeum.*

## × MUIRIO-GIBBAEUM

Jacobs. in *Die Sukkulenten* 164, 1933.

= *Gibbaeum* × *Muiria.*

1 wild hybrid.

## NANANTHUS

N. E. Brown in *Gard. Chron.* 78: 433, 1925.

Typ. *N. vittatus* N.E. Br.

SYN. *Aloinopsis, Rabiea.*

Medium-sized S. African genus of dwarf, compact plants with a thick taproot bearing many tufts of variously flattened, keeled or truncate leaves which are commonly pubescent or rough and dotted near the tip. The flowers are yellow to pink, and have 6–14 stigmas and cells.

JACOBSEN: **Keys** to species (under *Aloinopsis, Nananthus* and *Rabiea).*

## NELIA

Schwantes in *Gartenflora* 77: 129, 1928.
Typ. *N. meyeri* Schwant.

Very small genus from the W. Cape. The plants form clumps of tightly packed rosettes of opposite, trigonous or subterete, elongated leaves shortly united at the base and smooth, glaucous and dotless. The small, long-lived, white to yellowish flowers have 5 stigmas and cells.

## NEOHENRICIA

L. Bolus in *J. S. Afr. Bot.* 4: 51, 1938.
Typ. *N. sibbettii* L. Bol.
SYN. *Henricia.*

Monotypic genus from the Central Cape. *N. sibbettii* is justly popular with collectors for its neat, miniature habit and tiny but intensely perfumed white flowers that open in the evening. In habit it is like a small *Titanopsis*, but its rhizomes form a close carpet of leaves, whose tips are rough with large white papillae. There are 5 stigmas and cells.

## ODONTOPHORUS

N. E. Brown in *Gard. Chron.* 81: 12, 1927.
Typ. *O. marlothii* N.E. Br.

Very small genus from the W. Cape, close to *Dracophilus*, except that in 1 species (*O. marlothii*) a stem develops with visible internodes. *Faucaria* differs in having less united leaves. The white or yellow flowers have 8–11 stigmas and cells.

HARTMANN, H. in *Bot. Jahrb. Syst.* 97: 161–225, 1976. Key to species in German.

## ORTHOPTERUM

L. Bolus in *S. Afr. Gard. & Country Life* 17: 281, 1927.
Typ. *O. waltoniae* L. Bol.

Very small genus from the E. Cape similar to *Faucaria* but distinguishable by the entire leaves and curious, erect, sail-like appearance of the cell roofs. The flowers are yellow, with 5–6 stigmas and cells.

OSCULARIA ─────────────────────────────────────────

Schwantes in *Möllers Deutsche Gärtnerz.* 42: 187, 1927.

Typ. *O. deltoides* (L.) Schwant.

Very small genus of shrublets from the W. Cape, horticulturally valued for the glaucous, blue-green foliage. The most noticeable feature of most leaves is the presence of horny teeth on the margins and keel. The small white or pink flowers have (4–)5(–7) stigmas and cells.


PLATYTHYRA ─────────────────────────────────────────

N. E. Brown in *Gard. Chron.* 78: 412, 1925.

Typ. *P. haeckeliana* (Bgr.) N.E. Br.

A sprawling perennial with fleshy roots, 3–4-angled stems and flat, elliptic to oblanceolate leaves, this monotypic genus is located in the E. Cape. The yellow flowers have 4 stigmas and cells. *Aptenia* differs in flower colour and terete stems; *Sceletium* in its broader, slightly connate leaves and persistent skeletons.


PLEIOSPILOS ─────────────────────────────────────────

N. E. Brown in *Gard. Chron.* 78: 433, 1925.

Typ. *P. bolusii* (Hook. f.) N.E. Br.

SYN. *Punctillaria.*

Medium-sized S. African genus nicknamed 'Living Granite' from the characteristic dark brown or reddish, spotted appearance of the chunky leaves. The shoots bear 1–2(–4) tightly packed pairs of large often isodiametric or subhemispherical leaves united below and rubbery to the touch (Fig. 7.5). The large, solitary, yellow to orange flowers commonly smell of coconut and have 9–15 stigmas and cells (Figs. 28.1–2).


PRENIA ─────────────────────────────────────────

N. E. Brown in *Gard. Chron.* 78: 412, 413, 1925.

Typ. *P. pallens* (Ait.) N.E. Br.

Very small flat-leaved genus scattered from S.W. Africa to the E. Cape, similar in habit to *Platythyra,* but without petioles or angles on the stems. The pink, purple, yellow or white flowers have 4–5 stigmas and cells.

## PSAMMOPHORA

Dinter & Schwantes in *Zeitschr. f. Sukk.* 2: 188, 1926.

Typ. *P. nissenii* Dint. & Schw.

SYN. *Arenifera.*

Very small genus of stemless or short-stemmed, tufted succulents from S.W. Africa to the N.W. Cape, readily recognizable by the dark brown sticky foliage that picks up a coating of dust and sand. The flowers are white to purplish and have 5–8 stigmas and cells.

## PSILOCAULON

N. E. Brown in *Gard. Chron.* 78: 433, 1925.

Typ. *P. articulatum* (Thunb.) N.E. Br. (Herre) or *P. acutisepalum* N.E. Br. (Index Nom. Gen.).

SYN. *Brownanthus, Trichocyclus.*

Large genus of highly xerophytic, much-branched shrublets, rare in cultivation, from S. and S.W. Africa. The rather thick green shoots have usually short nodes that may be ± jointed after the fashion of *Monilaria* (q.v.). The small, opposite, subterete leaves soon wither to a stub, the sheath sometimes being laciniate. The small flowers have 4–5 stigmas and cells.

## RHINEPHYLLUM

N. E. Brown in *Gard. Chron.* 81: 92, 1927.

Typ. *R. muirii* N.E. Br.

SYN. *Neorhine, Peersia.*

Small, rather poorly defined genus from the Cape, with the habit of *Nananthus* and doubtfully separable from it on stigma and cell number (5) and nectary form. The stigmas are small and stalked, and the flowers white to yellow and scented.

JACOBSEN: **Key** to species.

## RHOMBOPHYLLUM

Schwantes in *Zeitschr. f. Sukk.* 3: 23, 1927.

Typ. *R. rhomboideum* (S.D.) Schwant.

Very small genus from the E. Cape with leaves vertically compressed at the tip and usually with 1–2 notches like some species of *Hereroa,* which differs in its more fruticose habit, prominent dots and small placental tubercle. The yellow flowers have 5 stigmas and cells.

## RUSCHIA

Schwantes in *Zeitschr. f. Sukk.* 2: 186, 1926.

Typ. *R. rupicola* (Engl.) Schwant.

SYN: *Amphibolia, Antimima, Enarganthe, Octopoma, Ottosonderia, Polymita, Scopelogena, Smicrostigma, Stayneria.*

Large and diverse genus, the largest in the Family, spread across S. Africa from S.W. Africa to Transvaal. Most frequent in cultivation are the twiggy shrublets with opposite, rather short, ± trigonous, grey leaves distinct from *Lampranthus* (q.v.) in their firmer, stiffer texture, united sheathing base and often sharp tip, sometimes with teeth on the keel also. A few more specialized species are heterophyllous, like a miniature *Mitrophyllum*, and the dried leaf sheaths protect the stem tips during the dormant season. The mostly small flowers have 4–5(–12) stigmas and cells, and usually a placental tubercle. *R. uncinata* is frost hardy.

JACOBSEN: Synopsis.

## SCELETIUM

N. E. Brown in *Gard. Chron.* 78: 412, 1925.

Typ. *S. tortuosum* (L.) N.E. Br.

Easily recognizable medium-sized genus from S. Africa in which the flat, soft, pale green leaves die away leaving persistent skeletons clothing the stem bases. The plants are short stemmed, ± prostrate perennials with whitish to yellowish or pink flowers having 4–5 stigmas and cells.

## SCHWANTESIA

Dinter in *Möllers Deutsche Gärtnerz.* 42: 234, 1927.

Typ. *S. ruedebuschii* Dint.

Small genus of faucaria-like plants from S.W. Africa and the N.W. Cape, distinguishable by the smoother surface of the leaves, which lack dots. *Carruanthus* differs in having a pair of bracts at the base of the pedicel distinct from foliage leaves, and nectar glands separate rather than in a ring. The yellow flowers have 5 stigmas and cells.

JACOBSEN: **Key** to species.

## SEMNANTHE

N. E. Brown in *Gard. Chron.* 81: 12, 1927.
Typ. *S. lacera* (Haw.) N.E. Br.

Monotypic genus of erect shrubs to 90 cm (3 ft.) tall from the S.W. Cape. The opposite, trigonous, pruinose leaves have rough cartilaginous edges and fine teeth on the keel. The 5 cm (2 in.) flowers are purple and have 10 stigmas and cells. The normal linear petals distinguish it from *Kensitia*; and the 10 minute stigmas from *Erepsia*.

## SPHALMANTHUS

N. E. Brown in *Gard. Chron.* 78: 433, 1925.
Typ. *S. canaliculatus* (Haw.) N.E. Br.
SYN. *Phyllobolus.*

Medium-sized genus of soft, herbaceous, prostrate perennials from the Cape and S.W. Africa. The elongated ± terete leaves begin opposite but may become alternate on the flowering shoots. The rootstock is fleshy and may even be caudiciform, with deciduous branches (*S. resurgens*). The yellowish, greenish or pink flowers have (4–)5 stigmas and cells and axile placentas. From *Aridaria* it is distinguished by being papillate on all green parts and less woody.
JACOBSEN: Synopsis.

## STOMATIUM

Schwantes in *Zeitschr. f. Sukk.* 2: 175, 1926.
Typ. *S. suaveolens* Schwant.
SYN. *Agnirictus.*

Medium-sized genus of compact, low-growing, many-headed, ± stemless plants from S. Africa. The habit is like a small *Faucaria*, with ± semiterete leaves usually broadened towards the tip and usually with small blunt teeth at the margins and a ± tuberculate surface. The yellow or rarely white or pink flowers have 5–6 stigmas and cells. It differs from *Faucaria* in having short stigmas and a less deep capsule.
JACOBSEN: Synopsis.

TITANOPSIS ──────────────────────────────

Schwantes in *Zeitschr. f. Sukk.* 2: 178, 1926.

Typ. *T. calcarea* (Marl.) Schwant.

Very small genus from the N. Cape and S.W. Africa, recognizable for the large, white papillae covering the tips of the spatulate leaves, making the whole plant seem encrusted in white and inconspicuous against its natural limestone background. The yellow flowers have 5–6 stigmas and cells.

TRICHODIADEMA──────────────────────────

Schwantes in *Zeitschr. f. Sukk.* 2: 187, 1926.

Typ. *T. barbatum* (L.) N.E. Br. (Herre) or *T. stelligerum* (Haw.) Schwant. (Index Nom. Gen.).

Medium-sized genus of shrublets from S. and S.W. Africa, characterized by the cluster of long or short radiating bristles at the tip of each leaf, recalling a cactus areole. The roots are woody or sometimes quite large and fleshy tubers. The white to purple or yellow flowers have 5–8 stigmas and cells. JACOBSEN: Synopsis.

VANHEERDEA ──────────────────────────────

L. Bolus *Notes on Mesemb.* I: 136, 1938.

Typ. *V. roodiae* (N.E. Br.) L. Bol.

SYN. *Rimaria* p.p.

Very small genus of gibbaeum-like plants from the W. Cape. From that genus it is distinguished by the pair of bracts visible at the base of the pedicel, the large number (7–15) of stigmas and cells, and the confluent nectar glands (6 and free in *Gibbaeum*). The flowers are yellow to orange. JACOBSEN: **Key** to species.

VANZIJLIA ──────────────────────────────

L. Bolus in *Fl. Pl. S. Afr.* 7 t. 262, 1927.

Typ. *V. annulata* (Bgr.) L. Bol.

Very small genus of heterophyllous shrublets from the W. Cape recalling *Mitrophyllum,* but with much thinner, wiry, straggling branches. The solitary, white to pink flowers have 10 stigmas and cells, and placental tubercles (lacking in *Mitrophyllum*).

# CHAPTER 29

# Moraceae

This medium-sized Family is most familiar from the mulberry (*Morus*) and the fig (*Ficus*). Characteristic of the tropics and subtropics, the Moraceae comprise trees and shrubs with minute, much-reduced, unisexual flowers packed into inflorescences of various shapes. In *Dorstenia*, for instance, we are confronted by weird, greenish, flower-like formations that comprise a circular or oddly shaped flat receptacle in which the minute flowers are immersed, the whole surrounded by tentacle-like bracts. The ripe seeds are catapulted some distance from the parent plant. In *Ficus* the receptacle is folded inwards so that the florets are inside a closed vessel: the fig, where pollination is by tiny wasps. Both these genera have evolved stem succulence of a type, but since *Ficus* ultimately becomes a tree, the interest is mainly on small specimens for the lover of bonsai.

## KEY TO GENERA INCLUDING SUCCULENTS

1  Receptacle ± flat                                                     **Dorstenia**
1  Receptacle globose or obovoid with a narrow orifice        **Ficus**

## DORSTENIA ——————————————————————

L. *Sp. Pl.* Edn. I: 121, 1753; *Gen. Pl.* Edn. V: 56, 1754 ('Dorstena').
Typ. *D. contrajerva* L.

Large genus of tropical herbs and shrubs readily recognized by the flat, fleshy, greenish receptacle surrounded by a variable number of usually linear bracts, the whole simulating a single flower. The shape can be circular, elliptical, cordate or stellate. The few succulent species have soft, very thick, irregularly branched stems and deciduous, flat leaves, and favour much warmth.

## FICUS

L. *Sp. Pl.* Edn. I: 1059, 1753; *Gen. Pl.* Edn. V: 482, 1754.
Typ. *F. carica* L.

This very large and remarkable genus includes the edible figs and some of the toughest and most indestructible of foliage shrubs for the home. A few xerophytes develop a swollen stem base, and young plants of, for example, *F. palmeri* are sought after for their bonsai appearance. The fruit is best interpreted as the flat receptacle of *Dorstenia* folded inwards to form a closed vessel with just a tiny orifice at the top.

---

## THE MANY TONGUES OF SCIENCE

By now you will have realized that the keen botanist has to face up to reading foreign languages, since many of the most useful reference works are in German, French and languages other than English. But, with the aid of a good science dictionary, minimal knowledge of them is needed to get the meaning of plant descriptions and keys.

For Latin, *Botanical Latin* by W. T. Stearn is the perfect primer.

# CHAPTER 30

# Oxalidaceae

A small Family, centred around the one very large genus of woodsorrels. It is related to the Geraniaceae, but distinguishable by the separate leaflets, details of flower structure, and by the explosive fruit that throws the seeds some distance from the parent plant. One species of *Oxalis* is native to Britain and several others are invasive and persistent weeds of gardens and glasshouses, spreading by means of catapulted seeds and, in some species, also by bulbils. Some of the hardy perennials are cultivated in the rock garden.

## General Reference

KNUTH, R. 1930. Oxalidaceae in ENGLER, A. *Das Pflanzenreich* 95.

Genus including Succulents: *OXALIS* only.

## OXALIS

L. *Sp. Pl. Edn.* I: 433, 1753; *Gen. Pl.* Edn. V: 198, 1754.

Typ. *O. acetosella* L.

A very large genus, mainly diversified in C. and S. America and in Africa, and easily recognizable by the long-stalked, trifoliate, clover-like leaves that mostly show sleep movements by lowering the leaflets at night. Of the 37 Sections into which the genus is divided by Knuth, one, Sect. Carnosae, includes a few species that claim attention as borderline stem-succulents, and one, *O. succulenta,* a curious shrublet in which each petiole is spindle-shaped and fleshy, and persists after the leaflets have fallen. The yellow flowers are borne on long stalks and are 5-partite with 10 stamens.

# CHAPTER 31

# Passifloraceae

The small passion-flower Family is made up mostly of tendril climbers, but there are herbs and shrubs as well. The leaves are alternate and the flowers 3–5-merous; the fruit is a capsule or—in the succulents—a berry. The one claim to succulence is among a few of the 92 species of *Adenia* in Africa, where we find various stages from a conical elongated main trunk to a full-scale caudex that may be strangely variegated, decorated with tubercles or crowned with prickly branches. The greenish or yellowish flowers, rarely seen in cultivation, have none of the splendour of the more familiar passion-flower, *Passiflora*.

## General Reference

HUTCHINSON, J. 1967. Passifloraceae in *The Genera of Flowering Plants II: 364–374*.

Genus including Succulents: *ADENIA* only.

**ADENIA** ─────────────────────────────────────────

Forskål *Fl. Aeg.-Arab.* 77, 1775, non Torrey 1843.
Typ. *A. venenata* Forsk.

Large genus of climbers from the tropics and sub-tropics of the Old World of which Jacobsen lists 19 as meriting consideration by lovers of succulents, by virtue of the curiously expanded and often ornately marked stems. Some climb by tendrils, some by stiff spines (*A. spinosa*); *A. globosa* and *A. pechuelii* have short, thick, perennial branches covered in stout prickles.
WILDE, W. J. J. O. De *A Monograph of the Genus Adenia Forsk. (Passifloraceae)*. Wageningen 1971. **Key** to species.

# CHAPTER 32

# Pedaliaceae

This is a small tropical Family centred in Africa and rarely encountered outside of botanical gardens and specialist collections. The plants are herbaceous or rarely shrubby, and typical of coastal and desert regions. They have opposite, often glandular hairy leaves, but in two genera large caudices are developed—reputedly 2 m (6½ ft.) or more across in *Sesamothamnus*. *Pterodiscus* is sometimes offered by nurserymen, but neither seems to live for long away from habitat. This is a pity because the large, bell-shaped flowers come in various colours and are showy. They may be succeeded by large, four-winged fruits.

## KEY TO GENERA INCLUDING SUCCULENTS

1 Plants unarmed; flowers solitary in the axils of leaves, not or only slightly spurred
**Pterodiscus**
1 Plants spiny; flowers in terminal and subterminal few-flowered racemes, spurred
**Sesamothamnus**

## PTERODISCUS ———————————————————————

Hooker in Curtis *Bot. Mag.* 1844 t. 4117.

Typ. *P. speciosus* Hook.

Small African genus of herbs or shrublets with the swollen caudex usually below ground, and aerial shoots bearing thin, flat leaves of various shapes. The showy flowers come in a range of colours.

## SESAMOTHAMNUS ———————————————————————

Welwitsch in *Trans. Linn. Soc.* 27: 49, 1869.

Typ. *S. benguellensis* Welw.

Very small genus of tropical African spiny xerophytes rarely seen in cultivation, with a habit not unlike some *Pachypodiums* and *Corallocarpus* (q.v.). Both trunk and branches are very thick, and the latter bear clusters of small, deciduous leaves from the axils of spines. The large and attractive flowers are white, pink or yellow.

---

### HOW LARGE IS 'LARGE'?

Size estimates for Families and genera as used in this book have a consistent numerical value.

Consult the chart on p. 77 if you want to know the actual range of taxa included.

# CHAPTER 33

# Peperomiaceae

As set out by Heywood (1978), this Family, a segregate from the peppers, Piperaceae, consists of 3 very small genera and one very large genus: *Peperomia,* with over 1000 species. It is centred in the tropics of South America but is widespread elsewhere, and all the species are more or less leaf-succulent. They form small, soft herbs or creepers and some are epiphytic. Window-leaves are developed in several species. Which to include in a succulent collection becomes a matter of personal choice, but the limiting factor is usually space and heating since all require much warmth. However, some are admirable house plants for a sunny window over a radiator, which does not suit most 'desert' succulents. The immediate distinction from all other leaf succulents is the peculiar flower spike that at first sight seems to have no flowers. These are microscopic, bisexual and immersed in the long, tail-like, yellowish green terminal axis.

Genus including Succulents: *PEPEROMIA* only

---

**PEPEROMIA** ————————————————————————

Ruiz & Pavon *Prodr.* 8, 1794.
Typ. *P. secunda* Ruiz & Pavon.
Very large pantropical genus of usually pale green, soft and brittle herbs as described above. A few die back to an underground tuber during the resting season. All are tender.
JACOBSEN: **Key** to 15 cultivated species p. 679.

### Figs. 34.1-34.4   Portulacaceae: *Portulaca grandiflora*

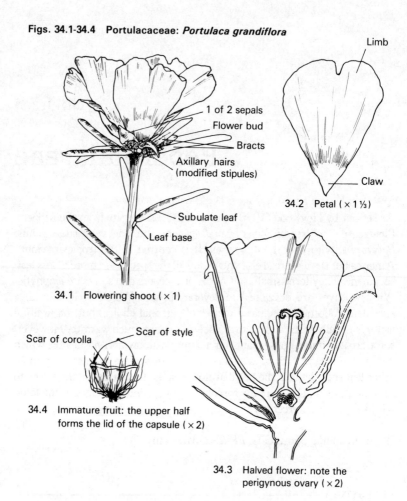

Limb

1 of 2 sepals

Flower bud

Bracts

Axillary hairs
(modified stipules)

Claw

34.2   Petal ( × 1⅓ )

Subulate leaf

Leaf base

34.1   Flowering shoot ( × 1 )

Scar of corolla

Scar of style

34.4   Immature fruit: the upper half
forms the lid of the capsule ( × 2 )

34.3   Halved flower: note the
perigynous ovary ( × 2 )

# CHAPTER 34

# Portulacaceae

A not-too-distant relative of Cactaceae and Mesembryanthemaceae, this small Family is worldwide in distribution although most prolific in the New World. All the plants are leaf-succulent to some degree, and a few have fleshy stems, but growers tend to ignore the small-flowered, weedy annuals, excepting *Portulaca oleracea,* which is grown locally as a potherb. Although predominantly small herbs, the Family also includes some sizeable shrubs (*Ceraria, Portulacaria*). Stipules are commonly present as hairs or scales. The flowers are actinomorphic and, in contrast to those of Crassulaceae and Liliaceae, markedly anisomerous: 2 green sepals (usually), (4–)5(–18) free, coloured petals, 1, 2 or more whorls of stamens and 3(–5) united carpels. The fruit is a dry capsule of one sort or another.

*Lewisia* species are hardy and popular with rock and alpine garden enthusiasts. *Portulaca grandiflora* is a very popular and colourful half-hardy annual.

## General References

McNEILL, J. 1974. Synopsis of revised Classification of the Portulacaceae in *Taxon* 23: 725–728.

PAX, F, and HOFFMANN, K. 1934 Portulacaceae in ENGLER and PRANTL *Die Natürlichen Pflanzenfamilien* Edn. II 16c. **Keys** to genera in German.

## KEY TO GENERA INCLUDING SUCCULENTS

1 Plants with visible internodes between the leaves
    2 Annual or perennial herbaceous leaf succulents, rarely woody or caudiciform, with all or most leaves alternate; fruit a dehiscent capsule
        3 Stipules usually present as hairs or scales; ovary half inferior to inferior; capsule opening by a lid                **Portulaca**

3 Stipules absent; ovary superior; capsule opening by valves          **Talinum**

NOTE: The closely related but scarcely succulent *Calandrinia* differs in having persistent rather than deciduous sepals, and the seed without an aril.

2 Perennial shrubs or shrublets, with succulent to woody stems, with all or most leaves opposite and without stipules; fruits (rarely seen in cultivation) indehiscent, with a single seed

    4 Flowers hermaphrodite, in small clusters along short, leafless branchlets; fruit 3-winged, dry          **Portulacaria**

    4 Flowers mostly unisexual, in clusters or axillary racemes; fruit wingless and fleshy when mature          **Ceraria**

1 Plant without visible internodes except in inflorescences (*Anacampseros australiana* excepted); leaves in sessile rosettes or densely overlapped up short stems

    5 Stipules absent; sepals (2–)5–8, persistent; petals 5–18; capsule opening by a lid; hardy plants          **Lewisia**

    5 Stipules present as hairs between the leaves or as white papery scales enveloping them; sepals 2, deciduous; petals (3–)5; capsule opening by valves which peel away leaving the winged seeds in a basket-like mesh of fibres; tender plants          **Anacampseros**

## ANACAMPSEROS

L. *Opera Varia* 232, 1758, Nom. cons.

Typ. *A. telephiastrum* A. DC.

Medium-sized genus of African leaf-succulents, with a single outlier in S.W. Australia. All are dwarf and compact in habit. Some have rosettes like *Sempervivum,* but with axillary white hairs (Fig. 37.74); in others the leaves are reduced to tiny green scales overlaid with large papery stipules (Fig. 37.75) so that each shoot appears as a cylinder of white. *A. alstonii,* the favourite among collectors, combines these slender, white shoots with a flat-topped caudex. The purple, pink or white flowers are ephemeral, sometimes cleistogamous. The unique fruit structure is the most characteristic feature. JACOBSEN: Synopsis and key to species.

## CERARIA

Pearson & Stephens in *Ann. S. Afr. Mus.* 9: 32, 1912.

Typ. *C. namaquensis* (Sond.) Pears. & Steph.

Very small genus of shrubs from S. and S.W. Africa with fleshy leaves that can be flat and obovate to almost terete and linear or minute and scale-like. Young plants have an attractive bonsai appearance. Distinctions from *Portulacaria* lie in the flowers, which are rarely seen in cultivation.

LEWISIA ────────────────────────────

Pursh in *Fl. Amer. Sept.* 368, 1814.

Typ. *L. rediviva* Pursh.

Small genus of typically alpine, xerophytic rosette plants from W. U.S.A. extending southwards to Bolivia. The flat to terete fleshy leaves spring direct from a thick rootstock and in some species are deciduous. The absence of stipules and higher number of flower parts distinguish it from other Portulacaceae. The plants are hardy, and most of those in cultivation are hybrid.

ELLIOT, R. C. *The Genus Lewisia.* Alpine Gdn. Soc. 1966.

JACOBSEN: **Key** to 10 cultivated species.


PORTULACA────────────────────────────

L. *Sp. Pl.* Edn. I: 445, 1753; *Gen. Pl.* Edn. V: 204, 1754.

Typ. *P. oleracea* L.

Large genus of fleshy annuals or small herbs centred in S. America but extending to Africa, Australia and some small islands. *P. oleracea*, purslane, has become widely naturalized as a result of cultivation as a potherb; descendants of *P. grandiflora* with large flowers of many colours are popular quick-growing annuals in gardens. A few portulacas forms a basal caudex, and stipules are nearly always present in the form of hairs, scales or bristles. The leaves are alternate, soft-fleshy and usually narrow. From all other Portulacaceae the perigynous to epigynous flower and capsule opening by a lid serve as distinction (Figs. 34.1–4).

POELLNITZ, K. V. in *Fedde Repert.* 37: 240–320, 1934. **Key** to species in German.


PORTULACARIA ────────────────────────

Jacquin *Collect.* 1: 160, 1786.

Typ. *P. afra* Jacq.

Monotypic genus from S. Africa. *P. afra* forms a much-branched shrub to 3.5 m (12 ft.) tall with thick, fleshy branches, not unlike some arborescent *Crassula* and *Tylecodon* species. The small, succulent, opposite leaves are obovate to subrotund and the flowers, rarely seen in cultivation, are minute and reddish.

## TALINUM

Adanson *Fam. Pl.* 2: 245, 1763 ('Talinium').

Typ. *T. triangulare* (Jacq.) Willd.

Medium-sized pantropical genus of herbs and annuals of little interest to collectors save for a few with an enlarged caudex. The alternate, flat or subterete leaves are ± fleshy and have no stipules; the flowers are ephemeral.

POELLNITZ, K. V. in *Fedde Repert.* 35: 1–34, 1934. **Key** to species in German.

---

## FINDING KEYS TO SPECIES

If, on referring to a particular genus, you find no further reference to keys or a monograph, turn back to the description of the Family. Some of the titles in the general reference list there may provide the answer. These are not separately cited after every genus.

# CHAPTER 35

# Vitaceae

This Family is small but nonetheless important: its type genus is *Vitis,* which includes the grapevine. Horticulturists will know *Parthenocissus,* the virginia creeper. The succulent representatives also bear bunches of grapes, but they are puny, scarcely juicy and inedible. Most Vitaceae are tendril climbers with alternate leaves and small, 4–5-merous, bisexual flowers in much-branched cymes. Originally all classified under *Vitis,* the two genera keyed out below include some succulents showing three different variations on a stem succulent theme: square-stemmed, jointed climbers; round-stemmed, non-jointed climbers with a gradually tapering axis, and massively thickened shrubs with peeling bark and no tendrils or climbing shoots.

## KEY TO GENERA INCLUDING SUCCULENTS

1 Climbers, sometimes pachycaul, with long, square, angled or terete stems bearing
   tendrils                                                              **Cissus**
1 Caudiciform plants without slender climbing shoots or tendrils     **Cyphostemma**

## CISSUS ─────────────────────────────────────────────

L. *Sp. Pl.* Edn. I: 117, 1753; *Gen. Pl.* Edn. V: 53, 1754.
Typ. *C. vitiginea* L.

Very large pantropical genus of tendril climbers with 4-merous flowers. *C. quadrangularis,* widespread from Africa to India, has thick, square, jointed, succulent stems; others have a long, tapering main axis like *Adenia* but distinct by the position of the tendril in relation to the leaf.

## CYPHOSTEMMA ─────────────────────────

(Planchon) Alston in Trimen *Handb. Fl. Ceylon* 6: 53, 1931.
Typ. *C. setosa* (Wall) Alst.

Small genus originally included in *Cissus,* but amply distinct on vegetative grounds. The massive lumpish caudex may reach 4 m (13 ft.) tall and half as thick at the base, with many branches; there are no thin annual shoots, and (except in seedlings) no tendrils. The smooth, soft stems are covered in yellowish, papery, peeling bark. The large, fleshy and often lobed leaves are deciduous.

---

## CONSERVATION IN THE GLASSHOUSE

Providing the correct name is only one aspect of the task of preserving in cultivation plants that are rapidly being exterminated in the wild. The true lover of nature can play a great part here. Treasure your labels, especially those with field data. Keep record files of the plants you grow, and propagate the rarities to ensure their survival.

# CHAPTER 36

# In Case of Failure

'Robinson Crusoe did not feel bound to conclude, from the single human footprint that he saw in the sand, that the maker of the impression had only one leg.'                                                            (*T. Huxley*)

1. If your plant fits equally well in either of two leads, the name should appear under both.
2. If your plant fits neither of two leads, suspect an error and check back step by step or start again at the beginning.
3. If you come to a halt through insufficient information—as, for instance, lack of fruits on a flowering specimen—try each lead in turn and decide between the answers.
4. If the blockage persists, it may be due to one of the following:
   (a) You are misinterpreting the key. Re-read the alternatives carefully, and check if you have missed out a lead or a third option following two.
   (b) You are misinterpreting the plant—as, for instance, calling the stems of *Schlumbergera* leaves.
   (c) The plant you are examining may indeed be a xerophyte and look cactus-like to you, but it is not a succulent in the commonly accepted sense used here. Bromeliads, cycads, saxifrages and prickly plants in general are commonly thought of as 'cacti' by the uninitiated.
   (d) You have a juvenile specimen that differs in habit, phyllotaxy, leaf form or other features from an adult.
   (e) You have an abnormal form of a succulent: a cristate or monstrous growth, or one so altered by bad cultivation that stemless rosettes have become elongated shoots, or large flowers have aborted in bad weather.

(f) You have an intergeneric hybrid, combining the characters of two genera: these are listed by name but are not included in the keys.

(g) You have a new or rare genus not included in the keys. Some extra names and borderline succulents will be found in the text. But before dashing off to name it as new, please read pp. 57–59!

Of course, it may be that you have caught the author out and uncovered an error or oversight, in which case he would be glad to be informed so that a correction can be made.

# CHAPTER 37

# Glossary

The language of botany has developed over the centuries into a beautiful and precise tool, capable of describing a plant clearly in the minimum number of words. These words are more specific than many in everyday usage. Some are familiar words used in a special, restricted sense: *succulent, family, form, spine, claw, limb, disc, inferior, superior* and so on. Readers familiar with classical languages will be at an advantage since many terms are derived from Latin or Greek and their meanings will be evident. Others will find much help from the works of Stearn (1966), Brown (1979), and Ivimey-Cook (1974).

Man recognizes the distinguishing features of plants and invents terms as a means of passing on information about them. As Linnaeus sagely remarked, it is the plants that make the characters, not the other way about. We try to fit animate nature into pigeon-holes of our own devising; the plants know no such artificial boundaries. To go on inventing new terms to cover every situation is no solution: terminology can suffer from inflation just as much as the naming of species. To describe every leaf shape encountered in the protean genus *Pelargonium,* for instance, would demand a never-ending stream of adjectives. However, much can be accomplished with a little ingenuity using existing terms, by combining them (ovate-elliptic), qualifying them (subglobose, semi-cylindrical), diminishing them (crenulate = finely crenate) or searching for comparisons with familiar objects (citriform = lemon-shaped; allantoid = sausage-shaped) and so on. More extensive glossaries are to be found in Lawrence (1955), Heywood (1978) and many botanical textbooks; for a systematic analysis of the shape and form of leaves see L. J. Hickey (1973).

**Figs. 37.1-37.6  Leaves: phyllotaxy**

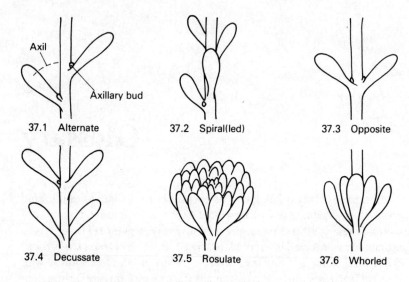

37.1  Alternate

37.2  Spiral(led)

37.3  Opposite

37.4  Decussate

37.5  Rosulate

37.6  Whorled

**Figs. 37.7-37.13  Leaves: type**

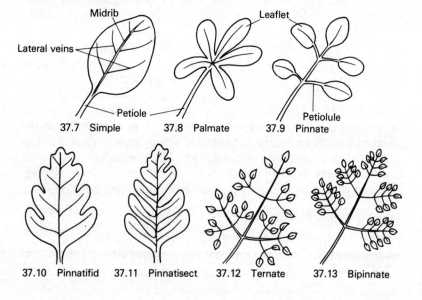

37.7  Simple

37.8  Palmate

37.9  Pinnate

37.10  Pinnatifid

37.11  Pinnatisect

37.12  Ternate

37.13  Bipinnate

# References

HEYWOOD, V. H. (Ed.) 1978 *Flowering Plants of the World* (Oxford: Oxford University Press).

HICKEY, L. J. 1973 *Amer. J. Bot.* 60(1): 17–33. Classification of the Architecture of Dicotyledonous leaves.

IVIMEY-COOK, R. B. 1974 *Succulents—A Glossary of Terms and Descriptions* (Oxford: Nat. Cact. Succ. Soc.).

LAWRENCE, G. H. M. 1955 *An Introduction to Plant Taxonomy* (New York: Macmillan).

McVAUGH, R., ROSS, R. and STAFLEU, F. A. 1968 *Regnum Vegetabile* Vol. 56 (Utrecht) An Annotated Glossary of Botanical Nomenclature.

SMITH, A. W. 1972 *A Gardener's Dictionary of Plant Names* (London: Cassell) Revised and enlarged by W. T. STEARN.

STEARN, W. T. 1966 *Botanical Latin* (London: Nelson).

# Abbreviations

| | |
|---|---|
| *Adj.* = Adjective | *q.v.* = Which see |
| *Ant.* = Antonym | S. = South, southern |
| *cf.* = Compare | *Syn.* = Synonym |
| *Dim.* = Diminutive | *V.* = Verb |
| E. = East, eastern | W. = West, western |
| *l.c.* = *loco citato;* in the place already cited. | × = Hybrid |
| N. = North, northern | ∅ = Diameter |
| *Pl.* = Plural | ± = More or less |

# Glossary

ACICULAR Needle-like (Fig. 4.3).

ACTINOMORPHY Radial symmetry; said of a flower that can be divided into two equal halves across many diameters (Fig. 18.2). *Adj.* ACTINOMORPHIC. *Ant.* ZYGOMORPHY.

ACUMINATE Tapering gradually to a point, with the sides ± concave (Fig. 37.42).

ADNATE Organically joined (said of dissimilar organs). *cf.* CONNATE.

ADVENTITIOUS Said of roots that arise anywhere other than from pre-existing roots.

ALKALOID Nitrogenous organic substance of basic character produced in certain plants and often protective by its poisonous nature.

ALTERNATE Inserted singly along an axis, successive members facing in opposite directions (Fig. 37.1). *cf.* SPIRALLED. *Ant.* OPPOSITE.

ANATOMY The study of the microscopic structure of plants.

ANDROECIUM The male organs of a flower; collectively, the stamens (Fig. 1.12).

ANISOMEROUS Unequal-parted; said of flowers having different basic numbers of sepals, petals, stamens and carpels (Figs. 34.1,3). *Ant.* ISOMEROUS.

ANNULUS A ring-like outgrowth, as from the corolla of *Orbea* (Figs. 11.1–3). *Adj.* ANNULAR.

ANTHER The top part of a stamen that contains the pollen (Fig. 1.13).

APETALOUS Lacking petals.

APICULATE Minutely spine-tipped (Fig. 37.40). *cf.* MUCRONATE.

APPENDICULATE Carrying an appendage or outgrowth of some sort.

APPRESSED Pressed tightly against.

ARBORESCENT Becoming tree-like.

AREOLE Spine cushion; the organ, as in a cactus, from which arise armature, leaf, lateral branch and flower (Figs. 4.3–6, 9–16, 37, 61).

ARIL A fleshy or bony outgrowth of a seed. *Adj.* ARILLATE.

**Figs. 37.14-37.28    Leaves (cont): shape (applicable also to other plane bodies like petals and solid bodies like fruits, seeds, caudices)**

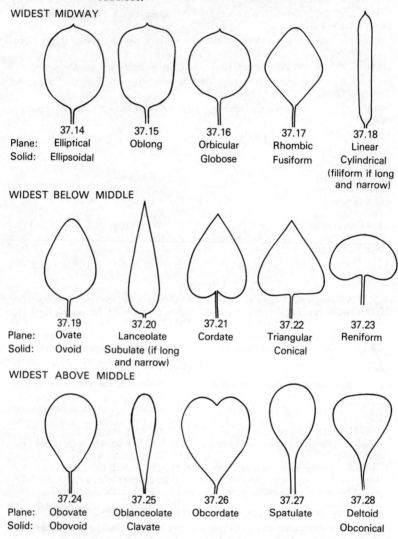

WIDEST MIDWAY

| | 37.14 | 37.15 | 37.16 | 37.17 | 37.18 |
|---|---|---|---|---|---|
| Plane: | Elliptical | Oblong | Orbicular | Rhombic | Linear |
| Solid: | Ellipsoidal | | Globose | Fusiform | Cylindrical (filiform if long and narrow) |

WIDEST BELOW MIDDLE

| | 37.19 | 37.20 | 37.21 | 37.22 | 37.23 |
|---|---|---|---|---|---|
| Plane: | Ovate | Lanceolate | Cordate | Triangular | Reniform |
| Solid: | Ovoid | Subulate (if long and narrow) | | Conical | |

WIDEST ABOVE MIDDLE

| | 37.24 | 37.25 | 37.26 | 37.27 | 37.28 |
|---|---|---|---|---|---|
| Plane: | Obovate | Oblanceolate | Obcordate | Spatulate | Deltoid |
| Solid: | Obovoid | Clavate | | | Obconical |

NOTE: In principle, -ate signifies a plane surface and -oid a solid body. But common usage allows a few exceptions.
Ob- indicates reversal in relation to point of attachment.

ARMATURE Plant defences: prickles, spines, thorns, etc.

AURICULATE Eared; having two rounded lateral lobes (Fig. 37.50). *cf.* SAGITTATE.

AWN A stiff, bristle-like appendage, usually borne at the tip of an organ (Fig. 28.5).

AXIL The upper angle between a stem and a leaf or tubercle (Fig. 37.1). *Adj.* AXILLARY.

AXILE A form of placentation in which the ovules arise from the centre of the ovary and face outwards. *Ant.* PARIETAL.

BASIONYM The earliest name of a taxon on which a later name has been founded.

BERRY An indehiscent fleshy fruit containing two or more seeds (Fig. 37.62). *Adj.* BACCATE. *cf.* DRUPE.

BETACYANIN A nitrogenous pigment found only in Caryophyllales and responsible for pink and purple colours.

BIFID Forking into two about halfway up.

BINOMIAL The two-part scientific name of a species, comprising a generic name followed by a specific epithet. *Adj.* BINOMIAL.

BIOCHEMISTRY The study of the chemical substances within an organism; the chemistry of life.

BIPINNATE Twice pinnate (Fig. 37.13).

BISEXUAL Said of a flower that includes both functional stamens and carpels (Fig. 18.2). *Ant.* UNISEXUAL. *cf.* HERMAPHRODITE.

BONSAI The Japanese art of dwarfing trees; said of a plant resembling such a miniature, gnarled tree.

BRACT A modified leaf at the base of a peduncle or pedicel (Fig. 37.59). *Dim.* BRACTEOLE.

BRACTEOLE A second-order bract subtending a single pedicel when the bract itself subtends a peduncle (Fig. 37.59).

BULB A usually underground storage organ comprising an enlarged bud with successive layers of fleshy leaves or leaf bases. *Adj.* BULBOUS. *Dim.* BULBIL.

CACTIFORM, CACTOID Having the general appearance of a globular cactus. *cf.* CEREIFORM, CEREOID.

CACTOPHILE A lover of cacti, but loosely applied to lovers of all succulent plants.

CACTUS A member of the Family Cactaceae (p. 103). As a generic name, *Cactus* L. is now treated as a synonym of *Melocactus.* Pl. CACTI, rarely CACTUSES.

C[A]ESPITOSE Forming tufted growth.

CALYX The outermost protective envelope of a flower, made up of usually greenish sepals (Fig. 1.10).

CAMPANULATE Shaped like a bell.

CAPITULUM A little head; especially a type of flower-head in which many small sessile flowers arise at the same level on a flattened axis, surrounded by a common involucre of bracts (Figs. 16.2, 37.55). *cf.* PSEUDANTHIUM.

CAPSULE A dry fruit composed of two or more carpels united laterally (Fig. 27.4). *Adj.* CAPSULAR.

CARPEL A modified leaf containing the ovules and with a stigma at the top (Fig. 1.15).

CARTILAGINOUS Flexible but tough and hard, like the skin around apple pips.

CAUDATE Tailed; with a long tapering terminal appendage (Fig. 37.43).

CAUDEX An enlarged storage organ at soil level, composed of a swollen stem base, or root, or both. *Adj.* CAUDICIFORM.

CAUDICIFORM Having a caudex with associated division of labour between short-lived photosynthesizing organs and a perennial water and food store; a plant of this nature (Figs. 1.7, 7.11–14).

CELL (1) The basic unit or 'brick' from which plant tissues are built.
(2) One chamber of an ovary, containing the ovules. *Syn.* LOCULE.

CELL WING In Mesembryanthemaceae, the membranous covering that roofs the cells in the capsule (Figs. 28.4–5).

CEPHALIUM A lateral or terminal crown of wool and/or bristles from which the flowers are borne in certain cacti.

CEREIFORM, CEREOID Having the general appearance of a columnar cactus. *cf.* CACTIFORM, CACTOID.

CHAMAEPHYTE A woody or herbaceous plant having its winter buds between soil

**Figs. 37.29-37.35 Leaves (cont): margins (applicable also to petals, sepals, etc.)**

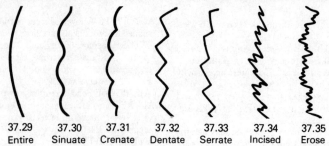

| 37.29 | 37.30 | 37.31 | 37.32 | 37.33 | 37.34 | 37.35 |
|-------|-------|-------|-------|-------|-------|-------|
| Entire | Sinuate | Crenate | Dentate | Serrate | Incised | Erose |

**Figs. 37.36-37.44  Leaves: tips**

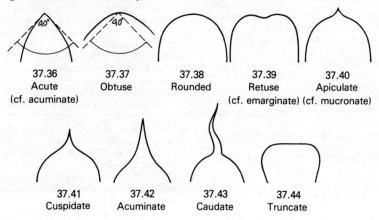

| 37.36 | 37.37 | 37.38 | 37.39 | 37.40 |
|-------|-------|-------|-------|-------|
| Acute | Obtuse | Rounded | Retuse | Apiculate |
| (cf. acuminate) | | | (cf. emarginate) | (cf. mucronate) |

| 37.41 | 37.42 | 37.43 | 37.44 |
|-------|-------|-------|-------|
| Cuspidate | Acuminate | Caudate | Truncate |

**Figs. 37.45-37.50  Leaves: bases**

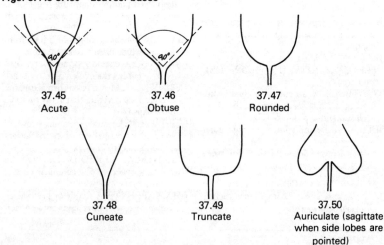

| 37.45 | 37.46 | 37.47 |
|-------|-------|-------|
| Acute | Obtuse | Rounded |

| 37.48 | 37.49 | 37.50 |
|-------|-------|-------|
| Cuneate | Truncate | Auriculate (sagittate when side lobes are pointed) |

level and 25 cm (10 ins.) above it. *cf.* GEOPHYTE, PHANEROPHYTE.

CHARACTER[ISTIC] Any feature of a plant selected for use in classification or identification.

CHIMAERA A plant composed of a mixture of two or more genetically different tissues.

CHROMOSOME An elongated structure in the cell nucleus which carries the genes in linear order.

CILIATE Fringed with hairs, like eyelashes (Fig. 37.72).

CINCINNUS A type of monochasium in which flowers arise alternately but spread out in different planes (Fig. 37.57).

CLADODE See PHYLLOCLADE.

CLAVATE Club-shaped (Fig. 37.25).

CLAW The tapered lower part of a petal or sepal. (Fig. 34.2) *cf.* LIMB.

CLEISTOGAMY Ability of a flower to set viable seed without opening. *Adj.* CLEISTOGAMOUS.

CLONE A group of genetically identical plants, such as those derived from vegetative propagation of one individual.

CLONOTYPE Descendant by vegetative propagation from the actual plant designated as type by the publishing author.

COLUMN An extension of the centre of a flower carrying up the gynoecium and sometimes also the androecium, as in Stapelieae (Fig. 1.18).

COMPOUND Subdivided into parts. *Ant.* SIMPLE.

CONNATE Organically joined (said of similar organs). *cf.* ADNATE.

CONNECTIVE The intervening tissue between the two lobes of an anther.

CONNIVENT Inclining together but not actually united. *cf.* DIFFUSE.

CONSERVATION In nomenclature, the authorized retention of a name despite its contravening the Code of Nomenclature. Such names are listed in full in an Appendix to the Code.

CONVERGENCE The evolutionary phenomenon whereby unrelated organisms come to look alike as a result of similar selection pressures—e.g. advance into desert habitats.

CONVOLUTE Rolled or wrapped in such a way that one margin is external, the other internal, as the bud of an *Adenium* (Fig. 10.1).

CORDATE Heart-shaped (Fig. 37.21).

COROLLA The inner of two perianth components, made up of usually coloured attractive petals (Fig. 1.11).

CORONA An extra crown-like whorl of appendages in a flower, as is found in *Adenium* and Stapelieae (Figs. 1.18, 11.1-3).

CORRECT Said of a plant name that is acceptable within the framework of a given classification. A plant can have two or more legitimate (*q.v.*) names, but only one is correct at a given time.

CORYMB A flat-topped inflorescence in which the flower stalks arise at different levels up the axis (Fig. 37.53). *Adj.* CORYMBOSE. *cf.* UMBEL.

COTYLEDON The first leaf produced by a seedling (Figs. 37.68-71).

CRENATE Having rounded teeth (Fig. 37.31). *Dim.* CRENULATE.

CREST, CRISTATE A fasciated stem or whole plant with fan-like growth. *Adj.* CRESTED, CRISTATE.

CRISPED Curled and wavy at the margins, like the leaves of parsley.

CROSSING Cross-pollination; transfer of pollen between two genetically dissimilar individuals. *Ant.* SELFING.

CULTIGEN A plant born in cultivation. *Ant.* INDIGEN.

CULTIVAR A taxonomic group of cultivated plants distinguishable by any characters that are stable and recognizable; a 'cultivated variety'. (See further details on pp. 18, 38-39.)

CUNEATE Wedge-shaped (Fig. 37.48).

CUSPIDATE Abruptly ending in a long sharp tip (Fig. 37.41).

CYATHIUM The unique inflorescence of Euphorbieae in which a single female flower, reduced to one ovary, is surrounded by several males, each reduced to a single stamen, the whole being enveloped in an involucre (Figs. 22.1-4). *cf.* PSEUDANTHIUM.

**Figs. 37.51-37.60   Inflorescences**

A. SIMPLE

a. Racemose

37.51   Raceme
(e.g. in *Haworthia*)

37.52   Spike
(e.g. in *Peperomia*)

37.53   Corymb
(e.g. in *Sedum spectabile*)

37.54   Umbel
(e.g. in *Brachystelma barberae*)

Involucre of bracts

b. Cymose

Scape

37.55   Capitulum
(e.g. in *Senecio*)

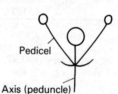

Pedicel

Axis (peduncle)

37.56   Simple cyme
(dichasial)
(e.g. in *Bergeranthus*)

37.57   Cincinnus
(monochasial)
(e.g. in *Pachyphytum*)

B. COMPOUND

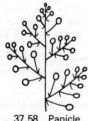

37.58   Panicle
(raceme of racemes)
(e.g. in *Aloe fosteri*)

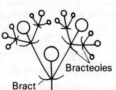

Bracteoles

Bract

37.59   Dichasium
(cyme of cymes)
(e.g. in *Hereroa*)

37.60   Thyrse
(raceme of cymes)
(e.g. in *Crassula multicava*)

*Special types:* See also Verticillaster, Cyathium.

CYME One of two basic types of inflorescence in which the oldest flower is at the centre and terminates the main axis, subsequent growth being from one or more branches beneath it (Fig. 37.56). *Adj.* CYMOSE. *Ant.* RACEME.

CYTOLOGY The study of cells, in particular the chromosomes within them.

DECUMBENT Growing with the base flat on the ground but the tip ascending. *cf.* PROCUMBENT.

DECUSSATE In crossed pairs, that is, with each pair at right angles to its predecessor (Fig. 37.4).

DEHISCENCE The way in which a fruit or anther splits to release its contents. *Adj.* DEHISCENT. *V.* DEHISCE.

DELTOID Triangular, attached by one corner (Fig. 37.28).

DENTATE Toothed, with symmetrical triangular teeth (Fig. 37.32). *Dim.* DENTICULATE. *cf.* SERRATE.

DICHASIUM A type of cymose inflorescence in which two opposite lateral branches grow out from beneath a terminal flower (Figs. 37.56,59). *Adj.* DICHASIAL. *Ant.* MONOCHASIUM.

DICHOTOMOUS Forking into two equal branches.

DICOTYLEDON A plant having two cotyledons; a member of one of the two major subdivisions of flowering plants. *cf.* MONOCOTYLEDON.

DIFFUSE Spreading away from one another. *Ant.* CONNIVENT.

DIGITATE See PALMATE.

DIMORPHISM Existence in two forms. *Adj.* DIMORPHIC.

DIOECIOUS Having separate male and female flowers on different plants. (Figs. 21.1–10) *cf.* MONOECIOUS.

DISC (1) The area surrounding the ovary, associated with nectar secretion.
(2) The flattened axis supporting the florets in a capitulum (Fig. 16.2).

DISC FLORET One of many small, actinomorphic flowers occupying the central area of a capitulum in Compositae (Fig. 37.66). *cf.* RAY FLORET.

DISTICHOUS In two opposite series, like a fishbone.

DRUPE An indehiscent fleshy fruit containing a single seed. *Adj.* DRUPACEOUS. *cf.* BERRY.

ECHINATE Covered in prickles like a hedgehog.

EFFECTIVE Said of a name that exists in printed form circulated to the general public. *cf.* CORRECT, LEGITIMATE, VALID.

ELLIPSOIDAL Shaped like an ellipse rotated about its longer axis (Fig. 37.14).

EMARGINATE Notched at the apex. *cf.* RETUSE.

ENDEMISM Occurrence in a smaller than average area in the wild. *Adj.* ENDEMIC. *cf.* WIDESPREAD.

ENTIRE Having a smooth, unbroken margin (Fig. 37.29).

EPICACTUS One of a range of hybrid cacti descended from epiphytic genera and grown primarily for the large and showy blooms; 'Epiphyllums' or 'Orchid Cacti' are misleading names for this group.

EPIDERMIS The skin of a plant, comprising the surface layer of cells. *Adj.* EPIDERMAL.

EPIGYNOUS Having an inferior ovary (Fig. 37.65). *Ant.* HYPOGYNOUS.

EPIPHYTE A plant growing upon the branches of another, but not parasitic upon it. *Adj.* EPIPHYTIC.

EPITHET In nomenclature, the second part of a binomial name, also referred to as the trivial name.

EQUILATERAL Said of an inflorescence whose branches spread equally in all directions. *Ant.* SECUND.

EROSE Jagged, as if bitten into at the margin (Fig. 37.35).

EVOLUTION The process whereby all living things descend from fewer and simpler ancestors.

EXPANDING KEEL In Mesembryanthemaceae, the hygroscopic margin of the capsule valve that expands when wetted and controls the opening and closing (Fig. 28.4–5).

EXSERTED Projecting beyond, as the stamens and style from a corolla tube (Fig. 27.3). *Ant.* INCLUDED.

**EXSTIPULATE** Lacking stipules. *Ant.* STIPULATE.

**FAMILY** A taxonomic grouping made up of related genera. Family names end in -aceae, with few exceptions (Compositae, Labiatae).

**FARINOSE** White and mealy.

**FASCIATION** An abnormal type of growth in which the stem apex broadens into a fan. *Adj.* FASCIATED. *cf.* CREST, CRISTATE, MONSTROUS.

**FASCICLE** A bunch or cluster in which there is a single point of origin.

**FILAMENT** The usually thread-like base of a stamen that bears the anther above. (Fig. 1.13).

**FILIFORM** Thread-like; cylindrical and elongated (Fig. 37.18).

**FIMBRIATE** Fringed.

**FLOCCOSE** Woolly.

**FLORET** A small flower, as in the flower heads of Compositae and Euphorbieae (Fig. 37.70).

**FOLLICLE** A dry fruit comprising a single carpel that dehisces longitudinally along one side (Figs. 18.4-5).

**FORM** A taxonomic subdivision of a variety; normally the smallest degree of differentiation meriting a name.

**FREE** Separate and not united with one another. *cf.* ADNATE, CONNATE.

**FRUIT** The seeds and their enclosing ovary at maturity, sometimes including other parts of the flower and axis.

**FRUTICOSE** Shrub-like.

**FUNICLE** The thread by which an ovule is attached to the placenta.

**FUSIFORM** Spindle-shaped; terete and tapered towards both ends (Fig. 37.17).

**GAMETE** A sex cell of a pollen grain or egg, containing the halved number of chromosomes. *cf.* MEIOSIS.

**GENUS** A taxonomic group composed of related species. *Pl.* GENERA *Adj.* GENERIC.

**GEOBOTANY** See PHYTOGEOGRAPHY.

**GEOPHYTE** Herb with winter buds situated below the surface of the soil. *cf.* CHAMAEPHYTE, PHANEROPHYTE.

**Fig. 37.61   The areole of a cactus (*Opuntia*)**

Subtending leaf

**Fig. 37.62 The berry of a *Mammillaria***

**Fig. 37.63 The hypanthium of a cactus flower**

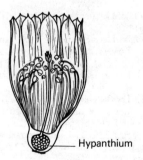

Hypanthium

GLABROUS With a smooth, hairless surface.

GLAND A secretory organ composed of one or more cells, often elevated upon a hair (Figs. 22.3–4). *Adj.* GLANDULAR.

GLAUCOUS With a fine waxy surface like a plum. *cf.* PRUINOSE.

GLOBOSE Spherical (Fig. 37.16).

GLOCHID The small, barbed, readily detachable spine of *Opuntia* (Figs. 4.6-7).

GREX A group of related cultivars, covered by a word or phrase name similar to that of a cultivar, e.g. × *Echinobivia* Paramount Hybrids.

GYNOECIUM The female organs of a flower; collectively the carpels (Fig. 1.14). *Syn.* PISTIL.

HALOPHYTE A salt-tolerant plant of maritime and saline areas. Most halophytes show a degree of succulence.

HERB A non-woody plant of which nothing persists above ground during the resting period. *Adj.* HERBACEOUS.

HERBARIUM A collection of preserved plants; the building in which such a collection is housed.

HERMAPHRODITE Possessing both male and female sex organs. *cf.* BISEXUAL.

HETEROGAMOUS Having flowers of more than one kind, as in the disc and ray florets of Compositae (Fig. 16.4). *Ant.* HOMOGAMOUS.

HETEROPHYLLY The state of having leaves of two or more basic types. *Ant.* HOMOPHYLLY.

HILUM The scar at one end of a seed where it was originally attached to the funicle.

HIRSUTE Coarsely hairy.

HISPID Rough from short bristles or stiff hairs.

HOLOTYPE The actual specimen designated as type by the publishing author.

HOMOGAMOUS Having flowers all of one kind (Fig. 16.2). *Ant.* HETEROGAMOUS.

HOMONYM A name duplicating that of another plant. *cf.* SYNONYM.

HOMOPHYLLY The state of having all leaves basically of one type. *cf.* HETEROPHYLLY.

HYGROSCOPIC Able to absorb water.

HYPANTHIUM The external part of a flower comprising the outside of an (epigynous) ovary and the perianth tube (Figs. 14.1, 37.63). *Syn.* RECEPTACLE TUBE; PERICARPEL.

HYPOCOTYL The part of a seedling between the radicle and the cotyledons, representing the transitional zone between root and stem (Fig. 37.69).

HYPOGYNOUS Having a superior ovary (Fig. 37.64). *Ant.* EPIGYNOUS.

INCISED Deeply and sharply cut into lobes (Fig. 37.34).

INCLUDED Wholly within, as stamens that do not overtop the corolla tube. *Ant.* EXSERTED.

INDEHISCENT Not breaking open at maturity. *Ant.* DEHISCENT.

INDIGEN A plant born in the wild. *cf.* CULTIGEN.

INDUMENTUM Any form of surface covering of hairs, glands, scales, etc. *Syn.* VESTITURE.

INFERIOR Growing below; said of an ovary when the perianth arises from its top (Fig. 37.65). *Ant.* SUPERIOR.

INFLORESCENCE The axis bearing flowers (Figs. 37.51-60).

INTERNODE That part of a stem between two nodes. *cf.* NODE.

INVOLUCRE A ring of protective, leaf-like organs, such as bracts surrounding a capitulum (Figs. 16.1, 37.55). *Adj.* INVOLUCRAL, INVOLUCRATE.

ISODIAMETRIC Having approximately the same diameter in all planes, and hence approaching spherical.

ISOMEROUS Equal-parted; said of flowers having the same basic number in each whorl of sepals, petals, stamens and carpels (Fig. 18.2). *Ant.* ANISOMEROUS.

ISOTYPE A duplicate of a holotype, taken from the same gathering.

KARYOTYPE The chromosome set, as distinct in size, shape and number.

KEY A mechanical aid for identification, usually dichotomous and posing a series of questions to proceed by a process of elimination.

LACINIATE Slashed into narrow lobes.

LAMINA The blade of a leaf.

LANCEOLATE Lance-shaped, that is, broadest near the base and tapered into a sharp tip (Fig. 37.20).

LATERAL On the side, as describing roots developed horizontally from a taproot. *Ant.* TERMINAL.

LATEX Liquid produced in special tubular vessels that exudes when a plant is cut, and is typically white and milky (as in *Euphorbia*).

LAX Loose; not packed tightly together.

LEAFLET One of two or more divisions of a compound leaf (Figs. 37.8–9).

LEAF SUCCULENT Having enlarged, fleshy, water-storing leaves; a plant of this type (Figs. 1.3–4, 7.1–6).

LECTOTYPE A 'chosen type'; a type selected from among the original material in the absence of a holotype.

LEGITIMATE Said of a name that is both effectively and validly published. *cf.* CORRECT.

LIMB The broad expanded upper part of a petal or sepal, or of the whole corolla or calyx (Fig. 34.2). *cf.* CLAW.

LINEAR Long and narrow, with parallel edges, like a grass leaf (Fig. 37.18).

LITHOPHYTE A plant that grows on the surface of rocks like a lichen.

LOBED Partially divided into two or more segments.

LOCULE See CELL (2).

LUMPER A botanist who classifies into few, broadly defined units. *Ant.* SPLITTER.

MEDUSIFORM Head-like with a crown of serpentine branches.

MEIOSIS Reduction division; a stage in the formation of gametes in which half of the original chromosomes passes to each pollen grain or egg cell. *Adj.* MEIOTIC. *cf.* MITOSIS.

MEMBRANOUS Thin, papery, non-green and translucent.

MERICARP A part-fruit comprising one or more seeds enclosed in an ovary segment and derived from the break-up of a schizocarp (Fig. 37.67).

—MEROUS -parted. Suffix referring to the number of parts in a flower. Hence DIMEROUS, TRIMEROUS, TETRAMEROUS, PENTAMEROUS etc. for 2-, 3-, 4-, 5-parted, etc. *cf.* ISOMEROUS, ANISOMEROUS.

MESOPHYTE A plant of average water requirements. *cf.* XEROPHYTE.

MITOSIS That part of cell division in which each chromosome duplicates and an identical set passes to each of the two daughter nuclei. *Adj.* MITOTIC. *cf.* MEIOSIS.

MONOCARPIC Flowering once and then dying. *Ant.* PLEIOCARPIC.

MONOCHASIUM A type of cymose inflorescence in which only one branch grows out from beneath the terminal flower (Fig. 37.57). *Adj.* MONOCHASIAL. *Ant.* DICHASIUM.

MONOCOTYLEDON A plant having one cotyledon; a member of one of the two major subdivisions of flowering plants. *cf.* DICOTYLEDON.

MONOECIOUS Having separate male and female flowers on the same plant (Figs. 22.1–4). *cf.* DIOECIOUS.

MONOGRAPH An overall systematic revision of a taxonomic group, including a synthesis of all previous work upon it.

MONOTYPIC Having only one subordinate unit; said of a Family containing only one genus, a genus of only one species, etc.

MONSTROUS In succulents, having an abnormal growth pattern arising from multiple growing points. *cf.* FASCIATED.

MORPHOLOGY The study of the form and development of parts.

MUCRONATE Abruptly ending in a small triangular tip. *cf.* APICULATE.

MUTATION A sport; a permanent genetic change. *v.* MUTATE.

NECTAR The sugary secretion produced by a nectary, associated with the attraction of pollinators.

**Figs. 37.64-37.65 Ovary levels**

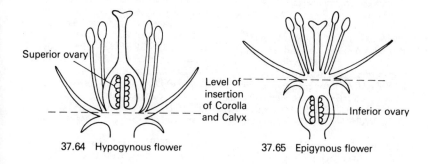

Superior ovary

Level of insertion of Corolla and Calyx

Inferior ovary

37.64   Hypogynous flower          37.65   Epigynous flower

NECTARY A gland that secretes nectar (Fig. 18.3).

NEOTYPE A 'new type'; a type selected from new material to serve in the absence of any original material.

NODE That portion of the stem from which the leaf arises. *cf.* INTERNODE.

NOMENCLATURE The names of things, and the pursuit of naming them.

NOMEN CONSERVANDUM A conserved name. *cf.* CONSERVATION.

NOMEN NOVUM A new name.

NOMEN NUDUM A 'naked name', that is, one lacking a published description or otherwise falling short of legitimate publication. Nomina nuda have no standing in botany.

NOTHOMORPH A subdivision of a 'hybrid species' equivalent to a variety of a non-hybrid species.

NUCLEUS The organizing body within a cell, in which the chromosomes are the most conspicuous feature. *Adj.* NUCLEAR.

OB- Prefix implying inverted in relation to the point of attachment (see p. 238).

OBCONICAL Shaped like an inverted cone (Fig. 37.28).

OBLIQUE-LIMBED Having the perianth slightly skewed in one plane; a first stage towards ZYGOMORPHY (*q.v.*).

OPPOSITE Inserted in pairs along an axis (Fig. 37.3). *cf.* ALTERNATE, DECUSSATE.

ORBICULAR Flat and circular in outline (Fig. 37.16). *Syn.* ROTUND.

ORDER A major taxonomic grouping made up of one or more related Families. Order names end in -ales.

OVARY The central female part of a flower made up of carpels containing ovules. (Figs. 1.15, 37.64-65).

OVATE Oval; flat and egg-shaped in outline (Fig. 37.19).

OVOID Solid and egg-shaped (Fig. 37.19).

OVULE The 'egg' of a plant, which on fertilization develops into a seed (Fig. 1.16).

PACHYCAUL Having a tapered swollen base to the main stem, as in *Pachypodium lealii* or *Adenia glauca*. *cf.* CAUDICIFORM.

PALMATE Diverging from a point of common origin, like the fingers on an outspread hand (Fig. 37.8) *Syn.* DIGITATE.

PANICLE A raceme of racemes (Fig. 37.58). *Adj.* PANICULATE.

PAPILLA A minute, rounded, usually glossy and blister-like projection from the epidermis. *Adj.* PAPILLATE, PAPULOSE.

PARIETAL A form of placentation in which the ovules arise from the outer wall of the ovary and face inwards. *Ant.* AXILE.

PECTINATE Set like the teeth of a comb (Fig. 4.14–15).

PEDICEL The ultimate stalk supporting a single flower (Fig. 37.56). *Adj.* PEDICEL-LATE. *cf.* PEDUNCLE.

PEDUNCLE The main axis of an inflorescence carrying the pedicels (Figs. 37.56–57). *Adj.* PEDUNCULATE.

PELTATE Having the petiole attached near the centre of the lower surface of the leaf blade.

PERIANTH The protective envelope of a flower, made up of uniform tepals or an outer calyx and an inner corolla. *Syn.* PERIGON.

PERICARPEL See HYPANTHIUM.

PERIGON See PERIANTH.

PERIGYNOUS Halfway between hypogynous and epigynous; that is, with the perianth arising midway up the ovary, as in *Portulaca* (Fig. 34.3).

PETAL One member of the corolla (Fig. 1.11). *Adj.* PETALOID.

PETIOLE The stalk of a leaf (Fig. 37.7). *Adj.* PETIOLATE. *Dim.* PETIOLULE (the stalk of a leaflet) (Fig. 37.9).

PHANEROPHYTE A woody plant having its winter buds 25 cm (10 in.) or more above soil level. *cf.* CHAMAEPHYTE, GEO-PHYTE.

PHENETIC Relating to form and general appearance; in particular applied to a classification based on overall similarities. *cf.* PHYLETIC.

PHYLLOCLADE A flattened stem that looks and functions like a leaf. *Syn.* CLADODE.

PHYLLOTAXY The arrangement of parts (leaves in particular) up an axis.

PHYLOGENY Race pedigree; the evolutionary history of a taxon. *Adj.* PHYLO-GENETIC, PHYLETIC. *cf.* PHENETIC.

PHYTOGEOGRAPHY The study of plants in relation to their world distribution. *Syn.* GEOBOTANY.

PICTOTYPE An illustration serving in place of an actual type specimen.

PINNATE Said of leaves that are compound, with two or more pairs of opposite leaflets (Fig. 37.9).

PINNATIFID Pinnately lobed, but not down as far as the midrib (Fig. 37.10). *cf.* PINNATISECT.

PINNATISECT Pinnately cut up, at least some of the divisions reaching right down to the midrib (Fig. 37.11). *cf.* PINNATIFID.

PISTIL See GYNOECIUM.

PLACENTA That part of the ovary from which the ovules arise (Fig. 1.16).

PLACENTATION The arrangement of placentas within an ovary.

PLEIOCARPIC Flowering more than once. *Ant.* MONOCARPIC.

PLUMOSE Feathery (Fig. 4.12).

POLLEN The dust-like grains produced by anthers and carrying the male gamete prior to fertilization.

POLLINIUM Pollen-mass; a structure comprising the whole contents of an anther lobe packaged for transfer as one unit, as in Stapelieae (Fig. 11.5). *Pl.* POLLINIA.

PRICKLE A pointed superficial outgrowth, not joined to the vascular system of a plant. *cf.* SPINE, THORN.

PRIORITY In nomenclature, the principle whereby the earliest valid name has precedence over all later ones.

PROCUMBENT Lying more or less flat on the ground; prostrate. *cf.* DECUMBENT.

PROLIFEROUS Unusually free in growth and differentiation, as from buds that normally remain dormant.

**Fig. 37.66**
**Ray (left) and disc (right)**
**florets of *Othonna***

PRUINOSE Having a pronounced waxy bloom. *cf.* GLAUCOUS.

PSEUDANTHIUM A 'false flower'; a much reduced inflorescence that simulates in appearance and function a single large bloom. Examples are the capitulum of Compositae (Fig. 16.4) and the cyathium of Euphorbieae (Fig. 22.2).

PUBESCENT Becoming downy.

PUSTULATE Puckered, blistered.

RACEME One of two basic types of inflorescence in which the axis has unlimited growth at the tip, the oldest flowers being at the bottom (Fig. 37.51). *Adj.* RACEMOSE. *Ant.* CYME.

RADICAL Arising from the root or from ground level.

RADICLE The first root developing from a seed (Figs. 37.68–71).

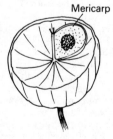

Mericarp

**Fig. 37.67**
**A schizocarp of *Hymenogyne***

RAY FLORET One of many small, zygomorphic flowers round the margin of a capitulum in Compositae (Fig. 37.66). *cf.* DISC FLORET.

RECEPTACLE The modified tip of the axis of a plant from which the flower parts (or whole florets) arise (Fig. 1.9).

RECURVED Curved back or downwards, more or less along the whole length. *cf.* REFLEXED.

REFLEXED Abruptly bent back or downwards. *cf.* RECURVED.

RENIFORM Kidney-shaped in outline (Fig. 37.23).

RETICULATE Intersecting like the meshes of a net.

RETUSE Having a rounded apex with a shallow curved central notch (Fig. 37.39). *cf.* EMARGINATE.

RHIZOME A modified underground stem.

ROSULATE Arranged in a rosette (Fig. 37.5).

ROTATE Spreading straight outwards like the spokes of a wheel.

ROTUND See ORBICULAR.

RUGOSE Rough from an uneven, wrinkled surface.

RUNNER A prostrate stem that produces a daughter plant at the tip.

SAGITTATE Shaped like the head of an arrow, with two lateral, backwardly directed points (Fig. 10.7). *cf.* AURICULATE.

SALVERFORM Having a long narrow tube abruptly flared above, as in a primrose flower.

SCAPE A conspicuous, almost or quite leafless peduncle.

SCHIZOCARP A dry fruit that breaks up at maturity into two or more mericarps (Fig. 37.67).

SECTION A taxonomic subdivision of a genus between subgenus and series.

SECUND Having branches all turned to one side. *cf.* EQUILATERAL.

SEED The end-product of a fertilized ovule. The 'seeds' of gardeners are often whole fruits or partial fruits, where the term is used more loosely.

**Figs. 37.68-37.71    Seedlings**

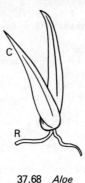

37.68    *Aloe*

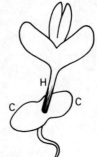

37.69    *Psilocaulon*

C = Cotyledon
H = Hypocotyl
R = Radicle
S = Seed coat remains

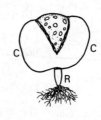

37.70    *Conophytum*

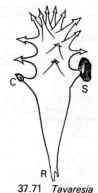

37.71    *Tavaresia*

SELF-COMPATIBLE Able to set viable seed as a result of selfing; self-fertile. *Ant.* SELF-INCOMPATIBLE.

SELF-INCOMPATIBLE Unable to set viable seed as a result of selfing; self-sterile. *Ant.* SELF-COMPATIBLE.

SELFING Self-pollination; transfer of pollen to stigmas on the same plant. *cf.* CROSSING.

SEMI- Half-.

SEPAL One member of the calyx (Fig. 1.10).

SERICEOUS Silky from soft, straight, appressed hairs.

SERIES A taxonomic subdivision of a genus below the level of section.

SERRATE Having an edge with lop-sided triangular teeth, like a saw (Fig. 37.33). *Dim.* SERRULATE. *cf.* DENTATE.

SESSILE Lacking a stalk.

SHRUB Woody perennial up to 5 m tall and without a dominant trunk. *Adj.* FRUTICOSE. *Dim.* SHRUBLET *cf.* SUBSHRUB, TREE.

SHRUBLET A miniature shrub. *cf.* SUBSHRUB.

SIMPLE Composed of a single entity; not subdivided or branched (Fig. 37.7). *cf.* COMPOUND.

SINUATE With a margin curving in and out (Fig. 37.30).

SPAT[H]ULATE Shaped like a spatula or narrow spoon (Fig. 37.27).

SPECIES A group of actually or potentially interbreeding plants more similar to each other than to plants of any other species, with which they usually show some barrier to free exchange of genes. As the basic unit of classification, species alone carry a binomial name. *Pl.* SPECIES. *Adj.* SPECIFIC.

**Figs. 37.72-37.75 Stipules**

37.72 *Pelargonium fulgidum*
Normal flat and acute
with ciliate margins

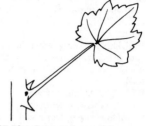

37.73 *Pelargonium spinosum*
Modified as spines

37.74 *Anacampseros rufescens*
Modified as brushes of hairs

37.75
*Anacampseros papyracea*
Modified as white, translucent,
overlapping scales enveloping
the minute green leaves beneath.

SPIKE A raceme in which the flowers are sessile (Fig. 37.52). *Adj.* SPICATE.

SPINE A leaf or part of a leaf modified into a sharp pointed structure (Figs. 4.2–15). *cf.* PRICKLE, THORN.

SPINESCENT Becoming spiny.

SPIRAL[LED] Inserted singly along an axis forming a helical series winding around it (Fig. 37.2). *cf.* ALTERNATE, OPPOSITE.

SPLITTER A botanist who classifies into many, finely divided units. *cf.* LUMPER.

SPORT See MUTATION.

SPUR Tubular or sac-like extension from the perianth or other parts of a flower, characteristically storing nectar.

STAMEN The male organ of a flower, comprising a filament bearing an anther at the top (Fig. 1.13).

STAMINODE A barren stamen, often modified to function as a petal or nectary.

STELLATE Star-shaped.

STEM SUCCULENT Having enlarged, fleshy, water-storing stems; a plant of this type (Figs. 1.5–6, 7.7–10).

STIGMA The receptive tip of a style on which the pollen alights and grows (Fig. 1.15).

STIPULE One of a pair of lateral outgrowths from the base of a petiole. In succulents these are mostly absent, or transformed into hairs or spines (Figs. 37.72–75). *Adj.* STIPULATE. *Ant.* EXSTIPULATE.

STOMA The breathing pore of a plant. *Pl.* STOMATA.

STYLE The extended tip of a carpel that bears the stigma (Fig. 1.15).

SUB- Somewhat; to some extent; of lower rank (as Subfamily, etc.).

SUBSHRUB A soft-wooded smallish shrub. *Adj.* SUFFRUTICOSE. *cf.* SHRUBLET.

SUBULATE Awl-shaped; narrow, terete and gradually tapering to a point (Fig. 37.20).

SUCCULENCE The quality of being succulent.

SUCCULENT Storing water in especially enlarged spongy tissue; a plant of this type.

SUCKER A shoot arising from below soil level.

SUFFRUTICOSE Subshrubby; woody at the base but otherwise herbaceous.

SUPERIOR Growing above; said of an ovary where the perianth arises from its base (Fig. 37.64). *Ant.* INFERIOR.

SYNONYM A surplus name for a taxon. *cf.* HOMONYM.

SYNOPSIS A tabular summary of a classification. *cf.* KEY.

SYSTEM A scheme of classification.

SYSTEMATICS See TAXONOMY.


TAPROOT A stout, vertical, anchoring root developed from the radicle.

TAXON A taxonomic unit of any rank. *Pl.* TAXA.

TAXONOMY The study of classification, including nomenclature.

TENDRIL A modified stem or leaf sensitive to touch and enabling a climbing plant to attach itself to a support.

TEPAL One member of the perianth. *cf.* SEPAL, PETAL.

TERETE Circular in cross-section.

TERMINAL At the end of an axis. *cf.* LATERAL.

TERNATE Divided into three, as in a compound leaf with three leaflets (Fig. 37.12).

TESSELLATE Divided up into polygonal areas, like tiles on a floor.

THORN Branch modified as a sharp pointed structure, and linked to the vascular system of the plant (Fig. 37.76). *cf.* PRICKLE, SPINE.

THYRSE A raceme of cymes (Fig. 37.60).

TISSUE Aggregate of cells similar in form and function.

**Fig. 37.76    Thorns of *Othonna euphorbioides***

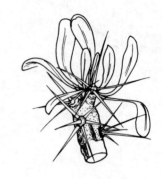

TOMENTOSE Densely clothed in soft matted hair.

TOPOTYPE A plant from the type locality.

TREE Woody perennial, typically more than 5 m tall, with a single trunk and usually a crown of radiating branches.

TRIBE A taxonomic subdivision of a Family containing related genera. Tribal names end in -eae.

TRIFOLIATE Having three leaflets arising from a common point of origin, like clover.

TRIGONOUS Three-angled in cross-section. *Syn.* TRIQUETROUS.

TRILOCULAR Three-chambered.

TRIQUETROUS See TRIGONOUS.

TRUNCATE Ending abruptly, as if sliced off (Figs. 37.44, 49).

TUBERCLE A conical outgrowth (Figs. 28.4–5). *Adj.* TUBERCULATE.

UTRICULAR Resembling a bladder or pouch.

**Fig. 37.77   A zygomorphic flower
of *Pelargonium***

VALID Said of a name that has been published effectively and in accordance with the Code of Nomenclature. *cf.* CORRECT, EFFECTIVE, LEGITIMATE.

VALVE One of two or more doors or lids by which a fruit opens (Figs. 28.4–5).

VARIEGATION Bicolour effect resulting from a localized failure of pigment to develop. *Adj.* VARIEGATED.

VARIETY A taxonomic subdivision of a species.

VASCULAR Provided with or pertaining to a conducting system made up of specialized tissues that transport fluid throughout the plant.

VERRUCOSE Rough from surface warts. *Dim.* VERRUCULOSE.

VERTICILLASTER An inflorescence consisting of compact dichasia at successive nodes, giving the impression of a series of whorls of flowers, as in Labiatae.

VESTITURE See INDUMENTUM.

VILLOUS Shaggy-haired.

TUNICATE Having two or more coats; specifically said of bulbs with concentric rings of leaf sheaths.

TURBINATE Top-shaped.

TYPE LOCALITY The locality from which the holotype came.

TYPE SPECIMEN The actual preserved specimen of a plant that serves as foundation for the name. *Syn.* HOLOTYPE. *cf.* CLONOTYPE, ISOTYPE, LECTOTYPE, NEOTYPE, PICTOTYPE, TOPOTYPE.

UMBEL A flat-topped inflorescence in which three or more pedicels arise from the same level (Fig. 37.54). *Adj.* UMBELLATE. *cf.* CORYMB.

UNISEXUAL Said of a flower that has functional stamens or carpels, but not both. (Figs. 21.2–7). *Ant.* BISEXUAL.

WHORLED Arranged three or more in a ring at the same level (Fig. 37.6).

WIDESPREAD Having a wider distribution than average. *cf.* ENDEMIC.

XEROMORPHY Possession of special features associated with water retention, and typical of xerophytes. *Adj.* XEROMORPHIC.

XEROPHYTE A plant adapted to survive with less than average available water. *cf.* MESOPHYTE.

ZYGOMORPHY Symmetry about one plane only, dividing into two mirror-image halves. *Adj.* ZYGOMORPHIC. *Ant.* ACTINOMORPHY.

# Succulent Plant Societies

A serious interest in classifying and identifying succulents cannot flourish in isolation. It demands comparison with plants in other collections and contact with other specialists. Science prospers from criticism and cross-fertilization of ideas; the hermit striving to do everything by himself comes to narrow and often very biased conclusions. As in all minority interests, succulent growers tend to be gregarious, seek out fellow addicts and thrive on social intercourse.

Out of this has grown up a body of flourishing amateur societies that offer lectures, tours of collections and nurseries, sales and exchanges of plants and seeds as well as public exhibitions and competitions. Most of them produce newsletters or journals ranging from a few mimeographed sheets to de-luxe printed format with colour plates.

Great Britain is especially rich in clubs and societies of this sort. One alone boasts a hundred branches, so nobody need feel cut off from kindred spirits. Membership of one or more of these societies is the ideal way of contacting specialists with interests similar to one's own, and an aid in searching out rare plants and literature. It also leads to valued contacts in one's travels abroad.

The list that follows is necessarily selective, and is biased towards those with better-class journals. Indeed, some are included that exist only through the medium of their periodicals or other publications. Addresses are the latest known to me at the time of writing.

## BRITAIN

National Cactus & Succulent Society
    Contact: 43 Dewar Drive, Sheffield S7 2GR.
    Journal: *National Cactus & Succulent Journal*, 1946 et seq.

Cactus & Succulent Society of Great Britain
    Contact:  67 Gloucester Court, Kew Road, Richmond, Surrey.
    Journal:  *Cactus & Succulent Journal of Great Britain*, 1932–39,
        1946 et seq.
Holly Gate Reference Collection
    Contact:  Holly Gate Nurseries Ltd., Ashington, Sussex
        RH20 3BA.
    Journal:  *Ashingtonia*, 1973 et seq.
The Exotic Collection
    Contact:  16–18 Franklin Road, Worthing, Sussex BN13 2PQ.
    Journal:  *Monthly Notes*, and *Photographic Reference Plates*
        1948 et seq.
Succulent Plant Club
    Contact:  Barleyfield, Southburgh, Thetford, Norfolk.
    Journal:  *The Xerophyte*, 1977 et seq.
The Chileans
    Contact:  5 Lyons Avenue, Hetton-le-Hole, Co. Durham
        DH5 0HS.
    Journal:  *The Chileans*, 1966 et seq.
The Mammillaria Society
    Contact:  26 Glenfield Road, Banstead, Surrey SM7 2DG.
    Journal:  *Journal of the Mammillaria Society*, 1960 et seq.
The Sempervivum Society
    Contact:  11 Wingle Tye Road, Burgess Hill, Sussex RH15 9HR.
    Journal:  *Journal of the Sempervivum Society*, 1970 et seq.
International Asclepiad Society
    Contact:  3 Annes Walk, Caterham, Surrey CR3 5EL.
    Journal:  *Asclepiadaceae*, 1974 et seq.
Succulent Plant Trust
    Contact:  72 Church Lane Avenue, Hooley, Coulsdon, Surrey
        CR3 3RT.
    Journal:  *Succulent Plant Trust Newsletter*, 1962 et seq.

## UNITED STATES OF AMERICA

Cactus & Succulent Society of America, Inc.
    Contact:  1675 Las Canoas Road, Santa Barbara, California
        93105.
    Journal:  *Cactus & Succulent Journal*, 1929 et seq.

Arizona Cactus & Native Flora Society
  Contact: Desert Botanical Garden, P.O. Box 5415, Phoenix,
    Arizona 85010.
  Journal: *Saguaroland Bulletin*, 1947 et seq.
Epiphyllum Society of America
  Contact: P.O. Box 1395, Monrovia, California 91016.
  Journal: *Bulletin of the Epiphyllum Society of America*, 1945 et
    seq.

## MEXICO
La Sociedad Mexicana de Cactologia
  Contact: Apartado Postal 979, Cuernavaca, Mor.
  Journal: *Cactaceas y Suculentas Mexicanas*, 1955 et seq.

## GERMANY (WESTERN)
Deutsche Kakteen-Gesellschaft
  Contact: Dr. Helmut-Junghans Strasse 81, D-7230 Schramberg
    11.
  Journal: *Kakteen und andere Sukkulenten*, 1891–1944, 1949
    et seq.
Verein der Kakteen-Freunde Frankfurt-M.
  Contact: 6 Frankfurt 1, Humboldstr. 1, Frankfurt am Main.
  Journal: *Der Frankfurter Kakteen-Freund*, 1973 et seq.
Arbeitskreis für Mammillarienfreunde e.V.
  Contact: Marientalstrasse 70/72, D-4400 Münster.
  Journal: *AFM (Mitteilungsblatt des Arbeitskreises für Mammil-*
    *larienfreunde e.V.)*, 1977 et seq.
Kakteen- und Orchideen-Rundschau
  Contact: Andersenring 87 f., D-2400 Lübeck 1.
  Journal: *Zeitschrift für Kakteen- und Orchideen-Liebhaberei und*
    *-Forschung,* 1975 et seq.

## GERMANY (EASTERN)
Fachgruppe für Kakteen und andere Sukkulenten im Kulturbund der DDR
  Contact: 801 Dresden, Pillnitzer Strasse 26.
  Journal: *Kakteen/Sukkulenten*, 1966 et seq.
Literaturschau Kakteen
  Contact: 1136 Berlin, Balatonstrasse 48.
  Journal: *Literaturschau Kakteen*, 1977 et seq.

# NETHERLANDS
Nederlands-Belgische Vereniging van Liefhebbers van Cactussen en andere Vetplanten
>Contact: Memlingstraat 9, 3817 DK Amersfoort.
>Journal: *Succulenta*, 1919–43, 1947 et seq.

# BELGIUM
Cactus
>Contact: Kasteellei 111, B-2110 Wijnegem.
>Journal: *Cactus—Tijdschrift voor Liefhebbers van Cactussen en andere Succulenten*, 1955 et seq.

Association Francaise pour Amateurs de Plantes de Serres et d'Acclimatation
>Contact: Avenue Victor Gilsoul 33, B 1200 Brussels.
>Journal: *Cactus*, 1976 et seq.

# FRANCE
Association Francophone des Amateurs de Plantes Succulentes
>Contact: Director, Jardin Exotique, B.P.105, Monte Carlo, Monaco.
>Journal: *Succulentes*, 1977 et seq.

# SOUTH AFRICA
South African Aloe & Succulent Society
>Contact: Box 1193, Pretoria 0001.
>Journal: *Aloe*, 1963 et seq.

Botanical Society of Southern Africa
>Contact: Kirstenbosch, Claremont 7735, Cape.
>Journal: *Veld & Flora*, 1927 et seq.

# ZIMBABWE
Aloe, Cactus & Succulent Society of Zimbabwe ( Rhodesia)
>Contact: P.O. Box 8514, Causeway, Salisbury.
>Journal: *Excelsa*, 1971 et seq.

In addition to the above, there are societies active in Australia, Canada, Czechoslovakia, Denmark, Hungary, India, Japan, Malta, New Zealand, Poland and elsewhere. Since almost all of these are run by volunteer labour—often in spare moments by a tiny band of fanatics—a measure of indulgence is needed if journals do not arrive on time, and the addresses of officers are apt to change often. Subscription rates frequently barely cover costs, and some are absurdly low: where else can one obtain equal value by modern standards? Finally, if you have difficulty in making a choice from the above societies, follow my example: join them all!

# General Bibliography

Included are encyclopaedic and other reference works covering cultivated ornamentals, their classification and identification in general.

BACKEBERG, C. 1978 Translated by L. GLASS *Cactus Lexicon* (Poole).

BAILEY, L. H. and E. Z. 1976 *Hortus 3* (New York: Macmillan).

BROWN, R. W. 1979 *Composition of Scientific Words* Washington D.C.: Smithsonian Inst.

CHITTENDEN, F. J. 1951 *Dictionary of Gardening* 4 vols (Oxford: Royal Horticultural Society); 1969 Supplement Vol. 5 2nd Edn. Ed. P. M. SYNGE Oxford: Royal Horticultural Society).

DAVIS, P. H. and HEYWOOD, V. H. 1963 *Principles of Angiosperm Taxonomy* (Harlow: Oliver & Boyd). 1951 et seq.

GRAF. A. B. 1963 *Exotica 3* (Rutherford, N.J.).

GRAF, A. B. 1978 *Tropica* (Rutherford, N.J.).

HUTCHINSON, J. 1959 *Families of Flowering Plants* 2nd Edn. 2 Vols. (Oxford: Clarendon Press).

JACOBSEN, H. 1960 *Handbook of Succulent Plants.* 3 Vols. (Poole: Blandford Press).

JACOBSEN, H. 1977 *Lexicon of Succulent Plants* 2nd Edn. (Poole: Blandford Press).

LAWRENCE, G. H. M. 1951 *The Taxonomy of Vascular Plants* (New York).

LEMÉE, A. 1929–59 *Dictionnaire descriptif et synonymique des genres de plantes phanéro-games* 10 Vols. (Brest).

RAUH, W. 1967 *Die grossartige Welt der Sukkulenten* (Hamburg).

RENDLE, A. B. 1930, 1938 *The Classification of Flowering Plants* 2 Vols. (Cambridge).

*Repertorium Plantarum Succulentarum 1951 et seq.* Ed. G. D. ROWLEY et al. (Richmond: I.O.S. British Section, 67 Gloucester Court, Kew Road).

ROWLEY, G. D. 1978 *Illustrated Encyclopedia of Succulents* (London: Salamander).

WILLIS, J. C. 1973 *A Dictionary of the Flowering Plants and Ferns* Ed. H. K. AIRY-SHAW 8th Edn. (London: Cambridge U.P.).

## Periodicals

*Baileya* 1953 et seq. (New York: Cornell University) Bailey Hortorium.

*Taxon* STAFLEU, F. A. *(Ed. 1951 et seq.) Journal of the International Association for Plant Taxonomy (Utrecht).*

# Index

NOTE: Family names are capitalized. Numbers in heavy type indicate an illustration. The Glossary, being alphabetical, is not separately indexed.